COLLECTED LETTERS

COLLECTED LETTERS

Cardiphonia, or The Utterance of the Heart in the Course of a Real Correspondence

John Newton

Edited by
Halcyon Backhouse

HODDER AND STOUGHTON

LONDON SYDNEY AUCKLAND TORONTO

British Library Cataloguing in Publication Data

Newton, John
Collected letters.
1. Christianity
I. Title II. Backhouse, Halcyon C.
200

ISBN 0–340–51294–6

 Typeset by Watermark, Hampermill Cottage, Watford WD1 4PL and printed in Great Britain for Hodder and Stoughton Limited, Mill Road, Dunton Green, Sevenoaks, Kent by Cox and Wyman Limited, Reading, Berks. Hodder and Stoughton Editorial Office: 47 Bedford Square, London WC1B 3DP.

CONTENTS

EDITOR'S INTRODUCTION

'Newton, John, a church of England divine, born 1725, sailed in the Guinea trade, and led a very irregular life for some years; but at last grew both serious and studious, and in 1764 was ordained to the curacy of Olney, in Buckinghamshire, where he became intimately acquainted with Cowper the poet, with whom he produced the *Olney Hymns*. In 1779 he obtained the rectory of St Mary Woolnoth, London, which he held till his death in 1807. He wrote *Cardiphonia . . .*' So reads John Newton's entry in Maunder's *Biographical Treasury* (Longmans, Green, 1889).

The life of John Newton makes gripping reading and the following quotations are all taken from his fourteen letters which make up a book he wrote entitled, *An Authentic Narrative of some Remarkable and Interesting Particulars in the Life of ———, in Fourteen Letters.* He was born in London in 1725, and also died there in 1807. His mother, a godly Nonconformist, trained her son in everything that was good, especially the Bible: 'The tender mercies of God towards me were manifested in the first moment of my life. I was born as it were in his house, and dedicated to him in my infancy. My mother (as I have heard from many) was a pious experienced Christian: she was a Dissenter; in communion with the late Dr Jennings. I was her only child; and as she was of a weak constitution, and a retired temper, almost her whole employment was the care of my education. I have some faint remembrance of her care and instruction. At a time when I could not be more than three years of age, she herself taught me English; and with so much success (as I had something of a forward turn) that when I was four years old I could read with propriety in any common book that offered. She stored my memory, which was then very retentive, with many valuable pieces, chapters, and portions of Scripture, catechisms, hymns, and poems.' Just before his seventh birthday Newton's mother died.

Newton's father, a stern, silent man, and a commander in the Merchant Service, took John to sea when he was only eleven years old and made six voyages with him. John became godless. Those were the days of the press-gang and young Newton was forced against his will aboard one of H M ships, where he was made a midshipman, but he soon deserted, only to be captured two days later: 'The small party of soldiers brought me back to Plymouth; I walked through the streets like a felon – my heart was full of indignation, shame and fear. I was confined two days in the guard-house, then sent on board my ship, kept a while in irons, then publicly stripped and whipped; after which I was degraded from my office and exposed to the insults of all. Whether I looked inward or outward, I could perceive nothing but darkness and misery.'

Soon after this he was put on board a slave-ship and taken to the coast of Sierra Leone. In this degraded position he endured a great deal of brutal treatment: 'My distress has been at times so great, as to compel me to go by night, and pull up roots in the plantation (though at the risk of being punished as a thief), which I have eaten raw upon the spot, for fear of discovery.' Newton's life fluctuated between being master of slave ships and being a lowly paid seaman. Later in his life Newton remembered the godless excesses of this part of his life with deep and heartfelt remembrance. Near the end of his life in 1805, aged eighty, he was being encouraged to give up preaching, as he could no longer read easily, and he replied, 'What, shall the old African blasphemer stop while he can speak!'

On his way home in 1748 Newton spent a night on a waterlogged boat, with death staring him in the face but found that this was the moment when God spoke to his conscience. Later Newton referred to this time as the 'Great Deliverance': 'I went to bed that night in my usual security and indifference; but was awakened from a sound sleep by the force of a violent sea, which broke on board us. The sea had torn away the upper timbers on one side, and made the ship a mere wreck in a few minutes. Taking in all the circumstances, it was astonishing, and almost miraculous, that any of us survived to relate the story. We had immediate recourse to the pumps; but the water increased against all our efforts: some of us were set to bailing in another part of the vessel, that is, to lade it out with buckets and pails. I continued doing this till noon, with almost every passing wave breaking over my head; but we made ourselves fast with ropes, that we might not be washed away. Although I dreaded death now, I thought, if the Christian religion was true, I could not be forgiven. The next day I began to pray. My prayer was like the cry of the ravens, which yet the Lord does not disdain to hear. I now began to think of that Jesus whom I had so often derided: I recollected the particulars of his life, and of his death; a death for sins not his own, but, as I remembered, for the sake of those who in their distress should put their trust in him. My companions in danger were either quite unaffected, or soon forgot it all: but it was not so with me; not that I was any wiser or better than they, but because the Lord was pleased to vouchsafe me peculiar mercy. I had a New Testament and was struck particularly by Prodigal, Luke chapter 15. Before we arrived in Ireland I had a satisfactory evidence in my own mind of the truth of the Gospel, as considered in itself, and its exact suitableness to answer all my needs. I saw that, by the way there pointed out, God might declare, not his mercy only, but his justice also, in the pardon of sin, on the account of the obedience and sufferings of Jesus Christ. My judgment at that time embraced the sublime doctrine of "God manifest in the flesh, reconciling the world to himself".'

After this Newton became master of a slave-ship, then a surveyor at Liverpool, where he came under the influence of Whitefield and Wesley. For nine years he studied theology with great care, including Greek and Hebrew, and also met and talked with such Christian leaders as Grimshaw, Venn, Berridge and Romaine. In 1764 he was ordained as curate of Olney. Three years later Cowper came to live there and the two men were scarcely apart for a single day. On the death of Cowper's brother the poet showed symptoms of another mental collapse and so Newton suggested that Cowper should compile the *Olney Hymns*. Cowper wrote sixty-eight of these and Newton two hundred and eighty, perhaps the most loved of which is 'How sweet the name of Jesus sounds'. Few men have ever lived who knew better, from personal experience, what they were writing than did John Newton, when he penned the words:

How sweet the Name of Jesus sounds
In a believer's ear!
It soothes his sorrows, heals his wounds,
And drives away his fear.

It makes the wounded spirit whole,
And calms the troubled breast;
'Tis manna to the hungry soul,
And to the weary rest.

Dear Name! the rock on which I build,
My shield and hiding-place,
My never-failing treasury filled
With boundless stores of grace.

Jesus! my shepherd, brother, friend,
My prophet, priest, and king,
My lord, my life, my way, my end
Accept the praise I bring.

Weak is the effort of my heart,
And cold my warmest thought;
But when I see thee as thou art,
I'll praise thee as I ought.

Till then I would thy love proclaim
With every fleeting breath;
And may the music of thy Name
Refresh my soul in death.

'Amazing grace' must rank as Newton's most well known hymn and takes on added significance when it is read as his spiritual autobiography:

Amazing grace! how sweet the sound
That saved a wretch like me;
I once was lost, but now am found;
Was blind, but now I see.

'Twas grace that taught my heart to fear,
And grace my fears relieved;
How precious did that grace appear,
The hour I first believed!

Through many dangers, toils and snares
I have already come:
'Tis grace that brought me safe thus far,
And grace will lead me home.

The Lord has promised good to me,
His word my hope secures;
He will my shield and portion be
As long as life endures.

Yes, when this heart and flesh shall fail,
And mortal life shall cease,
I shall profess within the veil
A life of joy and peace.

When we've been there a thousand years,
Bright shining as the sun,
We've no less days to sing God's praise
Than when we first begun.

Out of the many hundreds of letters Newton wrote, his collection entitled *Cardiphonia* is his most widely known. The first section, and longest one, is taken up with twenty-six letters to a nobleman and these are unabridged in this edition, while a selection has been made from the rest of the letters. They cover a wide range of topics – advice to a student going to college; counsel for the ill, dying and bereaved; and discussion on important theological topics. When in theological debate Newton has a gentle approach, and seems to have a had a special gift to point people to the One who had and continued to help him in his own Christian life. At all times he seeks to base his advice on the teaching of the Bible. He was keen to stress the sinful nature of mankind and the amazing love and grace of Jesus Christ. While some will read his letters so that they can derive benefit from them for themselves, others will do so in order to be better used as advisers and counsellors in God's service. In *Cardiphonia* Newton quotes 2 Corinthians chapter one verses 3–5 since this summarises so well his intention in writing so many letters: 'Praise be to the God and Father of our Lord Jesus Christ, the Father of compassion and the God of all comfort, who comforts us in all our troubles, so that we can comfort those in any trouble with the comfort we ourselves have received from God. For just as the sufferings of Christ flow over into our lives, so also through Christ our comfort overflows.' David Russell's Introductory Essay and Newton's own Introduction to *Cardiphonia* are both included in this edition so that readers of Newton's letters can derive maximum benefit from them.

One Sunday morning, this sailor-preacher with failing

eyesight, a few years before his death, was preaching and came to the words: 'Jesus Christ is precious', which he repeated. His helper thought that he was confused and whispered, 'Go on, go on; you have said that before'. Newton looked round and replied, 'John, I said that twice, and I am going to say that again', then, in an even louder voice he said, 'Jesus Christ is precious'.

Newton's epitaph, written by himself, underlines how precious Jesus Christ was to him, and this basic theme overflows from his *Cardiphonia*.

> John Newton, Clerk,
> Once an infidel and libertine,
> A servant of slaves in Africa:
> Was by the rich mercy of our Lord and Saviour,
> Jesus Christ,
> Preserved, restored, pardoned,
> And appointed to preach the Faith
> He had long laboured to destroy.
> Near sixteen years at Olney in Bucks:
> And twenty-seven years in this Church.

Halcyon Backhouse
Hampermill, 1988

INTRODUCTORY ESSAY

The Letters of John Newton have been long and justly esteemed. His chief excellence as a writer, seems to lie in the easy and natural style of his epistolary correspondence. He esteemed *Cardiphonia* as the most useful of his writings. It consists of letters which were actually written to his friends, and returned to him that they might be printed. They were confidential letters, and are indeed 'the utterance of the heart'. They breathe a tone of seriousness, affection and tenderness, which commends itself to the conscience, while it gains the confidence of the reader. You cannot fail to perceive that he speaks the language of firm persuasion, and of deep personal experience. There is nothing of cold theoretical speculation. You feel that you are listening to a man who is telling you what he has himself seen, and felt, and tasted, of the goodness of that God, whose Word and service he commends. His heart goes along with all his instructions, for 'he speaks because he believes'; it is seen in all his exhortations, for he evidently takes them home to himself; and it breaks forth in all his consolatory addresses, for he is but telling what God has done for his own soul; and, happy himself in fellowship with God, and sympathising with others in their sorrow and their wants, he is commending to them those springs of consolation which have calmed and purified his conscience, and which continue to cheer and gladden his heart. His social affections were remarkably warm; and when hallowed by the grace of God, the result was a tenderness of feeling, an expansion of heart, and an outflow of affection, admirably calculated to exhibit the amiableness of genuine religion, to overcome prejudice, and to win over men to the truth. He spoke from the heart to the heart; and powerfully indeed have his writings interested the hearts of all classes of his readers.

The narrative which Mr Newton published of his early years, serves to throw considerable light on many important subjects in religion; and that eventful portion of his history accounts for much of what continued to distinguish him in his after-life. His mother was a pious woman; and though she died before he was seven years of age, he derived considerable benefit from her instructions. She stored his mind with passages of Scripture, and with religious catechisms and hymns, and often commended him with many tears and prayers unto God. After her death, however, he was permitted to mingle with careless and profane children, and he soon learned their ways. The instructions of his mother, however, could not always be forgotten, and he was often disturbed with convictions. And from this let parents learn to be assiduous in instructing their children. It is no small matter to make the path of guilt unpleasant. Should no fruit appear at the time, should the young even plunge into profligacy, yet the instructions of a father or a mother will at times rise before them like departed ghosts, will imbitter the ways of transgression, and make conviction to flash upon the conscience, in spite of all their efforts against it, and may ultimately be the means of reclaiming them.

The convictions which disturbed Mr Newton, coupled with a natural fondness for reading, led him to peruse some religious books; and, from a wish to obtain peace to his mind, he began to pray, to read the Scriptures, and to keep a diary. He then thought himself religious. But alas, this seeming goodness had no solid foundation. He soon became weary of it, he gave it up entirely, and even became worse than before. Several alarming and affecting providences produced successively a temporary effect. He took up and laid aside a religious profession three or four different times before he was sixteen years of age. The last reformation of this kind was indeed very remarkable. It continued for more than two years. He then spent the greater part of the day in reading the Scriptures, and in meditation and prayer. He fasted often; he bemoaned his former evils, and he was careful, not only of his external conduct, but of every word of his tongue, and of the workings of his heart. But, after all this, he sunk into infidelity and profligacy.

How true it is, that when the heart of a sinner is penetrated with convictions of guilt, if he does not believe in the work of the Saviour, and thus obtain rest to his soul, he will either sink into despair and give himself up to melancholy, or he will engage in a course of formal and self-righteous obedience and devotion. If the former, then, finding the burden of distress intolerable, he will seek peace to his soul in stifling conviction, and in endeavouring to persuade himself that religion is all a dream. And, if the latter, then finding no enjoyment of escaping hell; being still under the power of his corrupt propensities; feeling his religion, such as it is, to be nothing but a system of restraints; in a word, being unable to get solid peace to his conscience, and being still haunted by dismal apprehensions, he will be prepared to embrace any system of error which, will serve to set his mind at rest. He becomes, as Mr Newton did, gloomy, and stupid, unsociable, and useless. He indulges in fruitless, inactive, and slothful wishes; for 'the soul of the sluggard desireth, and hath nothing' (Prov. 13:4). In times of trouble he sinks into sullen and proud, resentment against the fancied authors of calamity, for he is destitute of inward support. 'The wicked, through the pride of his countenance, will not seek God' (Psa. 10:4). 'They cry out because of the arm of the mighty, but none saith, Where is God my maker, who giveth songs in the night?' (Job 35:9–10). The man has just as much religion as makes him miserable; and not being happy in it, he easily gives it up. He knows not the blessedness of the man who is resting his hope for eternity on the work of the Saviour, and who has found rest to his soul where the justice of heaven found it, but is going about to establish his own righteousness. When the force of conviction obliges to abandon beloved ways, they are given up with reluctance, and with some secret reserve. Though a struggle is maintained with the evil workings of the heart, there is still an aversion to true spirituality of mind. He is kept from open pollution, and may even be attentive to the secret services of piety; knowing that a Christian should be heavenly-minded, he may endeavour to work up his heart to a heavenly frame; but there being no proper root in him, he soon becomes weary of this heavy constraint; or, fancying that he has obtained the victory over sin, he has a gleam of joy, arising from the notion that now God has accepted him: but his hopes are soon darkened, for there being no abiding principle within him, his goodness is 'like the morning cloud and like the early dew, which soon pass away.' He has recourse to vows and resolutions of amendment, but they are weakness itself before the power of temptation.

Now, in this state of mind, a man is prepared to say, 'It is vain to serve God: and what profit is it that I have kept his ordinances, and that I have walked mournfully before him?' Being forced to seek shelter from an accusing conscience, and being quite disappointed by all the means which he has tried, the poison of error and infidelity finds him a proper subject for its influence. And if books or companions of such a character come in his way, their principles are readily imbibed. He believes the fatal lie; and now, being free from restraint, he plunges into all manner of excess. Such, in substance, was the case with Mr Newton.

What more clear than that convictions of guilt will not of themselves turn a sinner to God? Every believer of the Gospel must have such convictions in a greater or less degree. For where there is no sense of guilt, there can be no sense of the need of forgiveness, and of course the import and glory of the Gospel cannot be discerned. But many are the subjects of convictions of sin, who never come to the Saviour. The question then is, have they excited us to flee for refuge to the cross, and to the wondrous work which was finished there on behalf of the ungodly? Have we come to this Saviour, guilty and unworthy as we see ourselves to be, and do we rest all our hope for eternity on that one perfect righteousness, through which God appears at once 'the just God and the Saviour?'

Mr Newton's case is at variance with the notion that it is absolutely necessary for sinners to be the subjects of a long and an exceedingly awful process of deep conviction of sin previously to their receiving the Gospel. Such a notion perplexes the minds of many anxious inquirers. It leads them to imagine that the process in question forms a kind of warrant to come to the Saviour, and a sort of recommendation to his mercy, or a qualification for obtaining the benefit of his work. But there is a wide difference between what excites a sinner to flee to the Redeemer, and that which is his warrant to do so in the confidence of obtaining mercy. Many indeed have been the subjects of severe convictions, and of great alarm and deep distress of mind, before they found peace in the cross. But others have been drawn in a more gentle way. The Lord, in his first call, and his following dispensations, has respect to the situation, temper, and talents of each of his people, and to the particular services or trials he has appointed them for. Why then make the case of some a standard to all? Must not this lead the sinner to busy himself with the inquiry, whether he has sufficiently long, or sufficiently in measure, been the subject of the process in question, and so turn his mind from the saving truth?

It is enough, then, that such a conviction of guilt be produced, as shall, by the grace of the divine Spirit, excite the sinner to come to Christ, that he may have life. God ought not to be limited; and accordingly experience decidedly shows that neither the same degree nor length of alarm is by any means always employed, even with the same class of characters.

Speaking of himself, Mr Newton says, 'Few, very few, have been recovered from such a dreadful state; and the few that have been thus favoured have generally passed through the most severe convictions; and after the Lord has given them peace, their future lives have been usually more zealous, bright, and exemplary, than common. Now as, on the one hand, my convictions were very moderate, and far below what might have been expected from the dreadful review I had to make, so, on the other, my first beginnings in a religious course were as faint as can be well imagined.'

The humility and modesty of our author are here apparent; but all who are acquainted with his history will acknowledge, that his life was as zealous, bright, and exemplary, as that of many who were led to God in the way he describes.

In the gracious providence of God, Mr Newton was brought, by means of certain circumstances of danger, to think of his former religious professions – of the extraordinary turns of his life – the calls, warnings, and deliverances with which he had met – the licentious course of his conversation – and his effrontery in making the Gospel history the subject of his ridicule, when he could not be sure that it was false. Being delivered from the present danger, he thought he saw in this the gracious hand of the Almighty, and, conscious of misery, he attempted to pray. He very properly compares his prayer to 'the cry of the ravens.' And certainly there is a wide difference between the formal, hypocritical, and self-righteous prayers which the Scriptures condemn, and which they declare that God will not hear, and the cries of wretched creatures for relief. The former must be sinful, but the latter are in themselves neither morally good nor morally evil, for they but express the instinctive feelings of every precipient being when in circumstances of pain. They contain nothing spiritually good, and therefore cannot be the object of complacency, but neither can they be the object of blame. And that God who pities the irrational animals in distress, and is represented as hearing their cry, is also represented as looking down from his throne in heaven to hear the groaning of the prisoner; to loose those that are appointed to death. Now in such a situation was Mr Newton at this time. His distress was employed as a means in the hand of heaven to lead him to the proper remedy. He felt himself wretched, but knew not how to get relief, and he looked up to God and implored deliverance. While he did this he applied himself to the Scriptures, and he did so, simply to discover what they taught. He was particularly struck with the parable of the prodigal – he saw it in his very case – he dwelt on the goodness of the father in receiving, nay in running to meet such a son – and he saw in this a designed representation of the goodness of God to returning sinners. And indistinct as his views were of the gospel of peace, there was a marked difference between his present views of the divine mercy and grace, and the self-righteous notions which predominated, when, as he said himself in the language of the apostle, 'after the strictest sect of our religion I lived a Pharisee.' God was drawing him with the cords of a man, and with bands of love. The apprehension he now had of the goodness of God encouraged him to cast himself upon him in the exercise of prayer for relief. That relief came. He was made to see the exact suitableness of the Gospel to answer all his wants. He saw how God might declare not his mercy only, but his justice also, in the pardon of sin, on account of the obedience and sufferings of Christ. His judgment, he says, 'embraced the sublime doctrine of God manifest in the flesh, reconciling the world unto himself.' But his views of this precious truth, and of others connected with it, were very imperfect.

Through unwatchfulness and temptation he greatly declined for a season. But by means of affliction, he was again awakened to a sense of his condition. Conscious of his weakness, he durst make no more resolves, but committed himself to the Lord. Divine goodness directed him to the cross of the Saviour. After this, the burden was removed from his conscience; and not only his peace but his health was restored, and though subject, as all are, to the effects and conflicts of indwelling sin, yet he was ever after delivered from its power and dominion. Thus did he soon experience the freeness and the suitableness of the Gospel to a sinner, when unable to view himself in any other light than that of an ungodly character.

Mr Newton did not consider himself to have been a believer in the full sense of the word until now; but certainly at the period formerly mentioned, he had embraced the substance of the saving truth. His views of the atonement of Jesus were much clearer than were those of the disciples in the days of our Lord, who did not clearly understand the design of his death, till after he was risen from the dead; and who yet were believers of the blessed truth, that in the goodness of God a way should be provided by which the exercise of mercy would be rendered compatible with the claims of justice. And the faith of many under the ancient economy certainly went no farther than this. Mistakes on this subject sometimes arise from dwelling too much on faith, as an exercise apart from its object, and also from dwelling almost exclusively on one particular vehicle of truth, to the neglect of the substance of the truth conveyed. It is not for us to say how small a portion of truth may in certain circumstances become the seed of genuine religion. So far as it goes, it does lead to a measure of confidence in the mercy of God; and it cherishes that humility and contrition of mind, which are opposed to the self-righteous hope of unbelievers.

The new perceptions of such a character are indeed

feeble and indistinct, compared with those of the man who is taught 'the way of God more perfectly'; and they are even in particular danger of being overborne and swallowed up, as they were in our author, in the tumult of natural passions, and in the conflict with natural slothfulness, and carnal propensities; but they constitute a leaven which will gradually diffuse its influence till the whole soul is leavened. The great defect in his views was, that while he acknowledged the divine mercy in the forgiveness of his past transgressions, he trusted chiefly in his own resolutions as to future obedience; not understanding that all our strength as well as our justifying righteousness must be sought in the Saviour. He had not the advantage of Christian fellowship, nor of hearing the Gospel preached; and the few books which came in his way were not of the best kind; while he was in the midst of the same course of evil company, and of bad examples as before. He, however, came gradually to learn more of the truth; and it becomes those who were brought to serious reflection in the midst of the means of grace, and surrounded by every external advantage and encouragement, not to despise such a day of small things as this, but to remember that their attainments, when compared with his, were perhaps far from being in proportion to their superior advantages. What a mercy that we have a Shepherd who gathers the lambs in his arms and carries them in his bosom, and gently leads those that are with young!

The declension into which Mr Newton unhappily fell, was overruled for the cure of his self-confidence, the deepening of his humility, and the enlargement of his views of the glory of divine grace. The Good Shepherd restored his soul. 'He gave me a distinct and a clear view of the way of forgiveness.' The character of God, as just, and yet the justifier of the ungodly, captivated his heart. The light of divine truth dissipated the darkness which had covered his mind, and put to flight the temptations which had formerly betrayed him. It calmed and composed his heart – it sweetly drew him to the Saviour as his only hope – and it satisfied his soul with unspeakable bliss. From that day forward, he lived in the firm persuasion of the Gospel. He walked humbly with God. He felt that he had neither wisdom nor strength in himself, but he also felt that at the same time he was connected with him who is infinitely wise and infinitely powerful. Often does he enlarge, in the following work, on the wisdom and the goodness displayed in the necessity under which, believers are laid, of coming daily to the Saviour, as they came at first. They have no such thing as a stock of sufficiency imparted at once. Even on the most common occasions they are constrained, by a sense of indigence, to have recourse to his fulness. He illustrates this by the life of the Israelites on their way to the promised country. They were fed with manna that they might be humbled. Not that this circumstance itself could humble them, but that as the manna could not be preserved, they were kept in a condition of constant absolute dependence from day to day, and were thus made to feel their littleness. Boasting was thus excluded, while gratitude ought to have been excited for the goodness manifested in the unwearied care, and the constant communications of heaven. They were naturally averse to this mode of life, and believers still manifest the folly and perverseness of the natural heart, by an unwillingness to be kept constantly in a state of dependence, and to be necessitated to the very last to come to the Saviour as they came to him at first. Daily are we offending, and daily do we need to apply to the God of all grace. This is indeed humbling. But unbelief, though it steals upon us under the semblance of humility, is the very essence of pride, when it keeps us from immediately applying to the only physician of the soul. There is indeed such a thing as a cold use of the precious promise of forgiveness, but this is not the spirit of genuine repentance. One of the greatest attainments in the life of godliness is, to be coming daily to the fountain which is opened for sin and uncleanness, and yet be so far from counting it a common thing, that every fresh instance of divine forgiveness yet more humbles and softens the heart, and increases our sense of the evil and demerit of sin: of this spiritual attainment the *Cardiphonia* discovers a very high degree.

Happy is that man who is such a case. It was a life of close walking by the faith of the Son of God, which maintained that settled peace and heavenly enjoyment which Mr Newton so signally experienced. He often speaks of the joy of the Lord as his strength. He felt and saw the evils of his heart, but though abased he did not suffer a spurious humility to mingle itself with the genuine, and to keep him from going afresh to the blood of sprinkling. He dwelt upon the dignity and righteousness, the faithfulness and mercy, of his great High Priest, and he committed his all to his care. And he found that the Gospel is indeed a glorious provision for the happiness of man. While it proclaims forgiveness, it heals the diseases of the soul, and communicates the purest enjoyment. In a sense the favour and the love of God, in fellowship with the Redeemer, and the love and the peace connected with the contemplation of unseen and eternal things, are a high anticipation of the bliss of heaven. We were formed for fellowship with the Father of spirits; and no other object, nor all other objects taken together, can fully occupy our powers, or satisfy our desires. The benevolent language of the Gospel is, 'Ho! every one that thirsteth for happiness, come to the fountain of enjoyment.' Why continue to pursue that which never can satisfy? In the most wonderful manner does the God of all grace express his regret, not only because of the rebellion, but also because of the misery of men. He feelingly complains that they have left him who is the fountain of life, for cisterns, yes, even for broken cisterns which can hold no water. It is as if he had said: 'If, in leaving me, ye had gone to a better, or even to an equal fountain of blessedness, I should not have complained. If ye will leave me, choose, if you can, an object which will make you happy, for your happiness is the desire of my heart. But why forsake a fountain for a cistern, and even for a broken cistern, which can yield you neither relief nor enjoyment? This is conduct not only deeply criminal, but most foolish and irrational; it is most dishonourable to me and fearfully ruinous to yourselves.'

In a similar way does he reason with Israel in Psalm 81. 'Hear, O Israel, if you will take my counsel, there shall no strange God be among you. Do not question my kindness, for I am thy best and thy tried friend; I am he who brought you from the land of bondage, and therefore you may well give me your confidence. Do not act as if another God could do more for you than I can, for all your wants I can and will fully supply. Open thy mouth wide and I will fill it.'

Such is the spirit breathed in the Gospel. And what has not God done, that he might gain our hearts? What love towards us, in delivering up his own Son for the ungodly and rebellious! Through him he proclaims forgiveness, peace, and eternal life, as the gifts of divine grace to all who believe. And why does he ask our hearts, but that he may fill them with pure, steady, and permanent bliss?

Throughout the letters of Newton, and in the narrative of his life, the most satisfactory reasons are given for his feelings of comfort and joy. His accounts of himself are not like those biographical writings which dwell almost entirely on the feelings of their subjects, to the exclusion of the causes which made them to feel. What is it to us, that an individual felt now in this way, and then in that, if we are not told what produced his varying sensations? How different are such writings from the Scriptures. When we read there of the hopes and the fears, of the joys and the sorrows of such as feared God, we read also of those truths or causes which produced them. Who, for instance, can read the Psalms of David, the Songs of Isaiah and Zechariah, of Simeon and Mary, or the Apostle's Epistles, without at once perceiving the spring and foundation of their feelings and exercises? How beautifully has Paul combined a clear view of the state of the workings of his heart, with the fullest displays of the glories of the Gospel. We see a man who feels most deeply the power of the truth, and who is sensibly alive to the varied events of the providence of heaven; and we are at no loss to understand the views and the motives which influence him. And when biography is written on this plan, it is of great utility. But when otherwise, it is calculated greatly to mislead an inquirer, and to cherish a sort of sentimental sickly piety.

The expression, sensible comfort, is sometimes employed to signify that enjoyment which a Christian has in a consciousness of the healing influence of the Gospel, and from the assurance of hope, as distinguished from the state of a man's mind, who, when viewing himself as a stranger to piety, goes to the Saviour, on the ground of the broad testimony and the unfettered invitations of mercy which are addressed to sinners indiscriminately. But it is incorrect to say, that the former is walking by sense and the latter by faith. Of what is the healing influence of the Gospel the fruit and the evidence, but of faith, in the very same testimony and unfettered invitations, which are the encouragement of the sinner when he first comes to the Redeemer, and of the backslider when he returns to him? And what is the peace which the latter obtains when he thus comes, but the fruit of confidence in the testimony and promise of heaven? It is not an unfounded persuasion, that he is a child of God; but it is that peace which arises from a proper view of the sufficiency of the work of Christ, to justify him, guilty as he is; and from a persuasion, founded on the promise, that through resting his eternity on that work, he shall obtain the blessings of salvation. He has not the same degree of enjoyment as the former; but let this be stated in plain language, and not in words which are apt to mislead. The phrase in question is also used to denote that flow of the spirits, which, in certain constitutions and circumstances, accompanies the gladdening influence of the truth; but this is in itself distinct from religious comfort. The latter may exist where, owing to constitutional causes, there is but little of the former. There may also be certain parts of the truth believed, which have the effect of producing a degree of confidence in the goodness of God, a persuasion that his favour is life, and a renunciation of false grounds of hope, while yet there is no joy; because other parts of the truth are not properly discerned. Such at one time was the case with Mr Newton; but even then there was a sensible change produced on his mind.

Having introduced this subject, it may be proper to add, that some have employed language, in relation to the confidence of faith, which would seem to imply that it is the duty of Christians to maintain the persuasion that they are such, even when they have not the least reason to conclude that they are living in the exercise of any Christian principle; and that to question this is the sin of unbelief. But unbelief is calling in question what God has said. The fact of our being believers, granting us to be such, is not the object of faith. Our persuasion of this fact is not properly faith, – it is rather a knowledge of the fact arising from our own immediate consciousness of believing.

In support of the notion in question, it has been argued that Christians are said to 'walk by faith and not by sight'. But the meaning of this obviously is, that while they are in this world, they have not the advantage of the actual and immediate vision of the Saviour, and of the glories with which he is surrounded, but derive all their knowledge of him and of them from testimony. It is only when 'absent from the body that we shall be present with the Lord' (2 Cor. 5:1–9).

The *Cardiphonia* is full of comfort to the afflicted and the tempted. Mr Newton was indeed 'a son of consolation.' He had a peculiar talent for entering into the feelings and the views of the distressed. Much of the Word of God is applicable to a state of trouble, and can only be understood in circumstances of trial. The Gospel of Christ throws light on the most mysterious events of time. He who so loved us as to give himself a sacrifice for our sins, when we were sunk, in rebellion, can never cease to care for us. In the midst of all the trials and conflicts of the wilderness, he is showing us the utter emptiness and vanity of the present world, and the insufficiency of the soul to its own happiness, that he may draw us to himself, and lead us to repose on him as our ultimate rest and satisfying portion. And what blessings are the most painful and complicated troubles, if the heart is thereby weaned from the transitory objects of sense, and if every stroke of affliction impels the soul more powerfully towards him who is the inexhaustible fountain of all genuine enjoyment. It is thus that we profit by the heaviest pressures which imbitter this state of tribulation. Such views of the wise and gracious, but often mysterious providences of God, in connection with the Gospel of peace, serve to dissolve many of those clouds of perplexity and error which mislead and depress the heart; and they free from that painful uncertainty which, by its distressful agitations, greatly injures at once the holiness and the peace of the soul. They serve to infuse courage, and to impart consolation when all human help is unavailing; when, in the last hours of weakness, languor, and pain, flesh and heart fail; and even in the dark vale of death, when nothing else could yield to the departing spirit, light and life, animation and joy. Whatever changes there may be in our lot, whatever afflictions we may be called to bear, if we live in fellowship with the friend and the Saviour of sinners, our rejoicing will be that he ever liveth; and that beyond the transitory scene, and the many clouds which now intervene, there is an unchanging paradise and an incorruptible inheritance, where 'our sun shall no more go down, where the Lord shall be our everlasting light, our God, our glory, and where the days of our mourning shall be ended!'

The wisdom of God appears in the production, if we may so speak, of the greatest power at the least possible expense of means. By a few strokes of affliction on a single individual he paves the way for the advancement of his holiness and joy, and thus fits him for extensive usefulness. 'While he muses, his heart burns'; he hears of the afflictions of others; his own sorrows are relieved in giving vent to his feelings; he rejoices in soothing the anguish of the bleeding heart; the comforted again seek the benefit of more; they request him to cast his gift into the public treasury for the general benefit; and as he does so, he says, with the blended feelings of pious gratitude and benevolent joy: 'Blessed be God, even the Father of our Lord Jesus Christ, the Father of mercies, and the God of all comfort, who comforteth us in all our tribulation, that we may be able to comfort them which are in any trouble by the comfort wherewith we ourselves are comforted of God.' Such were the feelings of the Apostle of the Gentiles, and such, in a measure, was the happiness of the author of the *Cardiphonia*.

The letters of Newton abound with references to a particular providence. Without any admixture of superstition, he habitually recognised in everything the overruling hand of the Almighty. He indeed walked with God, for in every object and event he traced his operations, and 'in all his ways he acknowledged him'. His faith in the providence and grace of his God maintained that composure and cheerfulness of mind for which he was distinguished in circumstances of the most gloomy and discouraging kind. The remarkable incidents in his own life tended to lead him to act at all times 'as seeing him who is invisible'.

And it is edifying indeed to read his reflections on the superintending care of that God 'who fainteth not, neither is weary', who is 'a present help in trouble,' and 'without whom not even a sparrow can fall to the ground'.

It seems strange that men should admit a general, and deny a particular providence. They speak as if the Almighty were too great to concern himself with the petty affairs of individuals, though in extraordinary cases he may interfere in what relates to the interests of nations. They even speak as if, amid the greatness and the multiplicity of the affairs of his government, he could not bend to the interests of individuals so mean and insignificant. But what strange ideas of greatness are these. Do they not degrade the Almighty, and lower our conceptions of his grandeur? Whatever it was worthy of his power to create, it cannot be unworthy of his greatness to preserve and to superintend. Does not true greatness consist in a capacity of lending the most particular attention to the minute, whilst it embraces the vast? It is this capacity surely, which presents the most overwhelming view of the omniscience, omnipresence, and omnipotence of God. How delightfully are greatness and goodness blended together, when we are told that he who counts the number of stars, and calls them all by their names, is the same who bindeth up the broken in heart, and healeth the wounded in spirit! (Ps. 147:2,3,4). While his eye and his arm are abroad upon all the world, he watches the steps of the wanderer, pities the bereaved mourner, visits the lonely cottage of affliction, and makes the bed of the afflicted sufferer. Soothing indeed is the reflection, that we are not overlooked in the crowd, but that our individual concerns are as much regarded as though we were the only care of the Almighty Jehovah. 'He knoweth the way that we take'; he is privy to every feeling of the heart, and he enters into our every trial; for 'the very hairs of our head are numbered'. And why should men presume to mark out what is great and what is little? Are not the most important events suspended on matters apparently trivial? Witness the histories of Joseph and Mordecai. And unquestionably the same providence which regulates the greater must necessarily regulate the smaller.

This is a doctrine fraught with the richest consolation, when connected with the infinite wisdom, the inviolable faithfulness, and the immutable love of 'the God and Father of our Lord Jesus Christ'. How sweet the repose of that heart which rests in the Lord! We are not left to be the sport of blind chance in a fatherless world; we are the objects of the care of him who is everywhere present, who orders the movements, and satisfies the wants of his innumerable offspring. This truth is in perfect harmony with the personal exertion which is requisite to our obtaining the end we have in view. The Almighty acts by natural means. We are not warranted to expect miraculous interferences. Such expectations cherish a wild enthusiasm, and give unbelievers occasion to ridicule the doctrine of a special providence as the fruit of credulity. Extraordinary visible deliverances, or benefits, serve to manifest the reality of such a providence; but it is not less real when, by the silent operations of nature, the Almighty accomplishes his will.

In the writings of Mr Newton the harmony of divine truth is uniformly maintained. It was his object to be influenced and governed by the whole of the doctrines and precepts, the promises and warnings of Scripture in their proper place, and for their several uses. He keeps clear, on the one hand, of the error of those who, confining their attention to the character of man as an accountable agent, dwell almost exclusively on the economy of heaven as a system of moral government, and exhort to the discharge of duty, without properly considering his capacity to be the subject of a heavenly influence; and on the other, he avoids the error of those who so represent the nature of the impotence of man and the nature of heavenly grace, as to set aside the commandment of God to believe in the Saviour, and to lull the sinner into a state of careless indifference. 'A man's "cannot"', he says, 'is not a natural but a moral inability; not an impossibility in the nature of things, as it is for me to walk on the water, or to fly in the air, but such an inability as, instead of extenuating, does exceedingly enhance and aggravate his guilt. He is so blinded by Satan, so alienated from God by nature and wicked works, so given up to sin, so averse from that way of salvation which is contrary to his pride and natural wisdom, that he will not embrace or seek after it; and, therefore, he cannot, till the grace of God powerfully enlightens his mind, and overcomes his obstacles.'

He invariably exhibits the practical design and tendency of the truth, while he never withholds the most unfettered declarations of mercy. He does not attack antinomianism in a controversial manner, but he states those principles which subvert its foundation. There are times and circumstances, however, in which error must be directly opposed, that the simple may be put upon their guard, and that the nature and glory of the truth may be displayed. Witness the tenor of the Epistles to the Galatians and Corinthians. The foundation of antinomianism is in the depravity of the heart; and when it shows itself as it is doing in the present day, it should be decidedly and openly met, that men may be warned of their danger and the attempts of the enemy be defeated.

It seems strange that any who profess to believe the Gospel, should question the obligation of Christians to observe the precepts of the law. The law of heaven is of essential service to believers. It shows them what is contrary to the will of God; it serves to deepen their sense of their innate depravity; it makes them cling to the work of Christ as their only refuge; it excites their admiration of the grace of God, and thus serves to cherish the love of him as the God of salvation; it tells how to express this love; it ascertains the progress which they are making in religion; it warns them of their errors and their danger when they wander from him; and it deepens their conviction of the necessity of abiding in Christ, as at once their Saviour from guilt, and the spring of their sanctification. So far from being set aside by the Gospel, it is thereby established (Rom. 3:31). While the law shows the necessity of such a salvation as the Gospel exhibits, the latter, on the other hand, strikingly illustrates the requirements of the former, as they regard both our temper towards God and our disposition towards man, while it enforces obedience to its precepts by the principles, at once awful and delightful, which are revealed in the cross.

By the 'law of God' in any given case, must certainly be understood that system of laws which is established for the time being. Each dispensation under which the creatures of God are placed, has peculiar institutions and laws adapted to its special nature and design. Thus the Mosaic economy had many peculiar institutions adapted to a typical dispensation, and to the peculiar character of Israel. All of them, however, were of use, and all of them had for their object some moral end. But there are certain moral principles which remain unalterably the same under every economy of heaven, and out of those principles certain moral precepts necessarily arise under every dispensation with which mankind in the present state can at all be connected. The abrogation of the Mosaic economy as such, could not therefore set aside those moral injunctions which arise out of the indissoluble relation between God and man. We never find that God left any of mankind to whom he revealed himself without a rule for the guidance of their love to him. He instructed Adam, even when in innocence, how he was to conduct himself; he instructed him after the revelation of mercy to him as a sinner; he instructed Noah, the founder of a new world; and so did he Abraham, the root of the Jewish people. To that people he, in a special manner, delivered his law; and to the Church of Christ, of which that nation was a figure, he hath given many commandments of a moral nature, and institutions adapted to the state of people called out of the world into holy fellowship with the Father, and with his Son, Jesus Christ. But all his positive appointments are designed to answer a moral purpose; they are but means to an end, namely, the promotion of love to God and to man, which is the sum of the divine law. None of them therefore, ought to be despised. And, indeed, none of them can be so without injuring ourselves, for there is, in all of them, an admirable fitness to promote our happiness.

Not only does the Saviour appeal to our love, he also interposes his authority. 'Ye are my friends', says he, 'if ye do whatsoever I command you.' (John 15:14). It is clear then, that while we are treated, not merely as servants, but as friends, we are enjoined obedience by authority. Hence such expressions as the following: 'Ye know what commandments we gave you by the Lord Jesus' (1 Thess. 4:2). 'Now them that are such we command and exhort by our Lord Jesus Christ' (2 Thess. 3:12). 'These things command and teach' (1 Tim. 4:11). 'Charge them that are rich in this world, that they do good, that they be rich in good works, ready to distribute, willing to communicate' (1 Tim. 6:17,18). Now, here a being ready and willing to do what is right is represented as a matter of charge or command, because, along with the charge, suitable and sufficient motives to obedience are suggested. Why then oppose the one to the other? The authority of God is not only blended with kindness, it is in fact itself a display of kindness, for it is employed the more effectually to preserve us from that which is our ruin.

To dispense with obedience, were to dispense with our happiness; for in holy likeness to God lies the true blessedness of man. When Christ is called Jesus, 'because he is to save his people from their sins', it is implied, that deliverance from that which is 'a transgression of the law' is the principal part of his salvation. He is 'sent to bless us, in turning everyone of us away from his iniquities.'

If we confine the Gospel to the proclamation of pardon, we rob it of its principal glory. Precious as pardon is, it is not to be viewed as an insulated blessing – it is a means to the moral end of our sanctification; and to the latter, it is subordinate. When Jesus said, 'The kingdom', that is, the reign or government of heaven, 'is at hand; repent ye, and believe the glad tidings' (Mark 1:15), his language evidently implies that one great design of his coming was to subject men to his dominion, and that this was a part of the good news which he had to announce to the world. No doubt he referred to the speedy accomplishment of that sacrifice on which his kingdom is founded, and to his investiture with supreme authority, as the great evidence of its acceptance, and the great security of all who should put their trust in it; but he evidently includes the establishment of his kingdom in the heart, and the exercise of his authority over a holy nation and a royal priesthood. And as the whole economy takes its name from this, it is evident that its great and ultimate object is to restore us to the image of God. 'The reign of heaven' could not be the appropriate designation of an economy, the only, or even the principal design of which was, the mercy which appears in forgiveness. On no other principle could Christ be denominated a king, than on that of his exercising authority, and ruling by means of laws. Objections to the idea of authority, as if it were associated with something stern and forbidding, betray the most unworthy notions of the law of God, and of the nature and design of obedience. The revelation of pardoning mercy is the foundation of other blessings. It is, in particular, the moral means by which we are delivered from the dominion of sin. A sense of unpardoned guilt, and the dread of vengeance, foster the enmity of the heart against God. Not that it ought to be so, or that this result is without blame; for this were to say, that a sinner, when condemned, has an excuse for his disaffection to God. Independently of the revelation of mercy, it is the duty of the sinner to obey the divine law; for, otherwise, no sin could have been committed after the first; whereas, men are represented as daily multiplying their transgressions, and their redemption is entirely ascribed to grace. The question, then, wholly respects a fact. And as it is a fact, that while the fear which hath torment prevails, the sinner does not return to God, it is a striking proof of his abundant goodness, that he not only has given his Son to be a propitiation for sin, but that while he makes use of his law to give the knowledge of sin, he employs the revelation of his mercy and his grace to subdue the enmity of the heart; and thus condescends, as it were, to meet the feelings and situation of the guilty and rebellious.

Now, if such be the previous obligation of the sinner, it is utterly inconsistent with the nature of moral government, and with the great design of mercy, that Christians should be freed from obligation to keep the law, the sum of which is love to God and to our neighbour. The requirement of love is founded in the nature of the relation between God and a rational creature. And the Gospel of Christ, while it exhibits him as a Saviour, does so, by showing how he magnified and made honourable the law of heaven, by suffering its penalty and obeying its precepts. His salvation consists in bringing the redeemed to be of one mind with himself; and since the law was written in his heart, it must also be written in theirs. The great object of heaven in the forgiveness of sin, is to impart and to cherish that filial temper which esteems duty a privilege, and which identifies obedience with happiness. When believers are said to be free from the law, the reference is to the abolition of the Mosaic economy, which has been superseded by the death of Christ, or to that deliverance from the condemning sentence of the unchangeable law of righteousness, which is obtained through forgiveness. But for this very reason, they are under increased obligations to obey its precepts. Accordingly, though freed from the Mosaic yoke, and from the law in general, as the rule or procuring cause of acceptance with God, 'they are under the law to Christ' (1 Cor. 9:21).

It is vain to deny the obligation of the law, by representing the Gospel as the rule of obedience; for the Gospel is not a rule of conduct, but a message of peace and of reconciliation. It is true, that it gives such transcendent discoveries of the character of God, as to call for higher degrees of love than could have been required before; but let it be remembered, that the divine law must ever require that Jehovah be loved according to the revelation given of his character at the time; so that perfect conformity to the law consists now in loving him as he is revealed in Christ.

It is also vain to say that the Spirit, and not the law, is our rule; for that which excites to obedience, as does the influence of the Spirit, is quite a distinct thing from the rule of obedience. The promise is that the law of God shall be written in the hearts of the subjects of the covenant of peace; and this is effected 'by the Spirit of the living God' (2 Cor. 3:3); but this supposes the previous existence and constant obligation of that very law.

It has been said that Christians are ruled by love, and not by the law. And it is true that they do not obey from a principle of slavish fear; but they are not so ruled by love, as to exclude the ideas of obligation on their part, and of authority on that of God. What indeed is conformity to the law, but the exercise of love? For there is not an act of obedience that is not comprehended in the general precept of love. So far from love to God being incompatible with subjection to authority, it is itself the subject of an express commandment. The precept which requires it, is given in the first and great commandment of the law. And this, so far from converting obedience into a task, is a powerful means of cherishing the warmest affection; for why does God ask the supreme love of our hearts, but because he himself loves us, and in this way seeks our highest blessedness and glory?

If it be said that the prevalence of love renders a law unnecessary, it is sufficient to say in reply, that the Scriptures expressly declare, that 'this is the love of God, that we keep his commandments' (1 John 5:3); and that those only are the friends of the Saviour, who do whatsoever he commands them (John 15:14). Love is indeed the great principle of Christian obedience; but it cannot be also the regulator. Love in creatures such as we are, is often like a ship with full sails, but without a pilot at the helm. The love which is required, is love to God with all our understanding, as well as with all the heart; and this certainly implies not only that our love should rest on just perceptions of his character as revealed to us, but that it should also be exercised in conformity to the revelation of his will (Mark 12:33). Even the angels in heaven, whose hearts certainly glow with love, are represented as doing his commandments, and hearkening to the voice of his Word, that they may know his will and do it with alacrity (Ps. 103:20,21). And, with reverence be it said, when the Saviour himself appeared in the form of a servant, his love to the Father was, in certain respects, regulated in its exercise by the divine commandment. And why then speak as if love were in itself incompatible with subjection to a rule, when Jesus himself was 'made under the law?' He was so, indeed, that he might redeem from its curse; but he could not be so to free from its claims of obedience; for in the keeping of God's commandments lies the happiness of man.

Love, indeed, will not require an explicit precept for everything, but still it will be guided by the spirit of the law; and it is the expressed regard for the will of God, which is contained in the services of his creatures, that renders them acceptable. Love will, no doubt, to a certain extent, dictate itself what is fit to be done; but then, what it thus dictates to be right, has really the force of a law, as though it had been, in express words, commanded. The common judgment of mankind, and of course, that of Christians, so far informs them what is right and what is wrong; but what right reason dictates, has the authority of a law, and is in fact at bottom but the application of a rule. We read of some, who, though destitute of a written revelation, were a law to themselves. They were not 'without law' in every sense; for their thoughts accused and excused them so that they must still have had a standard to judge by, though not a written one (Rom. 2:14,15).

But though love, in connection with the judgment, will, to a certain extent, dictate what is right to be done, it cannot do so in every case. There are many circumstances and dispensations, in which the path of duty cannot be ascertained, without an explicit revelation. Hence the necessity and the advantage of those particular rules, which are laid down for our guidance in the various relations and conditions of life. And in regard to things, about which we have only general principles and rules to walk by, the prevalence of holy tempers and dispositions will lead to a proper decision. Love, in a word, will prompt us to do whatever is pleasing to God. Yet we must, by some means or other, know what is pleasing to him, before we can thus properly express our affection (1 Thess. 4:1). No matter in what way the will of God be made known; for in whatever way it is revealed, its obligation is the same, so far as the revelation extends. And the appeals which are made to love, are made to it as the exciting principle to action, rather than its rule.

The laws given to sinful creatures must certainly differ from those given to perfectly holy beings; but still a rule is given even to the latter; for the holiness of angels is a doing of the will of our Father who is in heaven. Angels, as well as mankind, must be bound by the eternal law of love; but the special manner in which they are called to express their affection, must, of course, correspond at once with their particular nature as creatures, and with the condition in which they exist. The particular prohibitions which have been given to mankind, are proofs of their being considered as depraved creatures; and hence the apostle has said that the law (meaning, of course, the law as it stands) is not made for a righteous man (1 Tim. 1:9). Such prohibitions, as he proceeds to mention, are very different from the original prohibition delivered to Adam, and would not have been issued, had man been in a state of innocence. But who would infer from this, that Adam was not under a law? And is it not a display of wisdom and of great kindness, that the law given to mankind in their present state, so distinctly warns them of their danger, by prohibitions which suppose the existence of corruptions which, if not restrained or mortified, will prove the death of all happiness?

Nothing can be more plain, than that the particular laws given by God for the regulation of his creatures, must correspond with their circumstances. The question then must be, are the precepts of the law of God suitable or unsuitable to the present circumstances of believers of Christ? And that they are really suited to their circumstances, is evident from the fact, that even the select disciples of the Saviour were addressed by him as not beyond the danger of falling into the most heinous offences, and are accordingly solemnly and affectionately warned against them (Luke 12:41–46). And that these admonitions were designed, not for them only, but for all his disciples in after ages, is clear from the consideration, that the primitive Christians were frequently admonished against similar evils, and even against crimes still more abominable (Rom. 13:13,14; 1 Cor. 5:9,10, and 10:6–14; Eph. 4:17–32; Col. 3:5–11). It is clear, then, that in the present state the renovation of believers is imperfect, and does not supersede the necessity of the law of God, as it presently stands, for their guidance. In the passages now referred to, an appeal is made to their fears, as well as to their gratitude and love. In our present imperfect state, our obedience is not wholly left to the more generous influence of the latter principles. It merits our attention, too, that when certain duties are enforced, there is an express recognition of the authority of the law. As for instance, in the duties of children to their parents, which are enforced, there is an express repetition of the fifth commandment – Ephesians 6:1,2,3. And when certain evils are condemned, the very form of the commandments is employed, as in James 2:8–13, where a number of offences are enumerated in the express language of the law, and where the evil of respecting persons is declared to be a sin against the law, and a solemn warning is given, that he shall have judgment without mercy, who hath showed no mercy. Hence such expressions as the following: – 'He that loveth another, hath fulfilled the law' (Rom. 13:8). 'Whosoever committeth sin, transgresseth also the law; for sin is the transgression of the law' (1 John 3:4). Now, if there be no sin that is not 'a transgression of the law', it follows that there can be no rule that is not comprehended in the law. In a word, let the commandments of the law be considered, and the conscience of every Christian will say, that there is not one of them which he can break without blame, or obedience to which is not connected with his happiness.

Christ declared that he had not come to destroy the law or the prophets, but to fulfil them; and having said this, he proceeded to explain the moral precepts of the law in their spirituality and extent, as reaching to the thoughts and the desires of the heart; and to enforce them on the consciences of his disciples (Matt. 5:17–32). He taught that all the law and the prophets hang on to two great commandments of love to God and love to our neighbour, thereby declaring that the moral injunctions of the law of Moses and also of the prophets continue to be binding (Matt. 22:37–40). And after enjoining the universal law of equity, that we do to others as we would that they should do to us, he enforces it by saying: 'For this is the law and the prophets' (Matt. 7:12).

Now since instead of representing himself as teaching and enjoining what is altogether new, he enforces the duties of piety and humanity, by referring to the law and the prophets, he obviously teaches, that the moral injunctions of the latter constitute the law of his kingdom. There is no necessity for confining the moral part of the divine law to the ten commandments; for granting that every moral precept may be deduced from them, yet there were many such precepts delivered by Moses and the prophets besides them. It was of importance that the people should not be left to ascertain their duty by mere inferential reasoning, however solid. And on this principle our Lord and his apostles have given many broad, and express commandments, in relation to moral conduct, without always marking their connection with the Decalogue, even where such connection cannot be questioned. It is the whole of the divine precepts collectively, which constitute the law of God. And though the fundamental principles of his law must ever be the same, yet those principles are applied according to the nature of the special dispensation under which his creatures are placed. Attention to this is of importance in reflecting on the law of heaven. And Mr Newton, in a letter on the right use of the law, has justly observed that 'clearly to understand the distinction, connection and harmony between the law and the gospel, and their mutual subserviency to illustrate and establish each other, is a singular privilege, and a happy means of preserving the soul from being entangled by errors on the right hand or the left'.

In a word, the law of God, though it be the language of authority, is also the voice of friendship. It is authority which is exercised for the more effectually influencing us to keep the only path which can lead to blessedness. And the man who, in the faith of the Gospel, walks humbly and obediently with God finds the truest liberty, and his greatest happiness, in serving his gracious Father and his rightful Sovereign.

David Russell
Dundee, September 28, 1824

ADVERTISEMENT

The deference due to the Public seems to require an apology for committing letters of private correspondence to the Press, while the writer is yet living. He is sensible, that sending them abroad without his name prefixed, will not of itself be sufficient to obviate the charge of egotism. The manner of expression and thinking, where an author has been repeatedly in print, will mark him out to good judges when they see him again, so as to render any farther description unnecessary.

The solicitation of friends, though a trite, is not always an improper plea, and would probably in the present case be admitted, if he had not determined to conceal the names of his correspondents likewise, and to suppress, as far as possible, every circumstance which might lead to discover them. For they certainly did recommend the publication, and return him their letters purposely that a selection might be made. But as he does not think himself at liberty to declare them, he must forgo the advantage of screening himself under the sanction of their judgment.

Posthumous Letters are usually published to a disadvantage. If it be supposed that the Author has friends, whose regard to his memory will make them willing to purchase what appears under his name, that circumstance has sometimes given occasion to an indiscriminate and injudicious publication of letters collected from all quarters, in which more attention is paid to the bulk than the value. For amongst a number of letters written to intimate friends, some will be too trivial to deserve notice, and others may be so intermingled with details of private or domestic concerns, as perhaps to give pain to those who are interested in them, when they see them in print.

The writer of the following Letters thought himself more competent to decide at present, which and how much of the papers before him might be not utterly unworthy of being preserved, than a stranger could be after his decease.

Farther, he finds, that between an increase of engagements on the one hand, and the unavoidable effects of advancing years on the other, he can expect but little leisure or ability for writing letters in future, except upon necessary business. By this method of sending to each of his correspondents many letters at once, he takes leave of them with the less regret, persuaded that he thus communicates the substance of all he could offer, if he was able to write them severally as often and as much at large as in times past.

Though some attention has been paid to variety, it was not practicable wholly to avoid what may be thought repetition, without destroying the texture and connection of many Letters; particularly in those which treat of affliction. But where the same subject recurs, it is usually placed in something of a different point of view, or illustrated in a different manner.

Thus much to bespeak the reader's favourable and candid perusal of what is now put into his hands. But the writer stands before a higher tribunal; and would be most to be pitied if he were not conscious, that in this publication he has no allowed aims, but to be subservient to the gracious designs of God by the Gospel, and to promote the good of his fellow-creatures.

November 29, 1780

CARDIPHONIA

TWENTY-SIX LETTERS TO A NOBLEMAN

Letter 1

My Lord, *March, 1765*

I remember, when I once had the pleasure of waiting on you, you were pleased to begin an interesting conversation, which, to my concern, was soon interrupted. The subject was concerning the causes, nature, and marks of a decline in grace; how it happens that we lose that warm impression of divine things, which in some favoured moments we think it almost impossible to forget; how far this change of frame is consistent with a spiritual growth in other respects; how to form a comparative judgment of our proficiency upon the whole; and by what steps the losses we sustain from our necessary connection with a sinful nature and a sinful world may be retrieved from time to time. I beg your Lordship's permission to fill up the paper with a view to these inquiries. I do not mean to offer a laboured essay upon them, but such thoughts as shall occur while the pen is in my hand.

The awakened soul (especially when, after a season of distress and terror, it begins to taste that the Lord is gracious) finds itself as in a new world. No change in outward life can be so sensible, so affecting. No wonder then, that at such a time little else can be thought of. The transition from darkness to light, from a sense of wrath to a hope of glory, is the greatest that can be imagined, and is oftentimes as sudden as wonderful. Hence the general characteristics of young converts are zeal and love. Like Israel at the Red Sea, they have just seen the wonderful works of the Lord, and they cannot but sing his praise; they are deeply affected with the danger they have lately escaped, and with the case of multitudes around them, who are secure and careless in the same alarming situation; and a sense of their own mercies, and a compassion for the souls of others, is so transporting, that they can hardly forbear preaching to every one they meet.

The emotion is highly just and reasonable with respect to the causes from whence it springs; and it is doubtless a proof, not only of the imperfection, but the depravity of our nature, that we are not always thus affected; yet it is not entirely genuine. If we examine this character closely, which seems at first sight a pattern and a reproof to Christians of longer standing, we shall for the most part find it attended with considerable defects.

1. Such persons are very weak in faith. Their confidence arises rather from the lively impressions of joy within, than from a distinct and clear apprehension of the work of God in Christ. The comforts which are intended as cordials to animate them against the opposition of an unbelieving world, they mistake and rest in as the proper evidences of their hope. And hence it comes to pass, that when the Lord varies his dispensations, and hides his face, they are soon troubled, and at their wits' end.

2. They who are in this state of their first love, are seldom free from something of a censorious spirit. They have not yet felt all the deceitfulness of their own hearts; they are not well acquainted with the devices or temptations of Satan; and therefore know not how to sympathise or make allowances, where allowances are necessary and due, and can hardly bear with any who do not discover the same earnestness as themselves.

3. They are likewise more or less under the influence of self-righteousness and self-will. They mean well; but not being as yet well acquainted with the spiritual meaning, and proper use of the law, nor established in the life of faith, a part (oftentimes a very considerable part) of their zeal spends itself in externals and non-essentials, prompts them to practise what is not commanded, to refrain from what is lawful, and to observe various and needless austerities and singularities, as their tempers and circumstances differ.

However, with all their faults, methinks there is something very beautiful and engaging in the honest vehemence of a young convert. Some cold and rigid judges are ready to reject these promising appearances on account of incidental blemishes. But would a gardener throw away a fine nectarine, because it is green and has not yet attained all that beauty and flavour which a few more showers and suns will impart? Perhaps it will hold for the most part in grace as in nature (some exceptions there are), if there is not some fire in youth, we can hardly expect a proper warmth in old age.

But the great and good Husbandman watches over what his own hand has planted, and carries on his work by a variety of different and even contrary dispensations. While their mountain stands thus strong, they think they shall never be moved; but at length they find a change. Sometimes it comes on by insensible degrees. That part of their affection which was purely natural, will abate, of course, when the power of novelty ceases; they will begin, in some instances, to perceive their own indiscretions; and an endeavour to correct the excesses of imprudent zeal will often draw them towards the contrary extreme of remissness; the evils of their hearts, which, though overpowered, were not eradicated, will revive again; the enemy will watch his occasions to meet them with suitable temptations; and, as it is the Lord's design that they should experimentally learn and feel their own weakness, he will, in some instances, be permitted to proceed. When guilt is thus brought upon the conscience, the heart grows hard, the hands feeble, and the knees weak; then confidence is shaken, the spirit of prayer interrupted, the armour gone; and thus things grow worse and worse, till the Lord is pleased to interpose. For though we can fall of ourselves, we cannot rise without his help. Indeed every sin, in its own nature, has a tendency towards a final apostasy; but there is a provision in the covenant of grace, and the Lord, in his own time, returns to convince, humble, pardon, comfort, and renew the soul. He touches the rock, and the waters flow. By repeated experiments and exercises of this sort (for this wisdom is seldom acquired by one or a few lessons), we begin at length to learn that we are nothing, have nothing, can do nothing but sin. And thus we are gradually prepared to live more out of ourselves, and to derive all our sufficiency of every kind from Jesus, the fountain of grace. We learn to tread more warily, to trust less to our own strength, to have lower thoughts of ourselves, and higher thoughts of him; in which two last particulars I apprehend what the Scripture means by a growth in grace does properly consist. Both are increasing in the lively Christian; every day shows him more of his own heart, and more of the power, sufficiency, compassion, and grace of his adorable Redeemer; but neither will be complete till we get to heaven.

I apprehend, therefore, that though we find an abatement of that sensible warmth of affection which we felt at first setting out; yet, if our views are more evangelical, our judgment more ripened, our hearts more habitually humbled under a sense of inward depravity, our tempers more softened into sympathy and tenderness, if our prevailing desires are spiritual, and we practically esteem the precepts, ordinances, and people of God, we may warrantably conclude, that his good work of grace in us is, upon the whole, on an increase.

But still it is to be lamented, that an increase of knowledge and experience should be so generally attended with a decline of fervour. If it was not for what has passed in my own heart, I should be ready to think it impossible. But this very circumstance gives me a still more emphatical conviction of my own vileness and depravity. The want of humiliation humbles me, and my very indifference rouses and awakens me to earnestness. There are, however, seasons of refreshment, ineffable glances of light and power upon the soul, which, as they are derived from clearer displays of divine grace, if not so tumultuous as the first joys, are more penetrating, transforming and animating. A glance of these, when compared with our sluggish stupidity when they are withheld, weans the heart from this wretched state of sin and temptation, and makes the thoughts of death and eternity desirable. Then this conflict shall cease. I shall sin and wander no more, see him as he is, and be like him for ever.

If the question is: 'How are these bright moments to be prolonged, renewed, or retrieved?' we are directed to faith and diligence. A careful use of the appointed means of grace, a watchful endeavour to avoid the occasions and appearances of evil, and especially assiduity in secret prayer, will bring as much of them as the Lord sees good for us. He knows best why we are not to be trusted with them continually. Here we are to walk by faith, to be exercised and tried; by and by we shall be crowned, and the desires he has given shall be abundantly satisfied. I am, etc.

Letter 2

My Lord, *April, 1766*

I shall embrace your permission to fill my paper. As to subject, that which has been a frequent theme of my heart of late, I shall venture to lay before your Lordship – I mean the remarkable and humbling difference which I suppose all who know themselves may observe, between their acquired and their experimental knowledge, or, in other words, between their judgment and their practice. To hear a believer speak his apprehensions of the evil of sin, the vanity of the world, the love of Christ, the beauty of holiness, or the importance of eternity, who would not suppose him proof against temptation? To hear with what strong arguments he can recommend watchfulness, prayer, forbearance, and submission, when he is teaching or advising others, who would not suppose but he could also teach himself, and influence his own conduct? Yet alas! The person who rose from his knees before he left his chamber, a poor, indigent, fallible, dependent creature, who saw and acknowledged that he was unworthy to breathe the air or to see the light, may meet with many occasions before the day is closed, to discover the corruptions of his heart, and to show how weak and faint his best principles and clearest convictions are in their actual exercise. And in this view, how vain is man, what a contradiction is a believer to himself! He is called a believer emphatically, because he cordially assents to the Word of God; but, alas, how often unworthy of the name! If I were to describe him from the Scripture character, I should say, he is one whose heart is athirst for God, for his glory, his image, his presence; his affections are fixed upon an unseen Saviour; his treasures, and consequently his thoughts, are on high, beyond the bounds of sense.

Having experienced much forgiveness, he is full of bowels of mercy to all around; and, having been often deceived by his own heart, he dares trust it no more, but lives by faith in the Son of God, for wisdom, righteousness, and sanctification, and derives from him grace for grace; sensible that, without him, he has not sufficiency even to think a good thought. In short, he is dead to the world, to sin, to self; but alive to God, and lively in his service. Prayer is his breath, the Word of God his food, and the ordinances more precious to him than the light of the sun. Such is a believer, in his judgment and prevailing desires.

But were I to describe him from experience, especially at some times, how different would the picture be. Though he knows that communion with God is his highest privilege, he too seldom finds it so; on the contrary, if duty, conscience, and necessity, did not compel, he would leave the throne of grace unvisited from day to day. He takes up the Bible, conscious that it is the fountain of life and true comfort; yet perhaps while he is making the reflection, he feels a secret distaste, which prompts him to lay it down, and give his preference to a newspaper. He needs not to be told of the vanity and uncertainty of all beneath the sun; and yet is almost as much elated or cast down by a trifle, as those who have their portion in this world. He believes that all things shall work together for his good, and that the most high God appoints, adjusts, and overrules all his concerns; yet he feels the risings of fear, anxiety, and displeasure, as though the contrary was true. He owns himself ignorant, and liable to be deceived by a thousand fallacies; yet is easily betrayed into positiveness and self-conceit. He feels himself an unprofitable, unfaithful, unthankful servant, and therefore blushes to harbour a thought of desiring the esteem and commendations of men, yet he cannot suppress it. Finally (for I must observe some bounds), on account of these and many other inconsistencies, he is struck dumb before the

Lord, stripped of every hope and plea, but what is provided in the free grace of God, and yet his heart is continually leaning and returning to a covenant of works.

Two questions naturally arise from such a view of ourselves. First: – How can these things be, or why are they permitted? Since the Lord hates sin, teaches his people to hate it and cry against it, and has promised to hear their prayers, how is it that they go thus burdened? Surely if he could not overrule evil for good, he would not then permit it to continue. By these exercises he teaches us more truly to know and feel the utter depravity and corruption of our whole nature, that we are indeed defiled in every part. His method of salvation is likewise hereby exceedingly endeared to us; we see that it is and must be of grace, wholly of grace; and that the Lord Jesus Christ, and his perfect righteousness, is and must be our all in all. His power, likewise, in maintaining his own work, notwithstanding our infirmities, temptations, and enemies, is hereby displayed in the clearest light – his strength is manifested in our weakness. Satan, likewise, is more remarkably disappointed and put to shame, when he finds bounds set to his rage and policy, beyond which he cannot pass; and that those in whom he finds so much to work upon, and over whom he so often prevails for a season, escape at last out of his hands. He casts them down, but they are raised again; he wounds them, but they are healed; he obtains his desire to sift them as wheat, but the prayer of their great Advocate prevails for the maintenance of their faith. Farther, by what believers feel in themselves they learn by degrees how to warn, pity, and bear with others. A soft, patient, and compassionate spirit, and a readiness and skill in comforting those who are cast down, is not perhaps attainable in any other way. And lastly, I believe nothing more habitually reconciles a child of God to the thought of death, than the wearisomeness of this warfare. Death is unwelcome to nature; but then, and not till then, the conflict will cease.

Then we shall sin no more. The flesh, with all its attendant evils, will be laid in the grave – then the soul, which has been partaker of a new and heavenly birth, shall be freed from every incumbrance, and stand perfect in the Redeemer's righteousness before God in glory.

But though these evils cannot be wholly removed, it is worth while to inquire, secondly: – How they may be mitigated. This we are encouraged to hope for. The Word of God directs and animates to a growth in grace. And though we can do nothing spiritually of ourselves, yet there is a part assigned us. We cannot conquer the obstacles in our way by our own strength, yet we can give way to them, and if we do, it is our sin, and will be our sorrow. The disputes concerning inherent power in the creature have been carried to inconvenient lengths; for my own part, I think it safe to use scriptural language. The apostles exhort us, to give all diligence to resist the devil, to purge ourselves to reading, meditation, and prayer, to watch, to put on the whole armour of God, and to abstain from all appearance of evil. Faithfulness to light received, and a sincere endeavour to conform to the means prescribed in the Word of God, with an humble application to the blood of sprinkling, and the promised Spirit will undoubtedly be answered by increasing measures of light, faith, strength, and comfort; and we shall know, if we follow on to know the Lord.

I need not tell your Lordship that I am an extempore writer. I dropt the consideration of whom I was addressing from the first paragraph; but I now return, and subscribe myself, with the greatest deference, &c.

Letter 3

My Lord, *April, 1770*

I have a desire to fill the paper, and must therefore betake myself to the expedient I lately mentioned. Glorious things are spoken of the city of God, or (as I suppose) the state of glory, in Revelation chapter 21 from verse 10. The description is doubtless mystical, and perhaps nothing short of a happy experience and participation will furnish an adequate exposition. One expression, in particular, has, I believe, puzzled wiser heads than mine to explain. The street of the city was pure gold, as it were transparent glass. The construction, likewise in the Greek is difficult. Some render it pure gold, transparent as glass: this is the sense but then it should be neuter. If our reading is right, we must understand it either to gold pure, bright and perspicuous as the finest transparent glass (for all glass is not transparent,) or else, as two distinct comparisons, splendid and durable as the purest gold, clear and transparent as the finest glass. In that happy world the beauties and advantages, which here are divided and incompatible, will unite and agree. Our glass is clear but brittle; our gold is shining and solid, but it is opaque, and discovers only a surface. And thus it is with our minds. The powers of the imagination are lively and extensive, but transient and uncertain. The powers of the understanding are more solid and regular, but at the same time more slow and limited, and confined to the outside properties of the few objects around us. But when we arrive within the veil, the perfections of the glass and the gold will be combined, and the imperfections of each will entirely cease. Then we shall know more than we can now imagine. The glass will be all gold. And then we shall apprehend truth in its relations and consequences; not (as at present) by that tedious and fallible process which we call reasoning, but by a single glance of thought, as the sight pierces in an instant through the largest transparent body. The gold will be all glass.

I do not offer this as the sense of the passage, but as a thought which once occurred to me while reading it. I daily groan under a desultory ungovernable imagination, and a palpable darkness of understanding, which greatly impede me in my attempts to contemplate the truths of God. Perhaps these complaints, in a greater or less degree, are common to all our fallen race, and exhibit mournful proofs that our nature is essentially depraved. The grace of God affords some assistance for correcting the wildness of the fancy, and enlarging the capacity of the mind; yet the cure at present is but palliative; but ere long it shall be perfect, and our complaints shall cease for ever. Now it costs us much pains to acquire a pittance of solid and useful knowledge; and the ideas we have collected are far from being at the disposal of judgment, and, like men in a crowd, are perpetually clashing and interfering with each other. But it will not be so, when we are completely freed from the effects of sin: confusion and darkness will not follow us into the world where light and order reign. Then, and not till then, our knowledge will be perfect, and our possession of it uninterrupted and secure.

Since the radical powers of the soul are thus enfeebled and disordered, it is not to be wondered at, that the best of men, and under their highest attainments, have found cause to make the acknowledgment of the apostle, 'When I would do good, evil is present with me.' But, blessed be God, though we must feel hourly cause for shame and humiliation for what we are in ourselves, we have cause to rejoice continually in Christ Jesus, who, as he is revealed unto us under the various names, character, relation, and offices, which he bears in the Scripture, holds out to our faith a balm for every wound, a cordial for every discouragement, and a sufficient answer to every objection which sin or Satan can suggest against our peace. If we are guilty, he is our Righteousness; if we are sick, he is our infallible Physician; if we are weak, helpless, and defenceless, he is the compassionate and faithful Shepherd who has taken charge of us, and will not suffer any thing to disappoint our hopes, or to separate us from his love. He knows our frame, he remembers that we are but dust, and has engaged to guide us by his counsel, support us by his power, and at length to receive us to his glory, that we may be with him for ever. – I am, with the greatest deference, &c.

Letter 4

My Lord, *February, 1772*

I have been sitting perhaps a quarter of an hour with my pen in my hand, and my finger upon my upper lip, contriving how I should begin my letter. A detail of the confused, incoherent thoughts which have successively passed through my mind, would have more than filled the sheet; but your Lordship's patience, and even your charity for the writer, would have been tried to the uttermost if I could have penned them all down. At length my suspense reminded me of the apostle's words (Gal. 5:17): 'Ye cannot do the things that ye would.' This is an humbling but a just account of a Christian's attainments in the present life, and is equally applicable to the strongest and to the weakest. The weakest need not say less – the strongest will hardly venture to say more. The Lord has given his people a desire and will aiming at great things; without this they would be unworthy of the name of Christians; but they cannot do as they would: their best desires are weak and ineffectual, not absolutely so (for he who works in them to will, enables them in a measure to do likewise,) but in comparison with the mark at which they aim. So that while they have great cause to be thankful for the desire he has given them, and for the degree in which it is answered, they have equal reason to be ashamed and abased under a sense of their continual defects, and the evil mixtures which taint and debase their best endeavours. It would be easy to make out a long list of particulars which a believer would do if he could, but in which, from first to last, he finds a mortifying inability. Permit me to mention a few, which I need not transcribe from books, for they are always present to my mind.

He would willingly enjoy God in prayer – he knows that prayer is his duty; but, in his judgment, he considers it likewise as his greatest honour and privilege. In this light he can recommend it to others, and can tell them of the wonderful condescension of the great God, who humbles himself to behold the things that are in heaven, that he should stoop so much lower, to afford his gracious ear to the supplications of sinful worms upon earth. He can bid them expect a pleasure in waiting upon the Lord, different in kind and greater in degree than all the world can afford. By prayer he can say, You have liberty to cast all your cares upon him that careth for you. By one hour's intimate access to the throne of grace, where the Lord causes his glory to pass before the soul that seeks him, you may acquire more true spiritual knowledge and comfort, than by a day or a week's converse with the best of men, or the most studious perusal of many folios. And in this light he would consider it, and improve it for himself. But, alas, how seldom can he do as he would. How often does he find this privilege a mere task, which he would be glad of a just cause to omit; and the chief pleasure he derives from the performance is to think that his task is finished: he has been drawing near to God with his lips while his heart was far from him. Surely this is not doing as he would when (to borrow the expression of an old woman here) he is dragged before God like a slave, and comes away like a thief.

The like may be said of reading the Scripture. He believes it to be the Word of God: he admires the wisdom and grace of the doctrines, the beauty of the precepts, the richness and suitableness of the promises; and therefore, with David, he accounts it preferable to thousands of gold and silver, and sweeter than honey or the honeycomb. Yet while he thus thinks of it, and desires that it may dwell in him richly, and be his meditation night and day, he cannot do as he would. It will require some resolution to persist in reading a portion of it every day; and even then his heart is often less engaged than when reading a pamphlet. Here again his privilege frequently dwindles into a task. His appetite is vitiated, so that he has but little relish for the food of his soul.

He would willingly have abiding, admiring thoughts of the personal love of the Lord Jesus Christ. Glad he is, indeed, of those occasions which recall the Saviour to his mind; and with this view, notwithstanding all discouragements, he perseveres in attempting to pray and read, and waits upon the ordinances. Yet he cannot do as he would. Whatever claims he may have to the exercise of gratitude and sensibility towards his fellow-creatures, he must confess himself mournfully ungrateful and insensible towards his best Friend and Benefactor. Ah, what trifles are capable of shutting him out of our thoughts, of whom we say, He is the Beloved of our souls, who loves us, and give himself for us, and whom we have deliberately chosen as our chief good and portion. What can make us amends for the loss we suffer here? Yet surely if we could, we would set him always before us; his love should be the delightful theme of our hearts. But though we aim at this good, evil is present with us; we find we are renewed but in part, and have still cause to plead the Lord's promise, to take away the heart of stone, and give us a heart of flesh.

He would willingly acquiesce in all the dispensations of

divine providence. He believes that all events are under the direction of infinite wisdom and goodness, and shall surely issue in the glory of God, and the good of those who fear him. He doubts not but the hairs of his head are all numbered, that the blessings of every kind which he possesses were bestowed upon him, and are preserved to him, by the bounty and special favour of the Lord whom he serves – that afflictions spring not out of the ground, but are fruits and tokens of divine love, no less than his comforts – that there is a reason, whenever for a season he is in heaviness. Of these principles he can no more doubt, than of what he sees with his eyes; and there are seasons when he thinks they will prove sufficient to reconcile him to the sharpest trials. But often when he aims to apply them in an hour of present distress, he cannot do what he would. He feels a law in his members warring against the law in his mind; so that, in defiance of the clearest convictions, seeing as though he perceived not, he is ready to complain, murmur, and despond. Alas, how vain is man in his best estate! How much weakness and inconsistency, even in those whose hearts are right with the Lord! and what reason have we to confess that we are unworthy, unprofitable servants!

It were easy to enlarge in this way, would paper and time permit. But blessed be God, we are not under the law, but under grace. And even these distressing effects of the remnants of indwelling sin are overruled for good. By these experiences the believer is weaned more from self, and taught more highly to prize and more absolutely to rely on him, who is appointed to us of God, Wisdom, Righteousness, Sanctification, and Redemption. The more vile we are in our own eyes, the more precious he will be to us; and a deep repeated sense of the evil in our hearts is necessary to preclude all boasting, and to make us willing to give the whole glory of our salvation where it is due. Again, a sense of these evils will (when hardly anything else can do it) reconcile us to the thoughts of death;

yes, make us desirous to depart, that we may sin no more, since we find depravity so deep rooted in our nature, that (like the leprous house) the whole fabric must be taken down before we can be freed from its defilement. Then, and not till then, we shall be able to do the thing that we would: when we see Jesus, we shall be transformed into his image, and have done with sin and sorrow for ever. I am with great deference, &c.

Letter 5

My Lord, *March, 1772*

I think my last letter turned upon the apostle's thought: 'Ye cannot do the things that ye would' (Gal. 5:17). In the parallel place there is another clause subjoined, 'The evil which I would not, that I do' (Rom. 7:19). This, added to the former, would complete the dark side of my experience. Permit me to tell your Lordship a little part (for some things must not, cannot be told), not of what I have read, but of what I have felt, in illustration of this passage.

I would not be the sport and prey of wild, vain, foolish, and worse imaginations; but this evil is present with me; my heart is like a highway, like a city without walls or gates. Nothing so false, so frivolous, so absurd, so impossible, or so horrid, but it can obtain access, and that at any time, or in any place: neither the study, the pulpit, nor even the Lord's table, exempt me from their intrusion. I sometimes compare my words to the treble of an instrument, which my thoughts accompany with a kind of bass, or rather anti-bass, in which every rule or harmony is broken, every possible combination of discord and confusion is introduced, utterly inconsistent with, and contradictory to, the intended melody. Ah, what music would my praying and preaching often make in the ears of the Lord of Hosts, if he listened to them as they are mine only! By men, the upper part only (if I may so speak) is heard; and small cause there is for self-congratulation, if they should happen to commend, when conscience tells me they would be struck with astonishment and abhorrence could they hear the whole.

But if this awful effect of heart depravity cannot be wholly avoided in the present state of human nature, yet at least I would not allow and indulge it; yet this I find I do. In defiance of my best judgment and best wishes, I find something within me, which cherishes and cleaves to those evils, from which I ought to start and flee, as I should if a toad or a serpent was put in my food or in my bed. Ah, how vile must the heart (at least my heart) be, that can hold a parley with such abominations, when I so well know their nature and their tendency. Surely he who finds himself capable of this, may, without the least affectation of humility (however fair his outward conduct appears) subscribe himself less, than the least of all saints, and of sinners the very chief.

I would not be influenced by a principle of self on any occasion; yet this evil I often do. I see the baseness and absurdity of such a conduct as clearly as I see the light of the day. I do not affect to be thought ten feet high, and I know that a desire of being thought wise or good is equally contrary to reason and truth. I should be grieved or angry if my fellow-creatures supposed I had such a desire; and, therefore, I fear the very principle of self, of which I complain, has a considerable share in prompting my desires to conceal it. The pride of others often offends me, and makes me studious to hide my own; because their good opinion of me depends much upon their not perceiving it. But the Lord knows how this dead fly taints and spoils my best services, and makes them no better than specious sins.

I would not indulge vain reasonings concerning the counsels, ways, and providences of God; yet I am prone to do it. That the Judge of all the earth will do right, is to me as evident and necessary as that two and two make four. I believe that he has a sovereign right to do what he will with his own, and that this sovereignty is but another name for the unlimited exercise of wisdom and goodness. But my reasonings are often such, as if I had never heard of these principles, or had formerly renounced them. I feel the workings of a presumptuous spirit, that would account of everything, and venture to dispute whatever it cannot comprehend. What an evil is this, for a potsherd of the earth to contend with its Maker! I do not act thus towards my fellow-creatures; I do not find fault with the decisions of a judge, or the dispositions of a general, because, though I know they are fallible, yet I suppose they are wiser in their respective departments than myself. But I am often ready to take this liberty when it is most unreasonable and inexcusable.

I would not cleave to a covenant of works: it should seem, from the foregoing particulars, and many others which I could mention, that I have reasons enough to deter me from this. Yet even this I do. Not but that I say, and I hope from my heart, Enter not into judgment with thy servant, O Lord; I embrace it as a faithful saying, and worthy of all acceptance, that Jesus Christ came into the world to save sinners; and it is the main pleasure and business of my life to set forth the necessity and all-sufficiency of the Mediator between God and man, and to make mention of his righteousness, even of his only. But here, as in everything else, I find a vast difference between my judgment and my experience. I am invited to take the water of life freely, yet often discouraged, because I have nothing wherewith to pay for it. If I am at times favoured with some liberty from the above mentioned evils, it rather gives me a more favourable opinion of myself, than increases my admiration of the Lord's goodness to so unworthy a creature; and when the returning tide of my corruptions convinces me that I am still the same, an unbelieving legal spirit would urge me to conclude that the Lord is changed: at least I feel a weariness of being beholden to him for such continued multiplied forgiveness; and I fear that some part of my striving against sin, and my desires after an increase of sanctification, arises from a secret wish that I might not be so absolutely and entirely indebted to him.

This, my Lord is only a faint sketch of my heart but it is taken from the life; it would require a volume rather than a letter to fill up the outlines. But I believe you will not regret that I choose to say no more upon such a subject. But though my disease is grievous, it is not desperate; I have a gracious and infallible Physician. I shall not die, but live, and declare the works of the Lord. – I remain, My Lord, &c.

Letter 6

My Lord, *April, 1772*

My two last letters turned upon a mournful subject, the depravity of the heart, which impedes us when we would do good, and pollutes our best intended services with evil. We have cause, upon this account, to go softly all our days; yet we need not sorrow as they who have no hope. The Lord has provided his people relief under those complaints, and teaches us to draw improvement from them. If the evils we feel were not capable of being overruled for good, he would not permit them to remain in us. This we may infer from his hatred of sin, and the love which he bears to his people.

As to the remedy, neither our state nor his honour are affected by the workings of indwelling sin, in the hearts of those whom he has taught to wrestle, strive, and mourn, on account of what they feel. Though sin wars, it shall not reign; and though it breaks our peace, it cannot separate from his love. Nor is it inconsistent with his holiness and perfection to manifest his favour to such poor defiled creatures, or to admit them to communion with himself; for they are not considered as in themselves, but as one with Jesus, to whom they have fled for refuge, and by whom they live a life of faith. They are accepted in the Beloved, they have an advocate with the Father, who once made an atonement for their sins, and ever lives to make intercession for their persons. Though they cannot fulfil the law, he has fulfilled it for them; though the obedience of the members is defiled and imperfect, the obedience of the Head is spotless and complete; and though there is much evil in them, there is something good, – the fruit of his own gracious Spirit. They act from a principle of love, they aim at no less than his glory, and their habitual desires are supremely fixed upon himself. There is a difference in kind between the feeblest efforts of faith in a real believer, while he is covered with shame at the thoughts of his miscarriages, and the highest and most specious attainments of those who are wise in their own eyes, and prudent in their own sight. Nor shall this conflict remain long, or the enemy finally prevail over them. They are supported by almighty power, and led on to certain victory. They shall not always be as they are now; yet a little while, and they shall be freed from this vile body, which, like the leprous house, is incurably contaminated, and must be entirely taken down. Then they shall see Jesus as he is, and be like him, and with him for ever.

The gracious purposes to which the Lord makes the sense and feeling of our depravity subservient, are manifold. Hereby his own power, wisdom, faithfulness, and love, are more signally displayed: his power in maintaining his own work in the midst of so much opposition, like a spark burning in the water, or a bush unconsumed in the flames: his wisdom in defeating and controlling all the devices which Satan, from his knowledge of the evil of our nature, is encouraged to practise against us. He has overthrown many a fair professor, and like Goliath, he challenges the whole army of Israel; yet he finds there are some against whom, though he thrusts sorely, he cannot prevail; notwithstanding any seeming advantage he gains at some seasons, they are still delivered, for the Lord is on their side. The unchangeableness of the Lord's love, and the riches of his mercy, are likewise more illustrated by the multiplied pardons he bestows upon his people, than if they needed no forgiveness at all.

Hereby the Lord Jesus Christ is more endeared to the soul; all boasting is effectually excluded, and the glory of a full and free salvation is ascribed to him alone. If a mariner is suprised by a storm, and after one night spent in jeopardy, is presently safe brought into port, though he may rejoice in his deliverance, it will not affect him so sensibly as if, after being tempest-tossed for a long season, and experiencing a great number and variety of hair-breadth escapes, he at last gains the desired haven. The righteous are said to be scarcely saved, not with respect to the certainty of the event, for the purpose of God in their favour cannot be disappointed, but in respect of their own apprehensions, and the great difficulties they are brought through. But when, after a long experience of their own deceitful hearts, after repeated proofs of their weakness, wilfulness, ingratitude, and insensibility, they find that none of these things can separate them from the love of God in Christ, Jesus becomes more and more precious to their souls. They love much, because much has been forgiven them. They dare not, they will not ascribe anything to themselves, but are glad to acknowledge that they must have perished (if possible) a thousand times over, if Jesus had not been their Saviour, their Shepherd, and their Shield. When they were wandering, he brought them back; when fallen, he raised them; when wounded, he healed them; when fainting, he revived them. By him out of weakness they have been made strong; he has taught their hands to war, and covered their heads in the day of battle. In a word, some of the clearest proofs they have had of his excellence, have been occasioned by the mortifying proofs they have had of their own vileness. They would not have known so much of him, if they had not known so much of themselves.

Farther, a spirit of humiliation, which is both the strength and beauty of our profession, is greatly promoted by our feeling, as well as reading, that when we would do good, evil is present with us. A broken and contrite spirit is pleasing to the Lord, – he has promised to dwell with those who have it; and experience shows that the exercise of all our graces is in proportion to the humbling sense we have of the depravity of our nature. But that we are so totally depraved is a truth which no one ever truly learned by being only told it. Indeed, if we could receive, and habitually maintain a right judgment of ourselves, by what is plainly declared in Scripture, it would probably save us many a mournful hour; but experience is the Lord's school, and they who are taught by him usually learn, that they have no wisdom by the mistakes they make, and that they have no strength by the slips and falls they meet with. Every day draws forth some new corruption which before was little observed, or at least discovers it in a stronger light than before. Thus by degrees they are weaned from leaning to any supposed wisdom, power, or goodness in themselves; they feel the truth of our Lord's words, 'Without me ye can do nothing'; and the necessity of crying with David, 'O lead me and guide me for thy name's sake.' It is chiefly by this frame of mind that one Christian is differenced from another; for though it is an inward feeling, it has very observable outward effects, which are expressively intimated (Ezek. 16:63), 'Thou shalt be dumb and not open thy mouth, in the day when I am pacified towards thee, saith the Lord God.' The knowledge of thy full and free forgiveness, of thy innumerable backslidings and transgressions, shall make thee ashamed, and silence the unruly workings of thine heart. Thou shalt open thy mouth in praise; but thou shalt no more boast in thyself, or censure others, or repine at my dispensations. In these respects we are exceedingly prone to speak unadvisedly with our lips. But a sense of great unworthiness and much forgiveness checks the evils. Whoever is truly humbled will not be easily angry, will not be positive and rash, will be compassionate and tender to the infirmities of his fellow-sinners, knowing that if there be a difference, it is grace that has made it, and that he has the seeds of every evil in his own heart. And under all trials and afflictions, he will look to the hand of the Lord, and lay his mouth in the dust, acknowledging that he suffers much less than his iniquities have deserved. These are some of the advantages and good fruits which the Lord enables us to obtain from that bitter root, indwelling sin. – I am, with great deference, &c.

Letter 7

My Lord, *September, 1772*

Weak, unskilful, and unfaithful as I am in practice, the Lord has been pleased to give me some idea of what a Christian ought to be, and of what is actually attainable in the present life, by those whom he enables earnestly to aspire towards the prize of their high calling. They who are versed in mechanics can, from a knowledge of the combined powers of a complicated machine, make an exact calculation of what it is able to perform, and what resistance it can counteract; but who can compute the possible effects of that combination of principles and motives revealed in the Gospel, upon a heart duly impressed with a sense of their importance and glory? When I was lately at Mr Cox's museum, while I was fixing my attention upon some curious movements, imagining that I saw the whole of the artist's design, the person who showed it touched a little spring, and suddenly a thousand new and unexpected motions took place, and the whole piece seemed animated from the top to the bottom. I should have formed but a very imperfect judgment of it, had I seen no more than what I saw at first. I thought it might in some measure illustrate the vast difference that is observable amongst professors, even amongst those who are, it is to be hoped, sincere. There are persons who appear to have a true knowledge (in part) of the nature of the Gospel religion, but seem not to be apprised of its properties, in their comprehension and extent. If they have attained to some hope of their acceptance, if they find at seasons some communion with God in the means of grace, if they are in a measure delivered from the prevailing and corrupt customs of the world, they seem to be satisfied, as if they were possessed of all. These are indeed great things. The profession of too many, whose sincerity charity would be unwilling to impeach, is greatly blemished, notwithstanding their hopes and their occasional comforts, by the breakings forth of unsanctified tempers, and the indulgence of vain hopes, anxious cares, and selfish pursuits. Far, very far, am I from that unscriptural sentiment of sinless perfection in fallen man. To those who have a due sense of the spirituality and ground of the divine precepts, and of what passes in their own hearts, there will never be wanting causes of humiliation and self-abasement on the account of sin; yet still there is a liberty and privilege attainable by the Gospel, beyond what is ordinarily thought of. Permit me to mention two or three particulars, in which those who have a holy ambition of aspiring to them shall not be altogether disappointed.

A delight in the Lord's all-sufficiency. To be satisfied in him as our present and eternal portion. This, in the sense in which I understand it, is not the effect of a present warm frame, but of a deeply rooted and abiding principle; the habitual exercise of which is to be estimated by the comparative indifference with which other things are regarded. The soul thus principled is not at leisure to take or to seek satisfaction in anything but what has a known subserviency to this leading taste. Either the Lord is present, and then he is to be rejoiced in; or else he is absent, and then he is to be sought and waited for. They are to be pitied, who, if they are at some times happy in the Lord, can at other times be happy without him, and rejoice in broken cisterns, when their spirits are at a distance from the fountain of living waters. I do not plead for an absolute indifference to temporal blessings; he gives us all things richly to enjoy; and a capacity of relishing them is his gift likewise; but then the consideration of his love in bestowing should exceedingly enhance the value and a regard to his will should regulate their use. Nor can they all supply the want of that which we can only receive immediately from himself. This principle likewise moderates that inordinate fear and sorrow to which we are liable upon the prospect or the occurrence of great trials, for which there is a sure support and resource provided in the all-sufficiency of infinite goodness and grace. What a privilege is this, to possess God in all things while we have them, and all things in God when they are taken from us!

An acquiescence in the Lord's will, founded in a persuasion of his wisdom, holiness, sovereignty, and goodness is one of the greatest privileges and brightest ornaments of our profession. So far as we attain to this, we are secure from disappointment. Our own, limited views and short-sighted purposes and desires may be, and will be, often overruled; but then our main and leading desire, that the will of the Lord may be done, must be accomplished. How highly does it become us, both as creatures and as sinners, to submit to the appointments of our Maker, and how necessary is it to our peace! This great attainment is too often unthought of, and overlooked; we are prone to fix our attention upon the second causes and immediate instruments of events; forgetting that whatever befalls us is according to his purpose, and therefore must be right and seasonable in itself, and shall in the issue be productive of good. From hence arise impatience, resentment, and secret repinings, which are not only sinful but tormenting. Whereas, if all things are in his hand; if the very hairs of our head are numbered; if every event, great and small, is under the direction of his providence and purpose; and if he has a wise, holy, and gracious end in view, to which everything that happens is subordinate and subservient, then we have nothing to do, but with patience and humility to follow as he leads, and then cheerfully to expect a happy issue. The path of present duty is marked out, and the concerns of the next day and every succeeding hour are in his hands. How happy are they who can resign all to him, see his hand in every dispensation, and believe that he chooses better for them than they possibly could for themselves!

O blessed man that thus fears the Lord, that delights in his Word, and derives his principles, motives, maxims, and consolations, from that unfailing source of light and strength! He shall be like a tree planted by the rivers of water, whose leaf is always green, and fruit abundant. The wisdom that is above shall direct his plans, inspire his counsels; and the power of God shall guard him on every side, and prepare his way through every difficulty: he shall see mountains sink into plains, and streams spring up in the dry wilderness. The Lord's enemies will be his; and they may be permitted to fight against him, but they shall not prevail, for the Lord is with him to deliver him. The conduct of such a one, though in a narrow and retired sphere of life, is of more real excellence and importance, than the most splendid actions of kings and conquerors, which fill the annals of history (Prov. 16:32). And if the God whom he serves is pleased to place him in a more public light, his labours and cares will be amply compensated, by the superior opportunities afforded him, of manifesting the power and reality of true religion, and promoting the good of mankind.

I hope I may say, that I desire to be thus entirely given up to the Lord; I am sure I must say, that what I have written is far from being my actual experience. Alas, I might be condemned out of my own mouth, were the Lord strict to mark what is amiss. But, O the comfort, we are not under the law but under grace. The Gospel is a dispensation for sinners, and we have an Advocate with the Father. There is the unshaken ground of hope: a reconciled Father, a prevailing Advocate, a powerful Shepherd, a compassionate Friend, a Saviour, who is able and willing to save to the uttermost. He knows our frame; he remembers that we are but dust, and has opened for us a new and blood-besprinkled way of access to the throne of grace that we may obtain mercy, and find grace to help in every time of need. – I am, &c.

Letter 8

My Lord, *December, 1772*

I lately employed some of my leisure hours (which when I am not indolent, are but few) in reading the Memoirs of the Duke of Sully, which occasionally came in my way. It afforded me matter for a variety of reflections. I pity the Duke of Sully, whose attachment to the name of a Protestant seems to have been little more than a point of honour, who drew all his resources from himself, and whose chief aim seems to have been to approve himself faithfully to an earthly master. He acted as well as could be expected from natural principles; and the Lord, who employed him as an instrument of his providence, rewarded his fidelity with success, honour, and riches; a reward which, though in itself a poor one, is suited to the desires of men who place their happiness in worldly things, and is so far a compensation of their services. It is given to your Lordship to act from nobler principles, and with more enlarged views. You serve a Master of whose favour, protection, and assistance, you cannot be deprived, who will not overlook or misconstrue the smallest service you attempt for him, who will listen to no insinuations against you, who is always near to comfort, direct, and strengthen you, and who is preparing for you such honours and blessings as he only can give, an inheritance (the reverse of all earthly good) incorruptible, undefiled, unfading. Thus animated and thus supported, assisted likewise by the prayers of thousands, may we not warrantably hope that your Lordship will be an instrument of great good, and that both church and state will be benefitted by your example, counsels, and care?

In another view, the Duke of Sully's history exhibits a comment upon the Psalmist's words: 'Surely man in his best estate is altogether vanity.' View him in one light, he seems to have possessed all that the most aspiring mind could aim at – the favour and confidence of his prince, accumulated wealth, great honours, and such power by his offices and influence with the kind, that he could almost do what he pleased. Yet he had so much to suffer from the fatigues and difficulties of his station, and the cabals and malice of his enemies, that in the midst of all his grandeur a dispassionate mind would rather pity than envy him. And how suddenly were his schemes broken by the death of the kind. Then he lost his friend, his protector, his influence. The remainder of his days were embittered by many inquietudes; he lived indeed (if that could afford any consolation) in much state and pageantry afterwards; but after having toiled through more than fourscore years, died at last almost of a broken heart from domestic uneasiness. And is this all that the world can do for those who are accounted most successful! Alas! 'Too low they build who build below the skies.' And what a picture of the instability of human things have we in his master, Henry! Admired, beloved, dreaded full of vast designs, fondly supposing himself born to be the arbiter of Europe, in an awful moment, and in the midst of his friends, suddenly struck from the height of his grandeur, and snatched into the invisible, unchangeable world. In that moment all his thoughts perished.

How unspeakably awful such a transition! How remarkable were his own forebodings of the approaching hour! O Lord, how dost thou pour contempt upon princes, and teach us that the great and the mean are equally in thy hands, and at thy disposal, as clay in the hands of the potter! Poor king, while he expected obedience to his own commands, he lived in habitual defiance of the commands of God. Men may respect his memory for his sincerity, benevolence, and other amiable qualities; but besides that he was engrossed by a round of sensual pleasures, (when business of state did not interfere,) his life was stained with adultery. Happy if, in the hours he spent in retirement, when the pre-intimation of his death hung heavy upon his mind, the Lord humbled and softened his heart, and gave him repentance unto life! I wish the history afforded a proof of this. However, in his death, we see an affecting proof that no human dignity or power can ward off the stroke of the Almighty, who, by such sudden and unexpected dispensations, often shows himself terrible to the princes and great men of the earth. O that they could see his hand, and wisely consider his doing in them!

But happy is the man who fears the Lord, and delights in his commandments; who sets God always before him, and acts under the constraining influence of redeeming love. He is the real friend and the best champion of his country, who makes not the vague notions of human wisdom and honour, but the precepts and example of the blessed Jesus the model and the motive of his conduct. He inculcates (as occasion offers) the great truths of religion in his conversation, and demonstrates them by his practice; yet the best part of his life is known only to God and himself. His time is divided between serving his country in public, and wrestling for it in private. Nor shall his labours or his prayers be lost. Either he shall have the desire of his heart, and shall see the religion and the liberty he so highly values transmitted to posterity; or if he should live when wrath is decreed, and there is no remedy, the promise and the providence of God shall seal him as the peculiar charge of angels, in the midst of public calamity. And when all things are involved in confusion, when the hearts of the wicked shall shake like the leaves of the forest, he shall be kept in perfect peace, trusting in the Lord. – I am, with the greatest deference, &c.

Letter 9

My Lord, *March, 1773*

Usually for some days before I purpose writing to your Lordship, my thoughts are upon the stretch for a subject; I do not mean all day long, but it is so more or less: but I might as well spare my inquiries, I can come to no determination, and for the most part begin to write at an absolute uncertainty how I am to proceed. Since I cannot premeditate, my heart prays that it may be given me in the same hour what I shall offer. A simple dependence upon the teaching and influence of the good Spirit of God, so as not to supersede the use of appointed means, would, if it could be uniformly maintained, make every part of duty easy and successful. It would free us from much solicitude, and prevent many mistakes. Methinks I have a subject in view already, a subject of great importance to myself, and which, perhaps, will not be displeasing to your Lordship; how to walk with God in the daily occurrences of life, so as to do everything for his sake and by his strength.

When we are justified by faith and accepted in the Beloved, we become heirs of everlasting life; but we cannot know the full value of our privileges till we enter upon the state of glory. For this, most who are converted have to wait some time after they are partakers of grace. Though the Lord loves them, hates sin, and teaches them to hate it, he appoints them to remain a while in a sinful world, and to groan under the burden of a depraved nature. He could put them in immediate possession of the heaven but he does not. He has a service for them here, an honour which is worth all they can suffer, and for which eternity will not afford an opportunity, namely, to be instruments of promoting his designs, and manifesting his grace in the world. Strictly speaking, this is the whole of our business here, the only reason why life is prolonged, or for which it is truly desirable, that we may fill up our connections and situations, improve our comforts and our crosses, in such a manner as that God may be glorified in us and by us. And he is a bountiful Master and a kind Father, he is pleased to afford a variety of temporal blessings, which sweeten our service, and, as coming from his hand, are very valuable, but are by no means worth living for, considered in themselves, as they can neither satisfy our desires, preserve us from trouble, nor support us under it. That light of God's countenance which can pervade the walls and dissipate the gloom of a dungeon, is unspeakably preferable to all that can be enjoyed in a palace without it. The true end of life is to live not to ourselves, but to him who died for us; and while we devote ourselves to his service upon earth, to rejoice in the prospect of being happy with him for ever in heaven. These things are generally known and acknowledged by professors; but they are a favoured few who act consistently with their avowed principles; who honestly, diligently, and without reserve, endeavour to make the most of their talents and strength in promoting the Lord's service, and allow themselves in no views or designs but what are plainly subordinate and subservient to it. Yea, I believe the best of the Lord's servants see cause enough to confess, that they are not only unprofitable in comparison of what they wish to be, but, in many instances, unfaithful likewise. They find so many snares, hindrances, and temptations, arising from without, and so much embarrassment from that which dwells within, that they have more cause for humiliation than self-complacence, when they seem most earnest and most useful. However, we have no scriptural evidence that we serve the Lord at all, any farther than we find an habitual desire and aim to serve him wholly. He is gracious to our imperfections and weakness; yet he requires all the heart, and will not be served by halves, nor accept what is performed by a divided spirit. I lately met with some profane scoffs of Voltaire upon the sentiment of doing all to the glory of God (such as might be expected from such a man); however, this is the true alchemy which turns everything into gold, and ennobles the common actions of life into acts of religion (1 Cor. 10:31). Nor is there a grain of real goodness in the most specious actions which are performed without a reference to God's glory. This the world cannot understand; but it will appear highly reasonable to those who take their ideas of God from the Scripture, and who have felt the necessity, and found the benefits of redemption. We are debtors many ways. The Lord has a right to us by creation, by redemption, by conquest, when he freed us from Satan's power, and took possession of our hearts by his grace; and, lastly, by our own voluntary surrender in the day when he enabled us to fix our choice on himself, as our Lord and our portion. Then we felt the force of our obligations, we saw the beauty and honour of his service, and that nothing was worthy to stand in the least degree of competition with it. This is always equally true, though our perceptions of it are not always equally strong. But where it has been once really known, it cannot be wholly forgotten, or cease to be the governing principle of life; and the Lord has promised to revive the impression in those who wait upon him, and thereby they renew their strength. For, in proportion as we feel by what ties we are his, we shall embrace his service as perfect freedom.

Again, when the eye is thus single, the whole body will be full of light. The principle of acting simply for God, will, in general, make the path of duty plain, solve a thousand otherwise dubious questions, lead to the most proper and obvious means, and preclude that painful anxiety about events, which upon no other plan can be avoided. The love of God is the best casuist; especially as it leads us to a careful attendance to his precepts, a reliance on his promises, and a submission to his will. Most of our perplexities arise from an undue, though perhaps unperceived, attachment to self. Either we have some scheme of our own too closely connected with our general view of serving the Lord, or lay some stress upon our own management, which, though we suspect it may possibly fail us, we cannot entirely help trusting to. In these respects the Lord permits his servants occasionally to feel their own weakness; but if they are sincerely devoted to him, he will teach them to profit by it, and bring them by degrees to a simplicity of dependence, as well as of intention. Then all things are easy. Acting from love, and walking by faith, they can neither be disappointed nor discouraged. Duty is their part, care is his; and they are enabled to cast it upon him. They know that, when their expedients seem to fail, he is still all-sufficient. They know that, being engaged in his cause, they cannot miscarry; and that though, in some things, they may seem to fall short of success, they are sure of meeting acceptance, and that he will estimate their services, not by their actual effects, but according to the gracious principle and desire he has put into their hearts (2 Chron. 6:7,8). – I am, with the greatest respect, &c.

Letter 10

My Lord, *April, 1773*

For five or six weeks past I have been a good deal indisposed. The ground of my complaint was a cold, attended with a slight fever, and for some time with a cough, which made me feel some inconvenience in preaching; to this succeeded a deafness so great as to cut me off from conversation; for I could not hear the sound of a voice, unless it was spoke loud in my ear. But the Lord has mercifully removed the fever and cough, opened my ears, and I am now nearly as well as usual. I had cause to be thankful, especially for two things under this dispensation: First, that I was enabled, though sometimes with a little difficulty, to go on with my public work. It is a singular favour I have to acknowledge, that for the space of almost nine years since I have been in the ministry, our Sabbath and weekly opportunities have not been once suspended; whereas I have seen many of the Lord's servants laid by for a considerable space within that time. My other great mercy was, that the Lord was pleased to preserve me in a peaceful resigned frame: so that when I was deaf, and could not be certain that I should recover my hearing any more, I was in general as cheerful and easy as at other times.

This was the effect of his goodness: for though I know enough of his sovereignty, wisdom, and faithfulness, of his right to do what he pleases, and the certainty that he does all things well, to furnish me with arguments enough to prove that submission to his will is our absolute duty; yet I am sensible, that when the trial actually comes, notwithstanding all the advice I may have offered to others, I should myself toss like a wild bull in a net; rebel and repine; forget that I am a sinner, and that he is sovereign: this I say would always and invariably be the case, unless he was graciously pleased to fulfil his word, that strength shall be according to the day. I hope my deafness has been instructive to me. The exercise of our senses is so easily and constantly performed, that it seems a thing of course; but I was then reminded how precarious the tenure is by which we hold those blessings which seem most our own, and which are most immediately necessary to the comfortable enjoyment of life. Outward senses, mental faculties, health of body, and peace of mind, are extremely valuable; but the continuance of them for a single moment depends upon him, who, if he opens, none can shut, and when he shuts, none can open. A minute is more than sufficient to deprive us of what we hold most dear, or to prevent us from deriving the least comfort from it if it is not taken away. I am not presuming to give your Lordship information, but only mentioning the thoughts that were much upon my mind while I was incapable of conversation. These are indeed plain and obvious truths, which I have long acknowledged as indisputable; but I have reason to be thankful when the Lord impresses them with fresh power upon my heart, even though he sees fit to do it by the medium of afflictions. I have seen of late something of the weight and importance of that admonition (Jer. 9:23,24) a passage which, though addressed to the wise, the mighty, and the rich, is of universal application; for self, unless corrected and mortified by grace, will find something whereof to glory, in the meanest characters and the lowest situation. And indeed, when things come to be weighed in the balance of the sanctuary, the lunatics in Bedlam, some of whom glory in their straw or their chains, as marks of splendour, or ensigns of royalty, have as much reason on their side, as any persons upon earth who glory in themselves. This alone is the proper ground of glory and joy, if we know the Lord. Then all is safe at present, and all will be happy for ever. Then, whatever changes may affect our temporal concernments, our best interests and hopes are secured beyond the reach of change: and whatever we may lose or suffer during this little span of time, will be abundantly compensated in that glorious state of eternity which is just at hand. – I am, &c.

Letter 11

My Lord, *June, 1773*

My old cast-off acquaintance, Horace, caught my eye this morning. I opened it at Section 3, p 29. Did I not know the proposal to be utterly impracticable, how gladly should I imitate it, and send your Lordship, in honest prose, if not in elegant verse, an invitation. But I must content myself with the idea of the pleasure it would give me to sit with you half a day under my favourite great tree, and converse with you, not concerning the comparatively petty affairs of human governments, but of the things pertaining to the kingdom of God. How many delightful subjects would suggest themselves in a free and retired conversation! The excellency of our King, the permanency and glory of his kingdom, the beauty of his administration, the privileges of his subjects, the review of what he has prepared for us in future: – and if, while we were conversing, he should be pleased to join us (as he did the disciples when walking to Emmaus), how would our hearts burn within us! Indeed, whether we are alone or in company, the most interesting topics strike us but faintly, unless he is pleased to afford his gracious influence; but when he is present, light, love, liberty, and joy, spring up in the hearts that know him.

All that is left for me is to use the liberty you allow me of offering a few hints upon these subjects by letter, not because you know them not, but because you love them. The hour is coming when all impediments shall be removed. All distinctions shall cease that are founded upon sublunary things, and the earth and all its works shall be burnt up. Glorious day! May our souls be filled with the thought, and learn to estimate all things around us now, by the view in which they will appear to us then! Then it will be of small moment who was the prince, and who was the beggar, in this life; but who in their several situations sought, and loved, and feared, and honoured the Lord. Alas, how many of the kings of the earth, and the rich men, and the chief captains, and the mighty men, will then say (in vain) to the mountains and the rocks, fall on us, and hide us! In this world they are for the most part too busy to regard the commands of God, or too happy to seek his favour; they have their good things here; they pleased themselves for a while, and in a moment they go down to the grave: in that moment their thoughts perish, their schemes are left unfinished, they are torn from their possessions, and enter upon a new, an untried, an unchangeable, a never-ending state of existence. Alas, is this all the world can afford! I congratulate you, my Lord, not because God has appointed you to appear in an elevated rank (this, abstracted from the opportunity it affords you of greater usefulness, would perhaps be a more proper subject of condolence), but that he has admitted you to those honours and privileges which come from him only, and which so few, in the superior ranks of life, think worthy of their attention. I doubt not but you are often affected with a sense of this distinguishing mercy. But though we know that we are debtors, great debtors to the grace of God, which alone has made us to differ, we know it but imperfectly at present. It doth not yet appear what we shall be, nor can we form a just conception of the misery from which we are redeemed, much less of the price paid for our redemption. How little do we know of the Redeemer's dignity, and of the unutterable distress he endured when his soul was made an offering for sin, and it pleased the Father to bruise him, that by his stripes we might be healed. These things will strike us quite in another manner when we view them in the light of eternity. Then – to return to the thought from which I have rambled – then and there I trust we shall meet to the highest advantage, and spend an everlasting day together in happiness and praise. With this thought I endeavour to comfort myself under the regret I sometimes feel that I can have so little fellowship with you in this life.

May the cheering contemplation of the hope set before us support and animate us to improve the interval, and fill us with an holy ambition of shining as lights in the world, to the praise and glory of his grace, who has called us out of darkness! Encompassed as we are with snares, temptations, and infirmities, it is possible (by his promised assistance) to live in some good measure above the world while we are in it; above the influence of its cares, its smiles, or its frowns. Our conversation, our citizenship, is in heaven. We are not at home, but only resident here for a season, to fulfil an appointed service; and the Lord, whom we serve, has encouraged us to hope that he will guide us by his wisdom, strengthen us by his power, and comfort us with the light of his countenance, which is better than life. Every blessing we receive from him is a token of his favour, and a pledge of that far more exceeding and eternal weight of glory which he has reserved for us. O, to hear him say at last: 'Well done good and faithful servant, enter thou into the joy of the Lord!' will be a rich amends for all that we can lose, suffer, or forbear, for his sake. – I subscribe myself, with great sincerity, &c.

Letter 12

My Lord, *February, 1774*

The first line of Horace's epistle to Augustus, when

rightly applied, suggests a grand and cheering idea. As addressed by the poet, nothing can be more blasphemous, idolatrous, and absurd; but with what comfort and propriety may a Christian look up to him to whom all power is committed in heaven and earth, and say: 'Surely a more weighty and comprehensive sentence never dropped from an uninspired pen.' And how beautifully and expressively is it closed by the word 'solus'! The government is upon his shoulders; and though he is concealed by a veil of second causes from common eyes, so that they can perceive only the means, instruments, and contingencies by which he works, and therefore think he does nothing; yet, in reality, he does all, according to his own counsel and pleasure, in the armies of heaven, and among the inhabitants of the earth.

If we consider the heavens, the work of his fingers, the moon and the stars, which he has ordained; if we call in the assistance of astronomers and glasses, to help us in forming a conception of the number, distances, magnitude, and motions of the heavenly bodies; the more we search, the more we shall be confirmed, that these are but a portion of his ways. But he calls them all by their names, upholds them by his power, and without his continual energy they would rush into confusion, or sink into nothing. If we speak of intelligences, he is the life, the joy, the sun of all that are capable of happiness. Whatever may be signified by the thrones, principalities and powers in the world of light, they are all dependent upon his power, and obedient to his command; it is equally true of angels as of men, that without him they can do nothing. The powers of darkness are likewise under his subjection and control. Though but little is said of them in Scripture, we read enough to assure us that their number must be immensely great, and that their strength, subtlety, and malice, are such as we may tremble to think of them as our enemies, and probably should, but for our strange insensibility to whatever does not fall under the cognizance of our outward senses. But he holds them all in a chain, so that they can do or attempt nothing but by his permission; and whatever he permits them to do (though they mean nothing less,) has its appointed subserviency in accomplishing his designs.

But to come nearer home, and to speak of what seems more suited to our scanty apprehensions – still we may be lost in wonder. Before this blessed and only Potentate, all the nations of the earth are but as the dust upon the balance, and the small drop of a bucket, and might be thought (if compared with the immensity of his works) scarcely worthy of his notice; yet here he presides, pervades, provides, protects, and rules. In him his creatures live, move, and have their being; from him is their food and preservation. The eyes of all are upon him; what he gives they gather, and can gather no more; and at his word they sink into the dust. There is not a worm that crawls upon the ground, nor a flower that grows in the pathless wilderness, nor a shell upon the sea-shore, but bears the impress of his wisdom, power, and goodness. With respect to men, he reigns with uncontrolled dominion over every kingdom, family, and individual. Here we may be astonished at his wisdom, in employing free agents, the greater part of whom are his enemies, to accomplish his purposes. But, however reluctant, they all serve him. His patience, likewise, is wonderful. Multitudes, yea, nearly our whole species, spend the life and strength which he affords them, and abuse all the bounties he heaps upon them, in the say of sin. His commands are disregarded, his name blasphemed, his mercy disdained, his power defied; yet still he spares. It is an eminent part of his government to restrain the depravity of human nature, and in various ways to check its effects, which, if left to itself, without his providential control, would presently make earth the very image of hell. For the vilest of men are not suffered to perpetrate a thousandth part of the evils which their hearts would prompt them to. The earth, though lying in the wicked one, is filled with the goodness of the Lord. He preserveth man and beast, sustains the young lion in the forest, feeds the birds of the air, which have neither store-house nor barn, and adorns the insects and the flowers of the field with a beauty and elegance beyond all that can be found in the courts of kings.

Still more wonderful is his administration in his kingdom of grace. He is present with all his creatures, but in a peculiar manner with his own people. Each of these are monuments of a more illustrious display of power, than that which spread abroad the heavens like a curtain, and laid the foundation of the earth; for he finds them all in a state of rebellion and enmity and makes them a willing people; and from the moment he reveals his love to them, he espouses their cause, and takes all their concerns into his own hands. He is near and attentive to every one of them, as if there was only that one. This high and lofty One, who inhabits eternity, before whom the angels veil their faces, condescends to hold communion with those whom men despise. He sees not as man seeth – rides on a cloud disdainful of a sultan or a czar, to manifest himself to an humble soul in a mud-walled cottage. He comforts them when in trouble, strengthens them when weak, makes their beds in sickness, revives them when fainting, upholds them when falling, and so seasonably and effectually manages for them, that, though they are persecuted and tempted, though their enemies are many and mighty, nothing that they feel or fear is able to separate them from his love.

And all this he does 'solus'. All the abilities, powers, and instincts, that are found amongst creatures, are emanations from his fulness. All changes, successes, disappointments – all that is memorable in the annals of history, all the risings and falls of empires, all the turns in human life, take place according to his plan. In vain men contrive and combine to accomplish their own counsels, unless they are parts of his counsel likewise; the efforts of their utmost strength and wisdom are crossed and reversed by the feeblest and most unthought-of circumstances. But when he has a work to accomplish, and his time is come, however inadequate and weak the means he employs may seem to a carnal eye, the success is infallibly secured; for all things serve him, and are in his hands as clay in the hands of the potter. Great and marvellous are thy works, Lord God Almighty, just and true are thy ways, thou King of saints.

This is the God whom we adore. This is he who invites us to lean upon his almighty arm, and promises to guide us with his unerring eye. He says to you, my Lord, and even to me: 'Fear not, I am with thee; be not dismayed, I am thy God; I will strengthen thee, yea, I will help thee, yea I will uphold thee with the right hand of my righteousness.' Therefore, while in the path of duty, and following his call, we may cheerfully pass on regardless of apparent difficulties; for the Lord, whose we are, and who has taught us to make his glory our highest end, will go before us, and at his word crooked things become straight, light shines out of darkness, and mountains sink into plains. Faith may and must be exercised, experience must and will confirm what this Word declares, that the heart is deceitful, and that man in his best estate is vanity. But his promises to them that fear him shall be confirmed likewise, and they shall find him, in all situations, a sun, a shield, and an exceeding great reward.

I have lost another of my people; a mother in our Israel; a person of much experience, eminent grace, wisdom, and usefulness. She walked with God forty years; she was one of the Lord's poor; but her poverty was decent, sanctified, and honourable; she lived respected, and her death is considered as a public loss. It is a great loss to me; I shall miss her advice and example, by which I have been often edified and animated. But Jesus still loves. Almost her last words were, The Lord is my portion, saith my soul. – I am, &c.

Letter 13

My Lord, *March 10, 1774*

For about six weeks past I have had occasion to spend several hours of almost every day with the sick and the dying. These scenes are to a minister like walking the hospitals to a young surgeon. The various cases which occur, exemplify, illustrate, and explain, with a commanding energy, many truths, which may be learned indeed at home, but cannot be so well understood, nor their force so sensibly felt, without the advantage of experience and observation. As physicians, besides that competent general knowledge of their profession which should be common to them all, have usually their several favourite branches of study, some applying themselves more to botany, others to chemistry, others to anatomy; so ministers, as their inclinations and gifts differ, are led more closely to consider some particular branch of the system of divine truth. Some are directed to state and defend the doctrines of the Gospel; some have a talent for elucidating difficult texts of Scripture; some have a turn of explaining the prophetical parts, and so of the rest. For myself, if it be lawful to speak of myself, and so far as I can judge, anatomy is my favourite branch; I mean the study of the human heart, with its working and counterworkings, as it is differently affected in a state of nature or of grace, in the different seasons of prosperity, adversity, conviction, temptation, sickness, and the approach of death. The Lord, by sending me hither, provided me a good school for these purposes. I know not where I could have had a better, or affording a greater variety of characters in proportion to the number of people; and as they are mostly a poor people, and strangers to that address which is the result of education and converse with the world, there is a simplicity in what they say or do, which gives me a peculiar advantage in judging of their cases.

But I was about to speak of death. Though the grand evidence of those truths upon which our hopes are built arises from the authority of God speaking them in his Word, and revealing them by his Spirit, to the awakened heart (for till the heart is awakened it is incapable of receiving this evidence); yet some of these truths are so mysterious, so utterly repugnant to the judgment of depraved nature, that, through the remaining influence of unbelief and vain reasoning, the temptations of Satan and the subtle arguments with which some men reputed wise attack the foundations of our faith, the minds even of believers are sometimes capable of being shaken.

I know no better corroborating evidence for the relief of the mind under such assaults than the testimony of dying persons, especially of such as have lived out of the noise of controversy, and who perhaps never heard a syllable of what has been started in these evil days against the Deity of Christ, his atonement, and other important articles. Permit me, my Lord, to relate, upon this occasion, some things which exceedingly struck me in the conversation I had with a young woman whom I visited in her last illness about two years ago. She was a sober, prudent person, of plain sense, could read her Bible, but had read little beside: her knowledge of the world was nearly confined to the parish; for I suppose she was seldom, if ever, twelve miles from home in her life. She had known the Gospel about seven years before the Lord visited her with a lingering consumption, which at length removed her to a better world. A few days before her death, I had been praying by her bed-side, and in my prayer I thanked the Lord, that he gave her now to see that she had not followed cunningly-devised fables. When I had finished, she repeated that word. 'No', she said, 'not cunningly-devised fables; these are realities indeed; I feel their truth; I feel their comfort. O tell my friends, tell my acquaintances, tell inquiring souls, tell poor sinners, tell all the daughters of Jerusalem (alluding to Solomon's Song, 5:16, from which she had just before desired me to preach at her funeral), what Jesus has done for my soul. Tell them that now in the time of need I find him my beloved and my friend, and as such I commend him to them.' She then fixed her eyes steadfastly upon me, and proceeded, as well as I can recollect, as follows:– 'Sir, you are highly favoured in being called to preach the Gospel. I have often heard you with pleasure; but give me leave to tell you, that I now see all you have said, or can say, is comparatively but little. Nor, till you come into my situation, and have death and eternity full in your view, will it be possible for you to conceive the vast weight and importance of the truths you declare. O, Sir, it is a serious thing to die; no words can express what is needful to support the soul in the solemnity of a dying hour.'

I believe it was the next day when I visited her again. After some discourse as usual, she said, with a remarkable vehemence of speech, 'Are you sure I cannot be mistaken?' I answered without hesitation, 'Yes, I am sure; I am not afraid to say, my soul for yours that you are right.' She paused a little, and then replied, 'You say true; I know I am right. I feel that my hope is fixed upon the Rock of Ages; I know in whom I have believed. Yet if you could see with my eyes you would not wonder at my question. But the approach of death presents a prospect, which is till then hidden from us, and which cannot be described.' She said much more to the same purpose; and in all she spoke there was a dignity, weight, and evidence, which I suppose few professors of divinity, when lecturing from the chair, have at any time equalled. We may well say with Elihu, 'Who teacheth like him?' Many instances of the like kind I have met with here. I have a poor girl near me who looks like an idiot, and her natural capacity is indeed very small; but the Lord has been pleased to make her acquainted alternately with great temptations and proportionably great discoveries of his love and truth. Sometimes, when her heart is enlarged, I listen to her with astonishment.

But I am rambling again. My attendance upon the sick is not always equally comfortable; but could I learn aright, it may be equally instructive. Some confirm the preciousness of a Saviour to me, by the cheerfulness with which, through faith in his name, they meet the king of terrors. Others no less confirm it by the terror and reluctance they discover when they find they must die; for though there are too many who sadly slight the blessed Gospel while they are in health, yet in this place most are too far enlightened to be quite thoughtless about their souls, if they retain their senses in their last illness. Then, like the foolish virgins, they say: 'Give us of your oil': then they are willing that ministers and professors should pray with them, and speak to them. Through the Lord's goodness, several whom I have visited in these circumstances have afforded me good hope; they have been savingly changed by his blessing upon what has passed at the eleventh hour. I have seen a marvellous and blessed change take place in their language, views, and tempers, in a few days. I now visit a young person, who is cut short in her nineteenth year by a consumption, and I think cannot live many days. I found her very ignorant and insensible, and she remained so a good while; but of late I hope her heart is touched. She feels her lost state, she seems to have some right desires, she begins to pray, and in such a manner as I cannot but hope the Lord is teaching her, and will reveal himself to her before she departs. But it is sometimes otherwise. I saw a young woman die last week; I had been often with her; but the night she was removed she could only say: 'Oh! I cannot live, I cannot live!' She repeated this mournful complaint as long as she could speak; for as the vital powers were more oppressed, her voice was changed into groans; her groans grew fainter and fainter, and in about a quarter of an hour after she had done speaking, she expired. 'Poor thing,' I thought, as I stood by her bed-side, 'if you were a duchess in this situation, what could the world do for you now!' I thought likewise how many things are there that now give us pleasure or pain, and assume a mighty importance in our view, which, in a dying hour, will be no more to us than the clouds which fly unnoticed over our heads. Then the truth of our Lord's aphorism will be seen, felt, and acknowledged, – 'One thing is needful'.

Your Lordship allows me to send unpremeditated letters. I need not assure you that is one. – I am, &c.

Letter 14

My Lord, *March 24, 1774*

What a mercy is it to be separated in spirit, conversation, and interest, from the world that knows not God, where all are alike by nature! Grace makes a happy and unspeakable difference. Believers were once under the same influence of that spirit who still worketh in the children of disobedience, pursuing different paths, but all equally remote from truth and peace, – some hatching cocatrice eggs, others weaving spiders' webs. These two general heads of mischief and vanity include all the schemes, aims, and achievements of which man is capable, till God is pleased to visit the heart with his grace. The busy part of mankind are employed in multiplying evils and miseries; the more retired, speculative, and curious, are amusing themselves with what will hereafter appear as unsubstantial and useless as a cobweb. Death will soon sweep away all that the philosophers, the virtuosi, the mathematicians, the antiquarians, and other learned triflers, are now weaving with so much self-applauded address. Nor will the fine-spun dresses in which the moralist and the self-righteous clothe themselves, be of more advantage to them, either for ornament or defence, than the produce of a spider. But it is given to a few to know their present state of future destination. Those build upon the immoveable Rock of Ages for eternity. These are trees springing from a living root, and bear the fruits of righteousness, which are by Jesus Christ to the glory and praise of God. These only are awake, while the rest of the world are in a sleep, indulging in vain dreams, from which, likewise, they will shortly awake; but, oh, with what consternation, when they shall find themselves irrecoverably divorced from all their delusive attachments, and compelled to appear before that God to whom they have lived strangers, and to whom they must give an account! O for a thousand tongues to proclaim in the ears of thoughtless mortals that important aphorism of our Lord, 'One thing is needful.' Yet a thousand tongues would be, and are employed in vain, unless so far as the Lord is pleased to send the watchman's warning, by the power and agency of his own Spirit. We are told that Cassandra had the gift of truly foretelling future events; but she was afterwards laid under a painful embarrassment, that nobody should believe her words. Such, with respect to the bulk of their auditories, is the lot of Gospel ministers; they are enlightened to see, and sent forth to declare, the awful consequences of sin; but, alas, how few believe their report! To illustrate our grief and disappointment, I sometimes suppose there was a dangerous water in the way of travellers, over which there is a bridge, which those who can be prevailed upon may pass with safety. By the side of this bridge watchmen are placed, to warn passengers of the danger of the waters; to assure them, that all who attempt to go through them inevitably perish; to invite, entreat, and beseech them, if they value their lives, to cross the bridge. Methinks this should be an easy task. Yet, if we should see, in fact, the greater part stopping their ears to the friendly importunity; many so much offended by it as to account the watchman's care impertinent, and only deserving of scorn and ill treatment; hardly one in fifty betaking themselves to the friendly bridge, the rest eagerly plunging into the waters, from which none return, as if they were determined to try who should be drowned first: this spectacle would be no unfit emblem of the reception the Gospel meets with from a blinded world. The ministers are rejected, opposed, vilified; they are accounted troublers of the world, because they dare not, cannot stand silent while sinners are perishing before their eyes; and if, in the course of many sermons, they can prevail but on one soul to take timely warning, and to seek Jesus, who is the way, the truth, and the life, they may account it a mercy and an honour, sufficient to overbalance all the labour and reproaches they are called to endure. From the most they must expect no better reception than the Jews gave to Jeremiah, who told the prophet to his face: 'As to the word thou has spoken to us in the name of the Lord, we will not hearken to thee at all, but we will certainly do whatsoever thing goeth forth out of our own mouth.' Surely, if the Lord has given us any sense of the worth of our souls, any compassion towards them, this must be a painful exercise; and experience must teach us something of the meaning of Jeremiah's pathetic exclamation: 'O, that my head were waters, and mine eyes fountains of tears, that I might weep day and night for the slain of the daughters of my people!' It is our duty to be thus affected. Our relief lies in the wisdom and sovereignty of God. He reveals his salvation to whom he pleases, – for the most part to babes; from the bulk of the wise and the prudent it is hidden. Thus it hath pleased him, and therefore it must be right. Yea, he will one day condescend to justify the propriety and equity of his proceedings to his creatures: then every mouth will be stopped, and none will be able to reply against their Judge. Light is come into the world, but men prefer darkness. They hate the light, resist it, and rebel against it. It is true, all do so; and therefore, if all were to perish under the condemnation, their ruin would be their own act. It is of grace that any are saved; and in the distribution of that grace he does what he will with his own, – a right which most are ready enough to claim in their own concerns, though they are so unwilling to allow it to the Lord of all. Many perplexing and acrimonious disputes have been started upon this subject; but the redeemed of the Lord are called, not to dispute, but to admire and rejoice, – to love, adore, and obey. To know that he loved us, and gave himself for us, is the constraining argument and motive to love him, and surrender ourselves to him; to consider ourselves as no longer our own, but to devote ourselves, with every faculty, power, and talent, to his service and glory. He deserves our all; for he parted with all for us. He made himself poor, – he endured shame, torture, death, and the curse for us, that we, through him, might inherit everlasting life. Ah, the hardness of my heart, that I am no more affected, astonished, overpowered with this thought. – I am, &c.

Letter 15

My Lord, *April 20, 1774*

I have been pondering a good while for a subject, and at last I begin without one, hoping that (as it has often happened) while I am writing one line, something will occur to fill up another. Indeed I have an inexhaustible fund at hand; but it is to me often like a prize in the hand of a fool, – I want skill to improve it. O for a warm, a suitable, a seasonable train of thought, that might enliven my own heart, and not be unworthy your Lordship's perusal! Methinks the poets can have but cold comfort, when they invoke a fabled muse; but we have a warrant, a right to look up for the influence of the Holy Spirit, who ordains strength for us, and has promised to work in us. What a comfort, what an honour is this, that worms have liberty to look up to God, and that he, the high and holy One who inhabiteth eternity, is pleased to look down upon us, to maintain our peace, to supply our wants, to guide us with his eye, and to inspire us with wisdom and grace suitable to our occasions! They who profess to know something of this fellowship, and to depend upon it, are by the world accounted enthusiasts, who know not what they mean, or perhaps hypocrites, who pretend to what they have not, in order to cover some base designs. But we have reason to bear their reproaches with patience.

Let them rage, let them, if they please, point at me for a fool as I walk the streets; if I do but take up the Bible, or run over in my mind the inventory of the blessings with which the Lord has enriched me, I have sufficient amends. Jesus is mine; in him I have wisdom, righteousness, sanctification, and redemption, – an interest in all the promises and in all the perfections of God; he will guide me by his counsel, support me by his power, comfort me with his presence, while I am here; and afterwards, when flesh and heart fail, he will receive me to his glory.

Let them say what they will, they shall not dispute nor laugh us out of our spiritual senses. If all the blind men in the kingdom should endeavour to bear me down, that the sun is not bright, or that the rainbow has no colours, I would still believe my own eyes. I have seen them both, they have not. I cannot prove to their satisfaction what I assert, because they are destitute of sight, the necessary medium; yet their exceptions produce no uncertainty in my mind; they would not, they could not, hesitate a moment, if they were not blind. Just so, those who have been taught of God, who have tasted that the Lord is gracious, have an experimental perception of the truth, which renders them proof against all the sophistry of infidels. I am persuaded we have many plain people here, who, if a wise man of the world was to suggest that the Bible is a human invention, would be quite at a loss how to answer him by arguments drawn from external evidences; yet they have found such effects from this blessed book, that they would be no more moved by the insinuation, than if they were told that a cunning man, or set of men, invented the sun, and placed it in the firmament. So, if a wise Socinian was to tell them that the Saviour was only a man like themselves, they would conceive just such an opinion of his skill in divinity, as a philosopher would do of a clown's skill in astronomy, who should affirm that the sun was no bigger than a cart wheel.

It remains therefore a truth, in defiance of all the cavils of the ignorant, that the Holy Spirit does influence the hearts of all the children of God, or, in other words, they are inspired, not with new revelations, but with grace and wisdom to understand, apply, and feed upon the great things already revealed in the Scriptures, without which the Scriptures are as useless as spectacles to the blind. Were it not so, when we become acquainted with the poverty, ignorance, and wickedness of our hearts, we must sit down in utter despair of being ever able to think a good thought, to offer a single petition aright in prayer, or to take one safe step in the path of life. But now we may be content with our proper weakness, since the power and Spirit of Christ are engaged to rest upon us; and while we are preserved in a simple dependence upon this help, though unable of ourselves to do anything, we shall find an ability to do everything that our circumstances and duty call for. What is weaker than a worm? Yet the Lord's worms shall, in his strength, thresh the mountains, and make the hills as chaff. But this life of faith, – this living and acting by a power above our own, is an inexplicable mystery, till experience makes it plain. I have often wondered that St Paul has obtained so much quarter at the hands of some people, as to pass with them for a man of sense; for surely the greatest part of his writings must be to the last degree absurd and unintelligible upon their principles. How many contradictions must they find, for instance, if they give any attention to what they read, in that one passage, 'I am crucified with Christ: nevertheless I live; yet not I, but Christ liveth in me: and the life which I now live in the flesh I live by faith in the Son of God, who loved me, and gave himself for me' (Gal. 2:20).

And as believers are they inspired by the Holy Spirit, who furnishes them with desires, motives, and abilities to perform what is agreeable to his will; so I apprehend, that they who live without God in the world, whom the apostle styles sensual, not having the Spirit, are in a greater or less degree, under what I may call a black inspiration. After making the best allowances I can, both for the extent of human genius and the deplorable evil of the human heart, I cannot suppose that one half of the wicked wit, of which some persons are so proud, is properly their own. Perhaps such a one as Voltaire would neither have written, nor have been read or admired so much, if he had not been the amanuensis of an abler hand in his own way. Satan is always near when the heart is disposed to receive him; and the Lord withdraws his restraints, to heighten the sinner's ability of sinning, and assisting him with such strokes of blasphemy, malice and falsehood, as perhaps he could not otherwise have attained. Therefore, I do not wonder that they are clever and smart, that they raise a laugh, and are received with applause among those who are like minded with themselves. But unless the Lord is pleased to grant them repentance (though it is rather to be feared some of them are given up to judicial hardness of heart), how much better would it have been for them had they been born idiots or lunatics, than to be distinguished as the willing, industrious, and successful instruments of the powers of darkness, in beguiling, perverting, and ruining the souls of men! Alas, what are parts and talents, or any distinctions which give pre-eminence in life, unless they are sanctified by the grace of God, and directed to the accomplishment of his will and glory! From the expression 'bind them in bundles and burn them', I have been led to think that the deceivers and the deceived, they who have prostituted their gifts or influence to encourage others in sin may in another world have some peculiar and inseparable connection, and spend an eternity in fruitless lamentations, that ever they were connected here.

Your Lordship, I doubt not, feels the force of that line: O to grace how great a debtor! Had not the Lord separated you for himself, your rank, your abilities, your influence, which now you chiefly value as enlarging your opportunities of usefulness, might, nay, certainly would, have been diverted into the opposite channel. I am, &c.

Letter 16

My Lord, *November 5, 1774*

I have not very lately had recourse to the expedient of descanting upon a text, but I believe it the best method I can take to avoid ringing changes upon a few obvious topics, which I suppose uniformly present themselves to my mind when I am about to write to your Lordship. Just now that sweet expression of David occurred to my thoughts: 'The Lord is my Shepherd!' Permit me, without plan or premeditation, to make a few observations upon it; and may your Lordship feel the peace, the confidence, the blessedness, which a believing application of the words is suited to inspire.

The Socinians and others, in their unhappy laboured attempts to darken the principal glory and foundation comfort of the Gospel, employ their critical sophistry against those texts which expressly and doctrinally declare the Redeemer's character; and affect to triumph, if in any manuscript or ancient version they can find a variation from the received copies which seems to favour their cause. But we may venture to waive the authority of every disputed or disputable text, and maintain the truth against their cavils, from the current language and tenor of the whole Scripture. David's words in Psalm 23 are alone a decisive proof that Jesus is Jehovah, if they will but allow two things, which I think they cannot deny.

1. That our Saviour assumes to himself the character of the Shepherd of his people.

2. That he did not come into the world to abridge those advantages which the servants of God enjoyed before his incarnation.

Upon these premises, which cannot be gainsaid without setting aside the whole New Testament, the conclusion is undeniable: for if Jehovah was David's Shepherd, unless Jesus be Jehovah, we who live under the Gospel have an unspeakable advantage, in being intrusted to the care of one who, according to the Socinians, is a mere man; and, upon the Arian scheme, is at the most a creature, and infinitely short of possessing those perfections which David contemplated in his Shepherd. He had a Shepherd whose wisdom and power were infinite, and might therefore warrantably conclude he should not want and need not fear. And we also may conclude the same, if our Shepherd be the Lord or Jehovah, but not otherwise. Besides, the very nature of the Shepherd's office respecting the state of such frail creatures as we are, requires those attributes for the due discharge of it which are incommunicably divine. He must intimately know every individual of the flock. His eye must be upon them every one, and his ear open to their prayers, and his arm stretched out for their relief, in all places and in all ages. Every thought of every heart must be open to his view, and his wisdom must penetrate, and his arm control and overrule, all the hidden and complicated machinations of the powers of darkness. He must have the administration of universal providence over all the nations, families, and persons upon earth, or he could not effectually manage for those who put their trust in him, in that immense variety of cases and circumstances in which they are found. Reason as well as Scripture, may convince us, that he who gathereth the outcasts of Israel, who healeth the broken in heart, who upholdeth all that fall, raiseth up all that are bowed down, and upon whom the eyes of all wait for their support, can be no other than he who telleth the number of the stars, and calleth them all by their names, who is great in power, and whose understanding is infinite. To this purpose likewise the prophet Isaiah describes this mighty Shepherd, chapter 40:9–17, both as to his person and office.

But is not this indeed the great mystery of godliness! How just is the apostle's observation, that 'no man can say Jesus Christ is Lord, but by the Holy Spirit'! How astonishing the thought, that the maker of heaven and earth, the Holy One of Israel, before whose presence the earth shook, the heavens dropped, when he displayed a faint emblem of his majesty upon Sinai, should afterwards appear in the form of a servant, and hang upon a cross, the sport and scorn of wicked men! I cannot wonder that to the wise men of the world this appears absurd, unreasonable, and impossible; yet to right reason, to reason enlightened and sanctified, however amazing the proposition be, yet it appears true and necessary, upon a supposition that a holy God is pleased to pardon sinners in a way suited to display the awful glories of his justice. The same arguments which prove the blood of bulls and goats insufficient to take away sin, will conclude against the utmost doings or sufferings of men or angels. The Redeemer of sinners must be mighty; he must have a personal dignity to stamp such a value upon his undertakings, as that thereby God may appear just, as well as merciful, in justifying the ungodly for his sake: and he must be all-sufficient to bless, and almighty to protect, those who come unto him for safety and life.

Such a one is our Shepherd. This is he of whom we, through grace, are enabled to say: 'We are his people and the sheep of his pasture.' We are his by every tie and right; he made us, he redeemed us, he reclaimed us from the hand of our enemies, and we are his by our own voluntary surrender of ourselves; for though we once slighted, despised, and opposed him, he made us willing in the day of his power; he knocked at the door of our hearts; but we (at least I) barred and fastened it against him as much and as long as possible. But when he revealed his love, we could stand out no longer. Like sheep, we are weak, destitute, defenceless, prone to wander, unable to return, and always surrounded with wolves. But all is made up in the fulness, ability, wisdom, compassion, care, and faithfulness of our great Shepherd. He guides, protects, feeds, heals, and restores, and will be our guide and our God even until death. Then he will meet us, receive us, and present us unto himself, and we shall be near him, and like him, and with him for ever.

Ah, my Lord, what a subject is this! I trust it is the joy of your heart. Placed as you are by his hand in a superior rank, you see and feel that the highest honours, and the most important concernments that terminate with the present life, are as trivial as the sports of children in comparison with the views and the privileges you derive from the glorious Gospel; and your situation in life renders the grace bestowed upon you the more conspicuous and distinguishing. I have somewhere met with a similar reflection of Henry the Fourth of France, to this purpose, that though many came into the world the same day with him, he was probably the only one among them that was born to be a king. Your Lordship is acquainted with many who, if not born on the same day with you, were born to titles, estates, and honours; but how few of them were born to the honour of making a public and consistent profession of the glorious Gospel! The hour is coming when all honours and possessions, but this which cometh from God only, will be eclipsed and vanish; and, like the baseless fabric of a vision, leave not a wreck behind. How miserable will they then be who must leave their all!

But grace and faith can make the lowest state of life supportable. Of the former I have many living proofs and witnesses around me. Your Lordship, I trust, will have sweet experience of the latter, when, after having fulfilled the will of God in your generation, you shall be called (I hope in some yet distant day) to enter into your Master's joy. In the meantime, how valuable are life, talents, influence, and opportunities of every kind, if we are enabled to improve and lay out all for him who has thus loved us – thus provided for us. As to myself, I would hope there are few who have so clear a sense of their obligations to him, who make such unsuitable and languid returns as I do. I think I have a desire to serve him better; but alas, evil is present with me. Surely I shall feel something like shame and regret for my coldness, even in heaven: – for I find I am never happier than when I am most ashamed of myself upon this account there. – I am, &c.

Letter 17

My Lord, *December 8, 1774*

How wonderful is the patience of God towards sinful mankind! In him they live, and move, and have their being; and if he were to withdraw his support for a single moment, they must perish. He maintains their lives, guards their persons, supplies their wants, while they employ the powers and faculties they receive from him in a settled course of opposition to his will. They trample upon his laws, affront his government, and despise his grace; yet still he spares. To silence all his adversaries in a moment, would require no extraordinary exertion of his power; but his forbearance towards them manifests his glory, and gives us cause to say: 'Who is a God like unto thee?'

Sometimes, however, there are striking instances of his displeasure against sin. When such events take place, immediately upon a public and premeditated contempt offered to him that sitteth in the heavens, I own they remind me of the danger of standing, if I may so speak, in the Lord's way: for though his long-suffering is astonishing, and many dare him to his face daily with seeming impunity, yet he sometimes strikes an awful and unexpected blow, and gives an illustration of that solemn word: 'Who ever hardened himself against the Lord and prospered?' But who am I, to make this observation? I ought to do it with the deepest humiliation, remembering that I once stood (according to my years and ability) in the foremost rank of his avowed opposers; and, with a determined and unwearied enmity, renounced, defied, and blasphemed him. 'But he will have mercy on whom he will have mercy' and therefore I was spared, and reserved to speak of his goodness.

Josephus, when speaking of the death of Herod Agrippa, ascribes it to a natural cause, and says he was seized with excruciating pains in his bowels. But Luke informs us of the true cause: an angel of the Lord smote him. Had we a modern history, written by an inspired pen, we should probably often be reminded of such an interposition where we are not ordinarily aware of it. For, though the springs of actions and events are concealed from us for the most part, and vain men carry on their schemes with confidence, as though the Lord had forsaken the earth, yet they are under his eye and control; and faith, in some measure, instructed by the specimens of his government recorded in the Scripture, can trace and admire his hand, and can see how he takes the wise in their own craftiness, stains the pride of human glory; and that when sinners speak proudly, he is above them, and makes everything bend or break before him.

While we lament the growth and pernicious effects of infidelity, and see how wicked men and seducers wax worse and worse, deceiving, and being deceived; what gratitude should fill our hearts to him who has been pleased to call us out of the horrid darkness in which multitudes are bewildered and lost, into the glorious light of his Gospel? Faint are our warmest conceptions of this mercy. In order to understand it fully, we should have a full and adequate sense of the evil from which we are delivered; the glory to which we are called; and especially of the astonishing means to which we owe our life and hope, the humiliation, sufferings, and death of the Son of God. But our views of these points, while in our present state, are and must be exceedingly weak and disproportionate. We know them but in part, we see them by reflection, rather the images than the thing themselves; and though they are faithfully represented in the mirror of God's Word, to us they appear indistinct, because we see them through a gross medium of ignorance and unbelief. Hereafter every veil shall be removed; we shall know, in another manner than we do now, the unspeakable evil of sin, and the insupportable dreadfulness of God's displeasure against it, when we see the world in flames, and hear the final sentence denounced upon the ungodly. We shall have other thoughts of Jesus when we see him as he is; and shall then be able to make a more affecting estimate of the love which moved him to be made a substitute and a curse for us; and we shall then know what great things God has prepared for them that love him. Then with transport we shall adopt the Queen of Sheba's language:

'It was a true report we heard in yonder dark world; but behold the half, the thousandth part, was not told us!' In the meantime, may such conceptions as we are enabled to form of these great truths, fill our hearts, and be mingled with all our thoughts, and all our concerns: may the Lord, by faith, give us abiding evidence of the reality and importance of the things which cannot yet be seen: so shall we be enabled to live above the world while we are in it, uninfluenced either by its blandishments or its frowns; and, with a noble simplicity and singularity, avow and maintain the cause of God in truth, in the midst of a crooked and perverse generation. He whom we serve is able to support and protect us; and he well deserves at our hands, that we should be willing to endure, for his sake, much more than he will ever permit us to be exercised with. The believer's call, duty, and privilege, is beautifully and forcibly set forth in Milton's character of Abdiel, at the end of the fifth book of *Paradise Lost*:

> Faithful found
> Among the faithless, faithful only he;
> Among innumerable false, unmoved,
> Unshaken, unsedue'd, unterrify'd,
> His loyalty he kept, his love, his zeal;
> Nor number, nor example, with him wrought
> To swerve from truth, or change his constant mind
> Though single.

Methinks your Lordship's situation particularly resembles that in which the poet has placed Abdiel. You are not indeed called to serve God quite alone; but amongst those of your own rank, and with whom the station in which he has placed you necessitates you to converse, how few are there who can understand, second, or approve, the principles upon which you act, or easily bear a conduct which must impress conviction, or reflect dishonour upon themselves! But you are not alone; the Lord's people (many of whom you will not know till you meet them in glory) are helping you here with their prayers; his angels are commissioned to guard and guide your steps; yea the Lord himself fixes his eye of mercy upon your private and your public path, and is near you at the right hand, that you may not be moved! That he may comfort you with the light of his countenance, and uphold you with the arm of his power, is my frequent prayer. I am, &c.

Letter 18

My Lord, *January 20, 1775*

We have entered upon another year! So have thousands, perhaps millions, who will not see it close! An alarming thought to the worldling, at least it should be so. I have an imperfect remembrance of an account I read when I was a boy, of an ice-palace, built one winter at Petersburgh. The walls, the roof, the floors, the furniture, were all of ice, but finished with taste; and everything that might be expected in a royal palace was to be found there; the ice, while in the state of water, being previously coloured, as that to the eye all seemed formed of proper materials; but all was cold, useless, and transient. Had the frost continued till now, the palace might have been standing; but with the returning spring it melted away, like the baseless fabric of a vision. The wind passes over them, and they are gone. In the midst of all their preparations, or at farthest, when they think they have just completed their designs, their breath goeth forth, they return to their earth; in that very day their thoughts perish.

How many sleep who kept the world awake! Yet this ice-house had something of a leisurely dissolution, though, when it began to decay, all the art of man was unable to prop it; but often death comes hastily, and, like the springing of a mine, destroys to the very foundations without previous notice. Then all we have been concerned in here (all but the consequences of our conduct, which will abide to eternity) will be no more to us than the remembrance of a dream. This truth is too plain to be denied; but the greater part of mankind act as if they were convinced it was false; they spend their days in vanity, and in a moment they go down to the grave. What cause of thankfulness have they who are delivered from this delusion, and who, by the knowledge of the glorious Gospel, have learned their true state and end, are saved from the love of the present world, from the heart-distressing fear of death; and know, that if their earthly house were dissolved, like the ice-palace, they have a house not made with hands, eternal in the heavens.

Yet even these are much concerned to realise the brevity and uncertainty of their present state, that they may be stimulated to make the most and the best of it; to redeem their time, and manage their precarious opportunities, so as may most tend to the praise and glory of him who has called them out of darkness into marvellous light. Why should any that have tasted that the Lord is gracious wish to live another day, but that they may have the honour to be fellow-workers with him, instrumental in promoting his designs, and of laying themselves out to the utmost of their abilities and influence in his service! To enjoy a sense of his loving-kindness, and to have the light of his countenance lifted up upon our souls, is indeed, respecting ourselves, the best part of life, yes, better than life itself; but this we shall have to unspeakably greater advantage, when we have finished our course, and shall be wholly freed from the body of sin. And therefore the great desirable while here seems to be grace, that we may serve him and suffer for him in the world. Our first wish for ourselves might be to depart and be with Jesus, which is yet a lively thought of our immense obligations to his redeeming love. This may reconcile us to a much longer continuance here, if we may by any means be subservient to diffuse the glory of his name, and the blessings of his salvation, which is God's great and principal end in preserving the world itself. When historians and politicians descant upon the rise and fall of empires, with all their professed sagacity in tracing the connection between causes and effects, they are totally unacquainted with the great master-wheel which manages the whole movement, that is, the Lord's design in favour of his church and kingdom. To this every event is subordinate; to this every interfering interest must stoop. How easily might this position be proved, by reviewing the history of the period about the Reformation. Whether Dr Robertson considers things in this light, in his history of Charles V, I know not, as I have not seen his book; but if not, however elaborate his performance may be in other respects, I must venture to say, it is essentially defective, and cannot give that light and pleasure to a spiritual reader of which the subject is capable. And I doubt not but some who are yet unborn will hereafter clearly see, and remark, that the present unhappy disputes between Great Britain and America, with their consequences, whatever they may be, are part of a series of events, of which the extension and interests of the church of Christ were the principal final causes. In a word, that Jesus may be known, trusted, and adored, and sinners, by the power of his Gospel, be rescued from sin and Satan, is comparatively the one great business, for the sake of which the succession of day and night, summer and winter, is still maintained; and when the plan of redemption is consummated, sin, which now almost fills the earth, will then set it on fire; and the united interest of all the rest of mankind, when detached from that of the people of God, will not plead for its preservation of a single day. In this view I congratulate your Lordship, that however your best endeavours to serve the temporal interests of the nation may fall short of your wishes; yet, so far as your situation gives you opportunity of supporting the Gospel cause, and facilitating its progress, you have a prospect both of a more certain and more important success. For instance, it was, under God, your Lordship's favour and influence that brought me into the ministry. And though I be nothing, yet he who put it into your heart to patronise me, has been pleased not to suffer what you then did for his sake to be wholly in vain. He has been pleased, in a course of years, by so unworthy an instrument as I am, to awaken a number of people, who were at that time dead in trespasses and sins; but now some of them are pressing on to the prize of their high calling in Christ Jesus; and some of them are already before the throne. Should I suggest in some companies, that the conversion of a hundred sinners (more or less) to God is an event of more real importance than the temporal prosperity of the greatest nation upon earth I should be charged with ignorance and arrogance; but your Lordship is skilled in scriptural arithmetic, which alone can teach us to estimate the value of souls, and will agree with me, that one soul is worth more than the whole world, on account of its redemption-price, its vast capacities, and its duration. Should we suppose a nation to consist of forty millions, the whole and each individual to enjoy as much good as this life can afford, without abatement, for a term of fifty years each – all this good, or an equal quantity, might be exhausted by a single person in two thousand millions of years, which would be but a moment in comparison of the eternity which would still follow. And if this good were merely temporal good, the whole aggregate of it would be evil and misery, if compared with that happiness in God, of which only they who are made partakers of a divine life are capable. On the other hand, were a whole nation to be destroyed by such accumulated miseries as attended the siege of Jerusalem, the sum total of these calamities would be but trifling, if set in competition with what every single person that dies in sin has to expect, when the sentence of everlasting destruction from the presence of the Lord, and the glory of his power, shall be executed.

What an unexpected round have my thoughts taken since I set out from the ice-palace. It is time to relieve your Lordship, and to subscribe myself, &c.

Letter 19

My Lord, *February 23, 1775*

I assent to our Lord's declaration: 'Without me ye can do nothing', not only upon the authority of the speaker, but from the same irresistible and experimental evidence, as if he had told me, that I cannot make the sun to shine, or change the course of the seasons. Though my pen and my tongue sometimes move freely, yet the total incapacity and stagnation of thought I labour under at other times, convinces me, that in myself I have not sufficiency to think a good thought; and I believe the case would be the same if that little measure of knowledge and abilities, which I am too prone to look upon as my own, were a thousand times greater than it is. For every new service I stand in need of a new supply, and can bring forth nothing of my supposed store into actual exercise, but by his immediate assistance. His gracious influence is that to those who are best furnished with gifts what the water is to the mill, or the wind to the ship, without which the whole apparatus is motionless and useless. I apprehend that we lose much of the comfort which might arise from a sense of our continual dependence upon him, and of course fall short of acknowledging, as we ought, what we receive from him, by mistaking the manner of his operation.

Perhaps we take it too much for granted, that communications from himself must bear some kind of sensible impression that they are his, and therefore are ready to give our own industry or ingenuity credit for those performances in which we can perceive no such impression; yet it is very possible that we may be under his influence when we are least aware; and though what we say, or write, or do, may seem no way extraordinary; yet that we should be led to such a particular turn of thought at one time rather than at another, has, in my own concerns, often appeared to me remarkable, from the circumstances which have attended, or the consequences which have followed. How often, in the choice of a text, or in the course of a sermon, or in a letter to a friend, have I been led to speak a word in season! And what I have expressed at large, and in general, has been so exactly suited to some case which I was utterly unacquainted with, that I could hardly have hit it so well, had I been previously informed of it. Some instances of this kind have been so striking, as hardly to admit a doubt of superior agency. And, indeed, if believers in Jesus, however unworthy in themselves, are the temples of the Holy Spirit; if the Lord lives, dwells, and walks in them; if he is their life and their light; if he has promised to guide them with his eye, and to work in them to will and to do of his own good pleasure; methinks what I have mentioned, and more, may be reasonably expected. This gracious assistance is afforded in a way imperceptible to ourselves, to hide pride from us, and to prevent us from being indolent and careless with respect to the use of appointed means; and it would be likewise more abundantly, and perhaps more sensibly afforded, were our spirits more simple in waiting upon the Lord. But alas, a divided heart, an undue attachment to some temporal object, sadly deadens our spirits (I speak for myself) and grieves the Lord's spirit; so that we walk in darkness and at a distance, and though called to great privileges, live far below them. But methinks the thought of him who is always near, and upon whom we do and must incessantly depend, should suggest a powerful motive for the closest attention to his revealed will, and the most punctual compliance with it; for so far as the Lord withdraws, we become as blind men, and with the clearest light, and upon the plainest ground, we are liable, or rather sure, to stumble at every step.

Though there is a principle of consciousness, and a determination of the will sufficient to denominate our thoughts and performances our own, yet I believe mankind in general are more under an invisible agency than they apprehend. The Lord, immediately from himself, and perhaps by the ministry of his holy angels, guides, prompts, restrains, or warns his people. So there undoubtedly is what I may call a black inspiration, the influence of the evil spirits who work in the hearts of the disobedient, and not only excite their wills, but assist their faculties, and qualify as well as incline them to be more assiduously wicked, and more extensively mischievous, than they could be of themselves. I consider Voltaire, for instance, and many writers of the same stamp, to be little more than secretaries and amanuenses of one who has unspeakably more wit and adroitness in promoting infidelity and immorality, than they of themselves can justly pretend to. They have, for a while, the credit (if I may so call it) of the fund from whence they draw; but the world little imagines who is the real and original author of that philosophy and poetry, of those fine turns and sprightly inventions, which are so generally admired. Perhaps many now applauded for their genius would have been comparatively dolts, had they not been engaged in a cause which Satan has so much interest in supporting.

But to return to the more pleasing subject. How great and honourable is the privilege of a true believer! That he has neither wisdom nor strength in himself is no disadvantage; for he is connected with infinite wisdom and almighty power. Though weak as a worm, his arms are strengthened by the mighty God of Jacob, and all things become possible, yes easy to him, that occur within the compass of his proper duty and calling. The Lord, whom he serves, engages to proportion his strength to his day, whether it be a day of service or of suffering; and though he be fallible and short-sighted, exceeding liable to mistake and imposition, yet, while he retains a sense that he is so, and, with the simplicity of a child, asks counsel and direction of the Lord, he seldom takes a wrong step, at least not in matters of consequence; and even his inadvertancies are overruled for good. If he forgets his true state, and thinks himself to be something, he presently finds he is indeed nothing; but if he is content to be nothing, and to have nothing, he is sure to find a seasonable and abundant communication of all that he wants. Thus he lives, like Israel in the wilderness, upon mere bounty; but then it is a bounty unchangeable, unwearied, inexhaustible, and all-sufficient. Moses, when speaking of the methods the Lord took to humble Israel, mentions his feeding them with manna, as one method. I could not understand this for a time. I thought they were rather in danger of being proud, when they saw themselves provided for in such an extraordinary way. But the manna would not keep, they could not hoard it up, and were therefore in a state of absolute dependence from day to day: this appointment was well suited to humble them. Thus it is with us in spirituals. We should be better pleased, perhaps, to be set up with a stock or sufficiency at once, – such an inherent portion of wisdom and power, as we might depend upon, at least for common occasions, without being constrained to have continual recourse to the Lord for everything we want. But his way is best. His own glory is most displayed, and our safety best secured, by keeping us quite poor and empty in ourselves, and supplying us from one minute to another, according to our need. This, if anything, will prevent boasting, and keep a sense of gratitude awake in our hearts. This is well adapted to quicken us in prayer, and furnishes us with a thousand occasions for praise, which would otherwise escape our notice.

But who or what are we, that the Most High should thus notice us! – should visit us every morning, and water us every moment! It is an astonishing thought, that God should thus dwell with men! That he, before whom the mightiest earthly potentates are less than nothing and vanity, should thus stoop and accommodate himself to the situation, wants, and capacities of the weakest, meanest, and poorest of his children! But so it hath pleased him. He seeth not as man seeth. – I am, &c.

Letter 20

My Lord, *August, 1775*

I have no apt preface or introduction at hand, and as I have made it almost a rule not to study for what I should offer your Lordship, I therefore beg leave to begin abruptly. It is the future promised privilege of believers in Jesus, that they shall be as the angels; and there is a sense in which we should endeavour to be as the angels now. This is intimated to us where we are taught to pray: 'Thy will be done on earth as it is in heaven'. I have sometimes amused myself with supposing an angel should be appointed to reside a while upon earth in a human body; not in sinful flesh like ours, but in a body free from infirmity, and still preserving an unabated sense of his own happiness in the favour of God, and of his unspeakable obligation to his goodness; – and then I have tried to judge, as well as I could, how such an angel would comfort himself in such a situation. I know not that I ever enlarged upon the thought, either in preaching or writing. Permit me to follow it a little in this paper.

Were I acquainted with this heavenly visitor, I am willing to hope I should greatly reverence him; and, if permitted, be glad in some cases to consult him. In some, but not in all; for I think my fear would be equal to my love.

Methinks I could never venture to open my heart freely to him, and unfold to him my numberless complaints and infirmities; for, as he could have no experience of the like things himself, I should suppose he would not know how fully to pity me, indeed hardly how to bear with me, if I told him all. Alas, what a preposterous, strange, vile creature should I appear to an angel, if he knew me as I am! It is well for me that Jesus was made lower than the angels, and that the human nature he assumed was not distinct from the common nature of mankind, though secured from the common depravity; and because he submitted to be under the law in our name and stead, though he was free from sin himself, yet sin and its consequences being (for our sakes) charged upon him, he acquired, in the days of his humiliation, an experimental sympathy with his poor people. He knows the effects of sin and temptation upon us, by that knowledge whereby he knows all things; but he knows them likewise in a way more suitable for our comfort and relief – by the sufferings and exercises he passed through for us. Hence arises encouragement. We have not a High Priest who cannot be touched with a feeling of our infirmities, but was in all points tempted even as we are. When I add to this, the consideration of his power, promises, and grace, and that he is exalted on purpose to pity, relieve, and save, I gather courage. With him I dare to be free, and am not sorry, but glad, that he knows me perfectly, that not a thought of my heart is hidden from him; for without this infinite and exact knowledge of my disease, how could he effectually administer to my cure? But whither am I rambling? I seem to have lost sight of the angel already. I am now coming back, that he cannot effectually pity me – he may at least animate and teach me.

In the first place, I take it for granted this angel would think himself a stranger and pilgrim upon earth. Surely he would look upon all the bustle of human life (farther than the design of his mission might connect him with it) with more indifference than we look upon the sports of children, or the amusements of idiots and lunatics, which give us an uneasiness, rather than excite a desire of joining in them. He would judge of everything around him by the reference and tendency it had to promote the will of him that sent him: and the most specious or splendid appearances, considered in any other view, would make no impression upon him.

Consequently all his aim and desire would be to fulfil the will of God. All situations would be alike to him; whether he was commanded, as in the case of Sennacherib, to destroy a mighty army with a stroke; or, as in the case of Hagar, to attend upon a woman, a servant, a slave. Both services would be to him equally pleasing his Lord; which would be his element and his joy, whether he was appointed to guide the reigns of empire or to sweep the streets.

Again, the angel would doubtless exhibit a striking example of benevolence; for, being free from selfish bias, filled with a sense of the love of God, and a knowledge of his adorable perfection, his whole heart and soul and strength would be engaged and exerted, both from duty and inclination, to relieve the miseries, and advance the happiness of all around him; and in this he would follow the pattern of him who doeth good to all, commanding his sun to rise, and his rain to fall, upon the just and the unjust; though, from the same pattern, he would show an especial regard to the household of faith. An angel would take but little part in the controversies and contentions which might happen in the time of his sojourning here, but would be a friend to all, so far as consistent with the general good.

The will and glory of God being the angel's great view, and having a more lively sense of the realities of an unseen world than we can at present conceive, he would certainly, in the first and chief place, have the success and spread of the glorious Gospel at heart. Angels, though not redeemed with blood, yet feel themselves nearly concerned in the work of redemption. They admire its mysteries. We may suppose them well informed in the works of creation and providence. But (unlike too many men, who are satisfied with the knowledge of astronomy, mathematics, or history) they search and pry into the counsels of redeeming love, rejoice at the conversion of a sinner, and think themselves well employed to be ministering spirits, to minister to the heirs of salvation. It would therefore be his chief delight to espouse and promote their cause, and to employ all his talents and influence in spreading the savour and knowledge of the name of Jesus, which is the only effectual means of bringing sinners out of bondage and darkness into the glorious liberty of the sons of God.

Lastly, though his zeal for the glory of his Lord would make him willing to continue here till he had finished the work given him to do, he would, I am persuaded, look forward with desire to the appointed moment of his recall, that he might be freed from beholding and mixing with the sin and vanity of those who know not God, render his account with joy, and be welcomed to heaven with a 'Well done, good and faithful servant'. Surely he would long for this, as a labourer for the setting sun; and would not form any connection with the things of time, which should prompt him to wish his removal protracted for a single hour beyond the period of his prescribed service.

Alas, why am I not more like an angel! My views in my better judgment are the same. My motives and obligations are even stronger; an angel is not so deeply indebted to the grace of God as a believing sinner, who was once upon the brink of destruction, has been redeemed with blood, and might justly have been, before now, shut up with the powers of darkness, without hope! Yet the merest trifles are sufficient to debase my views, damp my activity, and impede my endeavours in the Lord's service, though I profess to have no other end or desire which can make a continuance in life worthy my wish. – I am, &c.

Letter 21

My Lord, *November, 1775*

In the midst of the hurries, and changes of this unsettled state, we glide along swiftly towards an unchangeable world, and shall soon have as little connection with the scenes we are now passing through, as we have with what happened before the flood. All that appears great and interesting in the present life, abstracted from its influence upon our internal character, and our everlasting allotment, will soon be as unreal as the visions of the night. This we know and confess; but though our judgments are convinced, it is seldom our hearts are duly affected by the thought. And while I find it easy to write in this moralising strain, I feel myself disposed to be seriously engaged about trifles, and trifling in the most serious concerns, as if I believed the very contrary. It is with good reason the Lord challenges, as his own prerogative, the full knowledge of the deceitfulness, desperate wickedness, and latent depths of the human heart, which is capable of making even his own people so shamefully inconsistent with themselves, and with their acknowledged principles.

I find, that when I have something agreeable in expectation (suppose, for instance, it were a few hours' conversation with your Lordship), my imagination paints and prepares the scene beforehand; hurries me over the intervening space of time, as though it were a useless blank, and anticipates the pleasure I propose. Many of my thoughts of this kind are mere waking dreams; for, perhaps, the opportunity I am eagerly waiting for never happens, but is swallowed up by some unforeseen disappointment; or if not, something from within or without prevents its answering the idea I had formed of it. Nor does my fancy confine itself within the narrow limits of probabilities; it can busy itself as eagerly in ranging after chimeras and impossibilities, and engage my attention to the ideal pursuit of things which are never likely to happen. In these respects my imagination travels with wings; so that if the wildness, the multiplicity, the variety of the phantoms which pass through my mind in the space of a winter's day were known to my fellow-creatures, they would probably deem me, as I am often ready to deem myself, only a more sober and harmless kind of lunatic. But if I endeavour to put this active roving power in a right track, and to represent to myself those scenes which, though not yet present, I know will soon be realised, and have a greatness which the most enlarged exercise of my powers cannot comprehend – if I would fix my thoughts upon the hour of death, the end of the world, the coming of the Judge, or similar subjects, then my imagination is presently tame, cold, and jaded, travels very slowly, and is soon wearied in the road of truth; though in the fairy fields of uncertainty and folly it can skip from mountain to mountain. Mr Addison supposes that the imagination alone, as it can be differently affected, is capable of making us either inconceivably happy or miserable. I am sure it is capable of making us miserable, though I believe it seldom gives us much pleasure, but such as is to be found in a fool's paradise. But I am sure, were my outward life and conduct perfectly free from blame, the disorders and defilement of my imagination are sufficient to constitute me a chief sinner in the sight of him to whom the thoughts and intents of the heart are continually open, and who is of purer eyes than to behold iniquity.

Upon this head I cannot but lament how almost universally education is suited, and as it were designed, to add to the stimulus of depraved nature. A cultivated imagination is commended and sought after as a very desirable talent, though it seldom means more than the possession of a large stock of other people's dreams and fables, with a certain quickness in compounding them, enlarging upon them, and exceeding them by inventions of our own. Poets, painters, and even historians, are employed to assist us from our early years, in forming an habitual relish for shadows and colourings, which both indispose for the search of truth, and even unfit us for its reception, unless proposed just in our own way. The best effect of the Belles Lettres upon the imagination seems generally expressed by the word Taste. And what is this taste but a certain disposition which loves to be humoured, soothed, and flattered, and which can hardly receive or bear the most important truths if they be not decorated and set off with such a delicacy and address as taste requires? I say the most important truths, because truths of a secular importance strike so closely upon the senses, that the decision of taste, perhaps, is not waited for. Thus, if a man be informed of the birth of his child, or that his house is on fire, the message takes up his thoughts, and he is seldom much disgusted with the manner in which it is delivered. But what an insuperable bar is the refined taste of many to their profiting by the preaching of the Gospel, or even to their hearing it. Though the subject of a discourse be weighty, and some just representation given of the evil of sin, the worth of the soul, and the love of Christ; yet if there be something amiss in the elocution, language, or manner of the preacher, people of taste must be possessed, in a good measure, of grace likewise, if they can hear him with tolerable patience. And, perhaps, three-fourths of those who are accounted the most sensible and judicious in the auditory, will remember little about the sermon, but the tone of the voice, the awkwardness of the attitude, the obsolete expressions, and the like; while the poor and simple, not being encumbered with this hurtful accomplishment, receive the messenger as the Lord's servant, and the truth as the Lord's Word, and are comforted and edified. But I stop. Some people would say that I must suppose your

Lordship to have but little taste, or else much grace, or I should not venture to trouble you with such letters as mine. – I am, &c.

Letter 22

My Lord,

The apostle speaks of a blessedness which it is the design of the Gospel to impart to those who receive it. The Galatians once had it, and spoke of it. The apostle reminds them of their loss, which is left upon record as a warning to us. His expression has led me sometimes to consider wherein a Christian's present blessedness consists – I mean that which is attainable in this state of trial, and the sense and exercise of which may be, and too often is, suspended and taken from us. It is a blessedness which, if we speak of man in his natural state, his eye hath not seen, nor his ear heard, so as to understand it, nor can the idea of it arise in his heart. It is no way dependent upon outward circumstances. Prosperity cannot impart it, preserve, or supply the want of it; nor can adversity put it out of our reach. The wise cannot acquire it by dint of superior abilities; nor shall the simple miss it for want of capacity.

The state of true believers, compared with that of others, is always blessed. If they are born from above, and united to Jesus, they are delivered from condemnation, and are heirs of eternal life, and may therefore well be accounted happy. But I consider now, not their harvest, but their first fruits; not their portion in reversion, but the earnest attainable in this life; not what they shall be in heaven, but what, in an humble attendance upon the Lord, they may be while upon earth. There is even at present a prize of our high calling set before us. It is much to be desired that we had such a sense of its value as might prompt us so to run that we might obtain. I have thought this blessedness may be comprised in five particulars, though, in order to take a succinct view of the subject, some of these might be branched out into several others; but I would not, by too many subdivisions, give my letter the air of a sermon.

In the first place, a clear, well-grounded, habitual persuasion of our acceptance in the Beloved is attainable; and though we may be safe, we cannot be said to enjoy blessedness without it. To be in a state of suspense and uncertainty in a point of so great importance is painful; and the Lord has accordingly provided, that his people may have strong consolation on this head. They are blessed, therefore, who have such views of the power, grace, and suitableness of Jesus, and the certainty and security of redemption in him, together with such a consciousness that they have anchored their hopes, and ventured their all upon his person, work, and promise, as furnishes them with a ready answer to all the cavils of unbelief and Satan, in the apostle's manner (Rom. 8:31–37). That Paul could thus challenge and triumph over all charges and enemies, was not an appendage of his office as an apostle, but a part of his experience as a believer; and it lies equally open to us; for we have the same Gospel and the same promises as he had; nor is the efficacy of the Holy Spirit's teaching a whit weakened by length of time. But many stop short of this. They have a hope, but it rather springs apprehension of the Redeemer's engagements and fulness, and therefore fluctuates and changes like the weather. Could they be persuaded to pray with earnestness and importunity, as the apostle prays for them (Eph. 1:17,18, and 3:16–19) they would find a blessedness which they have not yet known; for it is said: 'Ask, and ye shall receive.' – And it is said likewise: 'Ye receive not, because ye ask not.'

Could this privilege be enjoyed properly the natural man would have no objection to it. He would (as he thinks) be pleased to know he should be saved at last, provided that while here he might live in his sins. But the believer will not, cannot think himself blessed, unless he has likewise a conscience void of offence. This was the apostle's daily exercise, though no one was farther from a legal spirit, or more dependent upon Jesus for acceptance. But if we live in any known sin, or allow ourselves in the customary omission of any known duty, supposing it possible, in such a case, to preserve a sense of our acceptance (which can hardly be supposed, for if the Spirit be grieved, our evidences decline of course,) yet we could not be easy. If a traveller was absolutely sure of reaching his journey's end in safety, yet he walked with a thorn in his foot, he must take every step in pain. Such a thorn will be felt in the conscience, till we are favoured with a simplicity of heart, and made willing in all things, great or small, to yield obedience to the authority of the Lord's precepts, and make them the standing rule of our conduct, without wilfully admitting a single exception. At the best, we shall be conscious of innumerable shortcomings, and shameful defilement; but these things will not break our peace, if our hearts are upright. But if we trifle with light, and connive at what we know to be wrong, we shall be weak, restless, and uncomfortable. How many, who we would hope they are the children of the King, are lean from day to day, because some right-hand, or right-eye evil, which they cannot persuade themselves to part with, keeps them halting between two opinions; and they are as distant from happiness as they are from the possibility of reconciling the incompatible services of God and the world. But happy, indeed, is he who condemneth not himself in that thing which he alloweth.

Real communion with the Lord in his appointed means of grace, is likewise an important branch of this blessedness. The Scriptures were instituted for this end, and are sufficient, by virtue of his power and Spirit, to answer it. I do not believe this enjoyment will be always equal, but I believe a comfortable sense of it, in some measure, is generally attainable. To read the Scripture, not as an attorney may read a will, merely to know the sense, but as the heir reads it, as a description and proof of his interest; to hear the Gospel as the voice of our Beloved, so as to have little leisure either for admiring the abilities, or censuring the defects of the preacher; and, in prayer, to feel a liberty of pouring out our hearts before the Lord, to behold some glances of his goodness passing before us, and to breathe forth before him the tempers of a child, the spirit of adoption; and thus, by beholding his glory, to be conformed more and more to his image, and to renew our strength, by drawing water out of the wells of salvation: herein is blessedness. They who have tasted it can say: 'It is good for me to draw nigh to God.' The soul, thus refreshed by the water of life, is preserved from thirsting after the vanities of the world; thus instructed in the sanctuary, comes down from the mount filled with heavenly wisdom, anointed with a holy unction, and thereby qualified to judge, speak, and act in character, in all the relations and occasions of secular life. In this way, besides the pleasure, a spiritual taste is acquired, something analogous to the meaning of the word taste, when applied to music or good breeding, by which discords and improprieties are observed and avoided, as it were by instinct, and what is right is felt and followed, not so much by the force of rules, as by a habit insensibly acquired, and in which the substance of all necessary rules are, if I may so say, digested. O that I knew more of this blessedness, and more of its effects!

Another branch of blessedness is a power of reposing ourselves and our concerns upon the Lord's faithfulness and care, and may be considered in two respects: a reliance upon him that he will surely provide for us, guide us, protect us, be our help in trouble, our shield in danger; so that however poor, weak, and defenceless in ourselves, we may rejoice in his all-sufficiency as our own

– and farther, in consequence of this, a peaceful, humble submission to his will, under all events, which, upon their first impression, are contrary to our own views and desires. Surely, in a world like this, where everything is uncertain, where we are exposed to trials on every hand, and know not but a single hour may bring forth something painful, yes dreadful, to our natural sensations, there can be no blessedness, but so far as we are thus enabled to entrust and resign all to the direction and faithfulness of the Lord our Shepherd. For want of more of this spirit, multitudes of professing Christians perplex and wound themselves, and dishonour their high calling, by continual anxieties, alarms, and complaints. They think nothing safe under the Lord's keeping, unless their own eye is likewise upon it, and are seldom satisfied with any of his dispensations: for though he gratify their desires in nine instances, a refusal in the tenth spoils the relish of all, and they show the truths of the Gospel can afford them little comfort, if self is crossed. But blessed is the man who trusteth in the Lord, and whose hope the Lord is. He shall not be afraid of evil tidings: he shall be kept in perfect peace, though the earth be moved, and the mountains cast into the midst of the sea.

The paper admonishes me it is time to relieve your Lordship. And I have not room to detain you long upon the fifth particular. It belongs to a believer's blessedness to feel his spirit cheerful and active for the Lord's service in the world. For to what other end should he wish to live? If he thought of himself only, it would be better to depart and be with Jesus immediately. But he is a debtor to his grace and love; and though strictly he can make no returns, yet he longs to show his thankfulness: and if the Lord give him a heart to redeem his time, to devote his strength and influence, and lay himself out for his service – that he may be instrumental in promoting his cause, in comforting his people – or enable him to let his light shine before men, that his God and Father may be honoured –

he will account it blessedness. This is indeed the great end of life, and he knows it will evidently appear so at the approach of death; and, therefore, while others are cumbered about many things, he esteems this the one thing needful. – I remain, my Lord, &c.

Letter 23

My Lord, *July, 1776*

That I may not weary you by a preamble, I oblige myself to take the turn of my letter from some passage of Scripture; and I fix upon that which just now occurred to my thoughts, a clause in that pattern of prayer which he who best knows our state has been pleased to leave for the instruction of his people, in their great concern of waiting at his throne of grace (Matt. 6:13), 'And lead us not into temptation.' This petition is seasonable at all times, and to all persons who have any right knowledge of themselves or their spiritual calling.

The word 'temptation', taken at large, includes every kind of trial. To tempt, is to try or prove. In this sense, it is said, the Lord tempted Abraham, that is, he tried him; for God cannot tempt to evil. He proposed such an act of obedience to him, as was a test of his faith, love, dependence, and integrity. Thus, all our afflictions, under his gracious management, are appointed to prove, manifest exercise, and purify the graces of his children. And not afflictions only; prosperity likewise is a state of temptation: and many who have endured sharp sufferings, and came off honourably, have been afterwards greatly hurt and ensnared by prosperity. To this purpose the histories of David and Hezekiah are in point. But by temptation we more frequently understand the wiles and force which Satan employs in assaulting our peace, or spreading snares for our feet. He is always practising against us, either directly and from himself, by the access he has to our hearts, or mediately, by the influence he has over the men and the things of this world. The words which follow confirm this sense – 'Lead us not into temptation; but deliver us from evil', from the evil one, as it might be properly rendered here, and in 1 John 5:19. The subtlety and power of this adversary are very great: he is an overmatch for us; and we have no hope of safety but in the Lord's protection. Satan's action upon the heart may be illustrated by the action of the wind upon the sea. The sea sometimes appears smooth; but it is always disposed to swell and rage, and to obey the impulse of every storm. Thus the heart may be sometimes quiet; but the wind of temptation will awaken and rouse it in a moment: for it is essential to our depraved nature to be unstable and yielding as the water; and when it is under the impression of the enemy, its violence can only be controlled by him who says to the raging sea: 'Be still, and here shall thy proud waves be stayed.' The branches of temptation are almost innumerable; but the principal may be reduced to the several faculties of the soul (as we commonly speak) to which they are more directly suited.

He has temptations for the understanding. He can blind the mind with prejudices and false reasonings, and ply it with arguments for infidelity, till the most obvious truths become questionable. Even where the Gospel has been received, he can insinuate error, which, for the suddenness and malignity of its effects, may be properly compared to poison. A healthy man may be poisoned in a moment; and if he be, the baneful drug is usually mixed with his food. Many, who for a while seemed to be sound in the faith, have had their judgments strongly and strangely perverted, and prevailed upon to renounce and oppose the truths they once prized and defended. Such instances are striking proofs of human weakness, and loud calls to watchfulness and dependence, and to beware of leaning to our own understandings. For these purposes he employs both preachers and authors, who, by fine words and fair speeches, beguile the hearts of the unwary. And, by his immediate influence upon the mind, he is able (if the Lord permits him) to entangle those who are providentially placed out of the reach of corrupt and designing men.

He tempts the conscience. By working upon the unbelief of our hearts, and darkening the glory of the Gospel, he can hold down the soul to the number, weight, and aggravation of its sins, so that it shall not be able to look up to Jesus, nor draw any comfort from his blood, promises, and grace. How many go burdened in this manner, seeking relief from duties, and perhaps spending their strength in things not commanded, though they hear and, perhaps, acknowledge the Gospel? Nor are the wisest and most established able to withstand his assaults, if the Lord withdraw, and give him leave to employ his power and subtlety unrestrained. The Gospel affords sufficient ground for an abiding assurance of hope: nor should we rest satisfied without it. However, the possession and preservation of this privilege depends upon the Lord's presence with the soul, and his shielding us from Satan's attacks; for I am persuaded he is able to sift and shake the strongest believer upon earth.

He has likewise temptations suited to the will. Jesus makes his people willing in the day of his power; yet there is a contrary principle remaining within them, of which Satan knows how to avail himself. There are occasions in which he almost prevails to set self again upon the throne, as Dagon was raised after he had fallen before the ark. How else should any who have tasted that the Lord is gracious, give way to a repining spirit, account his dispensations hard, or his precepts too strict, so as to shrink from their observance through the fear of men, or a regard to their worldly interest?

Farther, he has snares for the affections. In managing these, he gains a great advantage from our situation in a world that knows not God. The Scripture gives Satan the title of 'god of this world'; and believers learn, by painful experience, how great his power is in and over the persons and things of it. So that to be stedfast in wisdom's ways requires unremitted efforts, like pressing through a crowd, or swimming against a stream. How hard is it to live in the midst of pitch and not be defiled. The air of the world is infectious. Our business and unavoidable connections are so interwoven with occasions of sin, and there is so much in our hearts suited to them, that unless we are incessantly upheld by almighty strength, we cannot stand a day nor an hour. Past victories afford us no greater security than they did Samson, who was shamefully surprised by enemies whom he had formerly conquered. Nor are we only tempted by compliances that are evil in themselves. With respect to these, perhaps, conscience may be awake, and we stand upon our guard, but we are still upon Satan's ground; and while he may seem to allow himself to be defeated, he can dexterously change his method, and come upon us where we do not suspect him. Perhaps our greatest danger rises from things in themselves lawful. He can tempt us by our nearest and dearest friends, and pervert every blessing of a kind Providence into an occasion of drawing our hearts from the Giver; yes, spiritual blessings, gifts, comforts, and even graces, are sometimes the engines by which he practises against us, to fill us with vain confidence and self-sufficiency, or to lull us into formality and indolence.

That wonderful power which we call the imagination, is, I suppose, rather the medium of the soul's perceptions during its present state of union with the body, than a spiritual faculty, strictly speaking; but it partakes largely of that depravity which sin has brought upon our whole frame, and affords Satan an avenue for assaulting us with the most terrifying, if not the most dangerous of his temptations. At the best, we have but an indifferent command over it. We cannot, by an act of our own will, exclude a thousand painful, wild, inconsistent, and hurtful ideas, which are ever ready to obtrude themselves upon our minds: and a slight alteration in the animal system, in the motion of the blood or nervous spirits, is sufficient to withdraw it wholly from our dominion, and to leave us like a city without walls or gates, exposed to the incursion of our enemy. We are fearfully and wonderfully made; and, with all our boasted knowledge of other things, can form no conception of what is so vastly interesting to us – the mysterious connection between soul and body, and the manner in which they are mutually affected by each other. The effects we too sensibly feel. The wisest of men would be accounted fools or mad, were they to express in words a small part of what passes within them; and it would appear that much of the soberest life is little better than a waking dream: but how dreadful are the consequences when the Lord permits some hidden pin in the human machine to be altered! Immediately a door flies open, which no hand but his can shut, and the enemy pours in, like a flood, falsehood and horror, and the blackness of darkness; the judgment is borne down and disabled, and the most distressing illusions seize us with all the apparent force of evidence and demonstration. When this is the case in a certain degree, we call it distraction; but there are various degrees of it, which leave a person in the possession of his senses as to the things of common life, and yet are sufficient, with respect to his spiritual concerns, to shake the very foundations of his hope, and deprive him of all peace and comfort, and make him a terror to himself. All the Lord's people are not called to navigate in these deep waters of soul distress; but all are liable. Ah, if we knew what some suffer, which excruciate the minds of those over whom Satan is permitted to tyrannise in this way, surely we should be more earnest and frequent in praying: 'Lead us not into temptation.' From some little sense I have of the malice and subtlety of our spiritual enemies, and the weakness of those barriers which we have to prevent their assaults, I am fully persuaded that nothing less than the continual exertion of that almighty power which preserves the stars in their orbits, can maintain our peace of mind for an hour or a minute. In this view, all comparative difference in external situations seems to be annihilated; for as the Lord's presence can make his people happy in a dungeon, so there are temptations which, if we felt them, would instantly render us incapable of receiving a moment's satisfaction from an assemblage of all earthly blessings, and make the company of our dearest friends tasteless, if not insupportable.

Ah! how little do the busy think of these things! How little indeed do they think of them who profess to believe them! How faint is the sense of our obligations to him, who freely submitted to the fiercest onsets of the powers of darkness, to free us from the punishment due to our sins; otherwise we must have been for ever shut up with those miserable and merciless spirits, who delight in our torment, and who, even in the present state, if they get access to our minds, can make our existence a burden! But our Lord, who knows and considers our weakness, of which we are so little aware, allows and directs us to pray: 'Lead us not into temptation.' We are not to expect an absolute freedom from temptation; we are called to be soldiers, and must sometimes meet with enemies, and perhaps with wounds; yet considering this prayer is provided by him who knows what we are, and where we are, it may afford us both instruction and consolation.

It calls to a constant reflection upon our own weakness. Believers, especially young ones, are prone to rest too much in grace received. They feel their hearts warm; and, like Peter, are ready to please themselves with thinking how they would act in such or such a state of trial. It is as if the Lord had said: 'Poor worms, be not high-minded, but fear and pray, that, if it may be, you may be kept from learning by bitter experience, how weak your supposed strength is.' It sweetly intimates that all our ways, and all our enemies, are in the hands of our great Shepherd. He knows our path. We are short-sighted, and cannot tell what an hour may bring forth: but we are under his protection: and if we depend upon him, we need not be anxiously afraid. He will be faithful to the trust we repose in him, and will suffer no temptation to overtake us, but what he will support us under and bring us through. But it becomes us to beware of security and presumption, to keep our eyes upon him, and not to think ourselves safe a moment longer than our spirits feel and breathe the meaning of this petition.

It implies, likewise, the duty of watchfulness on our part, as our Lord joins them elsewhere: 'Watch and pray.' If we desire not to be led into temptation, surely we are not to run into it. If we wish to be preserved from error, we are to guard against a curious and reasoning spirit. If we would preserve peace of conscience, we must beware of trifling with the light and motions of the Holy Spirit, for without his assistance we cannot maintain faith in exercise. If we would not be ensnared by the men of the world, we are to keep at a proper distance from them. The less we have to do with them the better, excepting so far as the providence of God makes it our duty, in the discharge of our callings and relations, and taking opportunities of doing them good. And though we cannot wholly shut Satan out of our imaginations, we should be cautious that we do not wilfully provide fuel for his flame; but entreat the Lord to set a watch upon our eyes and our ears, and to teach us to reject the first motions and the smallest appearances of evil.

I have been so intent upon my subject, that I have once and again forgot I was writing to your Lordship, otherwise I should not have let my lucubration run to so great a length, which I certainly did not intend when I began. I shall not add to this fault, by making an apology. I have touched upon a topic of great importance to myself. I am one among many who have suffered greatly for want of paying more attention to my need of this prayer. O that I could be wiser hereafter, and always act and speak as knowing that I am always upon a field of battle, and beset by legions! – I am, with great respect, &c.

Letter 24

My Lord, *September, 1776*

Without any preamble, I purpose now to wait on your Lordship, with a few thoughts on the meaning of that name which first obtained at Antioch, in other words, what it is to be a Christian. What are the effects which (making allowance for the unavoidable infirmities attending upon the present state of mortality) may be expected from a real experimental knowledge of the Gospel? I would not insinuate that none are Christians who do not come up to the character I would describe, – for then I fear I should unchristian myself; but only to consider what the Scripture encourages us to aim at as the prize of our high calling in this life. It is generally allowed and lamented, that we are too apt to live below our privileges, and to stop short of what the spirit and the promises of the Gospel point out to us as attainable.

Mr Pope's admired line: 'An honest man's the noblest work of God', may be admitted as a truth when rightly explained. A Christian is the noblest work of God in this visible world, and bears a much brighter impression of his glory and goodness than the sun in the firmament; and none but a Christian can be strictly and properly honest; all others are too much under the power of self, to do universally to others as they would others should do unto them: and nothing but an uniform conduct upon this principle deserves the name of honesty.

The Christian is a new creature, born and taught from

above. He has been convinced of his guilt and misery as a sinner, has fled for refuge to the hope set before him, has seen the Son and believed on him; his natural prejudices against the glory and grace of God's salvation have been subdued and silenced by almighty power; he has accepted the Beloved, and is made acceptable in him: he now knows the Lord; has renounced the confused, distant, uncomfortable notions he once formed of God; and beholds him in Christ, who is the way, the truth, and the life, the only door by which we can enter to any true satisfying knowledge of God, or communion with him. But he sees God in Christ reconciled, a Father, a Saviour, and a Friend, who has freely forgiven him all his sins, and given him the spirit of adoption: he is now no longer a servant, much less a stranger, but a son; and because a son, an heir already interested in all the promises, admitted to the throne of grace, and an assured expectant of eternal glory. The Gospel is designed to give us not only a peradventure or a probability, but a certainty both of our acceptance and our perseverance, till death shall be swallowed up in life. And though many are sadly fluctuating and perplexed upon this head, and perhaps all are so for a season, yet there are those who can say: 'We know that we are of God', and therefore they are stedfast and unmoveable in his way; because they are confident and their labour shall not be in vain, but that when they shall be absent from the body they shall be present with the Lord. This is the state of the advanced experienced Christian, who, being enabled to make his profession the chief business of his life, is strong in the Lord and in the power of his might. Every one who has this hope in Christ purifieth himself even as he is pure. I would now attempt a sketch of the Christian's temper, formed upon these principles and hopes, under the leading branches of its exercise, respecting God, himself, and his fellow-creatures.

The Christian's temper Godward is evidenced by humility. He has received from Gethsemane and

Golgotha such a sense of the evil of sin, and of the holiness of God, combined with his matchless love to sinners, as has deeply penetrated his heart; he has an affecting remembrance of the state of rebellion and enmity in which he once lived against this holy and good God: and he has a quick perception of the defilements and defects which still debase his best services. His mouth is therefore stopped as to boasting; he is vile in his own eyes, and is filled with wonder that the Lord should visit such a sinner with such a salvation. He sees so vast a disproportion between the obligations he is under to grace, and the returns he makes, that he is disposed, yes, constrained, to adopt the apostle's words without affectation, and to account himself less than the least of all saints; and, knowing his own heart while he sees only the outside of others, he is not easily persuaded there can be a believer upon earth so faint, so unfruitful, so unworthy as himself. Yet, though abased, he is not discouraged, for he enjoys peace. The dignity, offices, blood, righteousness, faithfulness and compassion of the Redeemer – in whom he rests, trusts, and lives, for wisdom, righteousness, sanctification, and redemption – are adequate to all his wants and wishes, provide him with an answer to every objection, and give him no less confidence in God, than if he were sinless as an angel; for he sees, that though sin has abounded in him, grace has much more abounded in Jesus. With respect to the past, all things are become new; with respect to the present and future, he leans upon an almighty arm, and relies upon the word and power which made and upholds the heavens and the earth. Though he feels himself unworthy of the smallest mercies, he claims and expects the greatest blessings that God can bestow; and being rooted and grounded in the knowledge and love of Christ, his peace abides, and is not greatly affected either by the variation of his own frames, or the changes of God's dispensations towards him while here. With such a sense of himself, such a heartfelt peace and heavenly hope, how can his spirit but breathe love to his God and Saviour? The love of Christ is the joy of his heart, and the spring of his obedience. With his Saviour's presence, he finds a heaven begun upon earth; and without it, all the other glories of the heavenly state would not content him. With his Saviour's presence he finds the excellence of Christ, his love to sinners, especially his dying love; his love to himself in seeking and saving him when lost, saving him to the uttermost – but I must stop. Your Lordship can better conceive than I can describe, how and why Jesus is dear to the heart that knows him. That part of the Christian's life which is not employed in the active service of his Lord, is chiefly spent in seeking and maintaining communion with him. For this he plies the throne, and studies the word of grace, and frequents the ordinances, where the Lord has promised to meet with his people. These are his golden hours; and when thus employed, how poor and trivial does all that the world call great and important appear in his eyes! Yes, he is solicitous to keep up a fellowship of heart with his Beloved in his busiest scenes; and so far as he can succeed, it alleviates all his labours, and sweetens all his troubles. And when he is neither communing with his Lord, nor acting for him, he accounts his time lost, and is ashamed and grieved. The truth of his love is manifested by submission. This is twofold, and absolute, and without reserve in each. He submits to his revealed will, as made known to him by precept, and by his own example. He aims to tread in his Saviour's footsteps, and made conscious of all his commandments, without exception and without hesitation. Again, he submits to his providential will; he yields to his sovereignty, acquiesces in his wisdom; he knows he has no right to complain of anything, because he is a sinner; and he has no reason because he is sure the Lord does all things well. Therefore his submission is not forced, but is an act of trust. He knows he is not more worthy than he is unable to choose for himself, and therefore rejoices that the Lord has undertaken to manage for him; and were he compelled to make his own choice, he could only choose that all his concerns should remain in that hand to which he has already committed them. And thus he judges of public as well as of his personal affairs. He cannot be an unaffected spectator of national sins, nor without apprehension of their deserved consequences; he feels, and almost trembles for others; but he himself dwells under the shadow of the Almighty, in a sanctuary that cannot be forced; and, therefore, should he see the earth shaken, and the mountains cast into the midst of the sea, his heart would not be greatly moved, for God is his refuge, – the Lord reigns! He sees his Saviour's hands directing every dark appearance, and overruling all to the accomplishment of his own great purposes: this satisfies him; and though the winds and waves should be high, he can venture his own little bark in the storm, for he has an infallible and almighty pilot on board with him. And indeed, why should he fear when he has nothing to lose? His best concerns are safe; and other things he holds as gifts from his Lord, to whose call he is ready to resign them in whatever way he pleases; well knowing that creatures and instruments cannot of themselves touch a hair of his head without the Lord's permission, and that if he does permit them, it must be for the best.

I might enlarge farther, but I shall proceed to consider the Christian's temper respecting himself. He lives godly and soberly. By sobriety we mean more than that he is not a drunkard; his tempers toward God of course form him to a moderation in all temporal things. He is not scrupulous or superstitious; he understands the liberty of the Gospel, that every creature of God is good if it be received with thanksgiving; he does not aim at being needlessly singular, nor practise self-devised austerities. The Christian is neither a Stoic nor a Cynic, yet he finds daily cause for watchfulness and restraint. Satan will not often tempt a believer to gross crimes; our greatest snares and sorest conflicts are usually found in things lawful in themselves, but hurtful to us by their abuse, engrossing too much of our time, or of our hearts, or somehow indisposing us for communion with the Lord. The Christian will be jealous of anything that might entangle his affections, damp his zeal, or straiten him in his opportunities of serving his Saviour. He is likewise content with his situation, because the Lord chooses it for him; his spirit is not eager for additions and alterations in his circumstances. If Divine Providence points out and leads to a change, he is ready to follow, even though it should be what the world would call from a better to a worse; for he is a pilgrim and a stranger here, and a citizen of heaven. As people of fortune sometimes, in travelling, submit cheerfully to inconvenient accommodations, very different from their homes, and comfort themselves with thinking they are not always to live so, so the Christian is not greatly solicitous about externals. If he has them, he will use them moderately. If he has but little of them, he can make a good shift without them; he is but upon a journey, and will soon be at home. If he be rich, experience confirms our Lord's words (Luke 12:15), and satisfies him that a large room, a crowd of servants, and twenty dishes upon his table, add nothing to the real happiness of life. Therefore he will not have his heart set upon such things. If he be in a humbler state, he is more disposed to pity than to envy those above him; for he judges they must have many incumbrances from which he is freed. However, the will of God, and the light of his countenance, are the chief things the Christian, whether rich or poor, regards; and therefore his moderation is made known unto all men.

A third branch of the Christian's temper respects his fellow creatures. And here, methinks, if I had not filled a sheet already, I could enlarge with pleasure. We have in this degenerate day, among those who claim and are allowed the name of Christian, too many of a narrow, selfish, mercenary spirit; but in the beginning it was not so. The Gospel is designed to cure such a spirit, but gives no indulgence to it. A Christian has the mind of Christ who went about doing good, who makes his sun to shine upon the good and the evil, and sendeth rain on the just and the unjust. His Lord's example forms him to the habit of diffusive benevolence; he breathes a spirit of good-will to mankind, and rejoices in every opportunity of being useful to the souls and bodies of others, without respect to parties or interests. He commiserates, and would, if possible, alleviate the miseries of all around him; and if his actual services are restrained by want of ability, yet all share in his sympathy and prayers. Acting in the spirit of his Master, he frequently meets with a measure of the like treatment; but if his good is requited with evil, he labours to overcome evil with good. He feels himself a sinner, and needs much forgiveness; this makes him ready to forgive. He is not haughty, captious, easily offended, or hard to be reconciled, for at the feet of Jesus he has learned meekness; and when he meets with unkindness or injustice, he considers, that though he has not deserved such things from men, they are instruments employed by his heavenly Father (from whom he has deserved to suffer much more) for his humiliation and chastisement, and is therefore more concerned for their sins than for his own sufferings, and prays, after the pattern of his Saviour: 'Father, forgive them, for they know not what they do.' He knows he is fallible, and therefore he cannot be positive. He knows he is frail, and therefore dares not be censorious. As a member of society he is just, punctual in the discharge of every relative duty, faithful to his engagements and promises, rendering to all their dues, obedient to lawful authority, and acting to all men according to the golden rule of doing as he would be done by. His conduct is simple, devoid of artifice, and consistent, attending to every branch of duty; and in the closet, the family, the church, and in the transactions of common life, he is the same man; for in every circumstance he serves the Lord, and aims to maintain a conscience void of offence in his sight. No small part of the beauty of his profession, in the sight of men, consists in the due government of his tongue. The law of truth, and kindness, and purity, is upon his lips. He abhors lying; and is so far from inventing a slander, that he will not repeat a report to the disadvantage of his neighbour, however true, without a proper call. His converse is cheerful, but inoffensive; and he will no more wound another with his wit (if he has a talent that way) than with a knife. His speech is with grace, seasoned with salt, and suited to promote the peace and edification of all around him.

Such is the Christian in civil life; but though he loves all mankind, he stands in a nearer relation, and bears an especial brotherly love to all who are partakers of the faith and hope of the Gospel. This regard is not confined within the pale of a denomination, but extended to all who love the Lord Jesus Christ in sincerity. He calls no man 'master' himself, nor does he wish to impose a shibboleth of his own upon others. He rejoices in the image of God, wherever he sees it, and in the work of God wherever it is carried on. Though tenacious of the truths which the Lord has taught him, his heart is open to those who differ from him in less essential points, and allows to others that right of private judgment which he claims for himself, and is disposed to hold communion in love with all who hold the Head. He cannot indeed countenance those who set aside the one foundation which God has laid in Zion, and maintain errors derogatory to the honour of his Saviour, or subversive of the faith and experience of his people; yet he wishes well to their persons, pities and prays for them, and is ready in meekness to instruct them that oppose; but there is no bitterness in his zeal, being sensible that it is dishonourable to the cause of truth, and quite unsuitable in the mouth of a sinner, who owes all that distinguishes him from the vilest of men to the free grace of God. In a word, he is influenced by the wisdom from above, which, as it is pure, is likewise peaceable, gentle and easy to be entreated, full of mercy, and good works, without partiality, and without hypocrisy.

I must just recur to my first head, and observe, that with this spirit and deportment, the Christian, while he is enabled to maintain a conscience void of offence towards God and man, is still sensible and mindful of indwelling sin; he has his eye more upon his rule than upon his attainments; and therefore finds and confesses, that in everything he comes exceedingly short, and that his best services are not only defective, but defiled; he accounts himself an unprofitable servant, is abased in his own eyes, and derives all his hope and comfort, as well as his strength, from Jesus, whom he has known, received, and trusted, to whom he has committed his soul, in whom he rejoices, and worships God in the spirit, renouncing all confidence in the flesh, and esteeming all things as loss, for the excellency of the knowledge of Christ Jesus his Lord.

If I have lately been rather tardy in making my payments to your Lordship, I have proportionably increased the quantity. It is high time I should now relieve your patience. I hope I long to be a Christian indeed; and I hope this hasty exemplification of my wishes will answer to your Lordship's experience better than I fear it does to my own. May I beg a remembrance in your prayers, that he who has given me to will and desire, may work in me to be and to do according to his own good pleasure. – I am, &c.

Letter 25

My Lord, *November, 1776*

My London journey, which prevented my writing in October, made me amends by an opportunity of waiting upon your Lordship in person. Such seasons are not only pleasant at the time, but afford me pleasure in the review. I could have wished the half-hour we were together by ourselves prolonged to half a day. The subject your Lordship was pleased to suggest has been often upon my mind, and glad should I be were I able to offer you anything satisfactory upon it. There is no doubt but first religious impressions are usually mingled with much of a legal spirit; and that conscience at such a time is not only tender, but misinformed and scrupulous; and I believe, as your Lordship intimated, that when the mind is more enlightened, and we feel a liberty from many fetters we had imposed upon ourselves, we are in danger of verging too far towards the other extreme. It seems to me that no one person can adjust the medium, and draw the line exactly for another. There are so many particulars in every situation, of which a stranger cannot be a competent judge, and the best human advices and models are mixed with such defects, that it is not right to expect others to be absolutely guided by our rules, nor is it safe for us implicitly to adopt the decisions or practices of others. But the Scripture undoubtedly furnishes sufficient and infallible rules for every person, however circumstanced; and the throne of grace is appointed for us to wait upon the Lord for the best exposition of his precepts. Thus David often prays to be led in the right way, in the path of judgment. By frequent prayer, and close acquaintance with the Scripture, and an habitual attention to the state of our hearts, there is a certain delicacy of spiritual taste and discernment to be acquired. Love is the clearest and most persuasive casuist; and when our love to the Lord is in lively exercise, and the rule of his Word is in our eye, we seldom make great mistakes. And I believe the overdoings of a young convert, proceeding from an honest simplicity of heart, and a desire of pleasing the Lord, are more acceptable in his sight than a certain coldness of conduct which frequently takes place afterward, when we are apt to look back with pity upon our former weakness, and secretly to applaud ourselves for our present greater attainments in knowledge, though perhaps (alas, that it should ever be so!) we may have lost as much in warmth as we have gained in light.

From the time we know the Lord, and are bound to him by the cords of love and gratitude, the two chief points we should have in view, I apprehend, are to maintain communion with him in our own souls, and to glorify him in the sight of men. Agreeably to these views, though the Scripture does not enumerate or decide, for or against many things which some plead for, and others condemn; yet it furnishes us with some general canons, which, if rightly applied, will perhaps go a good way towards settling the debate, at least to the satisfaction of those who would rather please God than man. Some of these canons I will just remark to your Lordship, (Rom. 12:1,2; 1 Cor. 7:13, and 10:31; 2 Cor. 6:17; Eph. 4:30, and 5:11,15,16; 1 Thess. 5:22; Eph. 6:18); to which I may add, as suitable to the present times, (Isa. 22:12; Luke 21:34). I apprehend the spirit of these and similar passages of Scripture (for it would be easy to adduce a larger number) will bring a Christian under such restrictions as follow.

To avoid and forbear, for his own sake, whatever has a tendency to damp and indispose his spirit in attendance upon the means of grace; for such things, if they be not condemned as sinful, if they be not absolutely unlawful, yes, though they be, when duly regulated, lawful and right (for often our chief snares are entwined with our blessings), yet if they have a repeated and evident tendency to deaden our hearts to divine things, of which each person's experience must determine, there must be something in them, either in season, measure, or circumstance, wrong to us; and let them promise what they will, they do but rob us of our gold to pay us with counters. For the light of God's countenance, and an open cheerfulness of spirit in walking with him in private, is our chief joy; and we must be already greatly hurt, if anything can be pursued, allowed, or rested in, as a tolerable substitute for it.

For the sake of the church, and the influence example may have upon his fellow Christians, the law of charity and prudence will often require a believer to abstain from some things, not because they are unlawful, but inexpedient. Thus the apostle, though strenuous for the right of his Christian liberty, would have abridged himself of the use, so as to eat no meat, rather than offend a weak brother, rather than mislead him to act against the present light of his conscience. Upon this principle, if I could, without hurt to myself, attend some public amusements, as a concert or oratorio, and return from thence with a warm heart to my closet, (the possibility of which, in my own case, I greatly question,) yet I should think it my duty to forbear, lest some weaker than myself should be encouraged by me to make the like experiment, though in their own minds they might fear it was wrong, and have no other reason to think it lawful but because I did it; in which case I should suspect, that though I received no harm, they would. And I have known and conversed with some who, I fear, have made shipwreck of their profession, who have dated their first decline from imitating others, whom they thought wiser and better than themselves, in such kind of compliance. And it seems that an obligation to this sort of self-denial rises and is strengthened in proportion to the weight and influence of our characters. Were I in private life, I do not know that I should think it sinful to kill a partridge or a hare; but, as a minister, I no more dare do it than I dare join in a drunken frolic, because I know it would give offence to some, and be pleaded for as a license by others.

There is a duty and a charity likewise, which we owe to the world at large, as well as a faithfulness to God and his grace, in our necessary converse among them. This seems to require, that though we should not be needlessly singular, yet, for their instruction, and for the honour of our Lord and Master, we should keep up a certain kind of singularity, and show ourselves called to be a separate people; that though the providence of God has given us callings and relations to fill up (in which we cannot be too exact,) yet we are not of the world, but belong to another community, and act from other principles, by other rules, and to other ends, than the generality of those about us. I have observed that the world will often leave professors in quiet possession of their notions and sentiments, and places of worship, provided they will not be too stiff in the matter of conformity with their more general customs and amusements. But I fear many of them have had their prejudices strengthened against our holy religion by such compliances, and have thought, that if there were such joy and comfort to be found in the ways of God as they hear from our pulpits, professors would not, in such numbers, and so often, run amongst them, to beg a relief from the burden of time hanging upon their hands. As our Lord Jesus is the great representative of his people in heaven, he does them the honour to continue a succession of them as his representatives on earth. Happy are they who are favoured with most of the holy unction, and best enabled to manifest to all around them, by their spirit, tempers, and conversation, what is the proper design and genuine effect of his Gospel upon the hearts of sinners.

In our way of little life in the country, serious people often complain of the snares they meet with from worldly people, and yet they must mix with them to get a livelihood. I advise them, if they can, to do their business with the world as they do it in the rain. If their business calls them abroad, they will not leave it undone for fear of being a little wet; but then, when it is done, they presently seek shelter, and will not stand in the rain for pleasure. So providential and necessary calls of duty, that lead us into the world, will not hurt us, if we find the spirit of the world unpleasant, and are glad to retire from it, and keep out of it as much as our relative duties will permit. That which is our cross is not so likely to be our snare; but if that spirit, which we should always watch and pray against, infects and assimilates our minds to itself, then we are sure to suffer loss, and act below the dignity of our profession.

The value of time is likewise to be taken into the account. It is a precious talent, and our Christian profession opens a wide field for the due improvement of it. Much of it has been already lost, and therefore we are exhorted to redeem it. I think many things which custom pleads for will be excluded from a suitableness to a Christian, for this one reason, that they are not consistent with the simplest notion of the redemption of time. It is generally said we need relaxation; I allow it in a sense; the Lord himself has provided it; and because our spirits are too weak to be always upon the wing in meditation and prayer, he has appointed to all men, from the king downwards, something to do in a secular way. The poor are to labour, the rich are not exempted from something equivalent. And when everything of this sort in each person's situation is properly attended to, I apprehend, if the heart be alive and in a right state, spiritual concernments will present themselves, as affording the noblest, sweetest, and most interesting relaxation from the cares and business of life; as, on the other hand, that business will be the best relaxation, and unbending of the mind from religious exercises; and between the two, perhaps there ought to be but little mere leisure-time. A life, in this sense, divided between God and the world, is desirable; when one part of it is spent in retirement, seeking after and conversing with him whom our souls love; and the other part of it employed in active services for the good of our family, friends, the church, and society, for his sake. Every hour which does not fall in with one or other of these views, I apprehend, is lost time.

The day in which we live seems likewise to call for something of a peculiar spirit in the Lord's people. It is a day of abounding sin, and I fear a day of impending judgment. The world as it was in the days of Noah and Lot, is secure. We are soon to have a day of apparent humiliation; but the just causes for it are not confined to one day, but will subsist and too probably increase every day. If I am not mistaken in the signs of the times, there never was, within the annals of the English history, a period in which the spirit and employment described in Ezekiel 9:4, could be more suitable than the present. The Lord calls for mourning and weeping, but the words of many are stout against him. New species of dissipation are invented almost daily, and the language of those who bear the greatest sway in what is called the polite circle, I mean the interpretative language of their hearts, is like that of the rebellious Jews (Jer. 44:16–17ff). As for the word which thou hast spoken, we will not hearken unto thee at all. In short, things are coming to a point, and it seems to be almost putting to the vote whether the Lord or Baal be God. In this state of affairs, methinks, we cannot be too explicit in avowing our attachment to the Lord, nor too careful in avoiding an improper correspondence with those who are in confederacy against him. We know not how soon we may greatly need that mark of providential protection which is restrained to those who sigh and cry for our abominations. Upon the whole, it appears to me, that it is more honourable, comfortable, and safe (if we cannot exactly hit the golden mean) to be thought by some too scrupulous and precise, than actually to be found too compliant with those things which, if not absolutely contrary to a divine commandment, are hardly compatible with the genius of the Gospel, or conformable to the mind that was in Christ Jesus, which ought also to be in his people. The places and amusements which the world frequent and admire, where occasions and temptations to sin are cultivated, where the sinful passions are provoked and indulged, where the fear of God is so little known or regarded, that those who do fear him must hold their tongues though they should hear his name blasphemed, can hardly be a Christian's voluntary chosen ground. Yet I fear these characters will apply to every kind of polite amusement or assembly in the kingdom.

As to family connections, I cannot think we are bound to break or slight them. But as believers and their friends often live as it were in two elements, there is a mutual awkwardness, which makes their interviews rather dry and tedious. But upon that account they are less frequent than they would otherwise be, which seems an advantage. Both sides keep up returns of civility and affection.

I have simply given your Lordship such thoughts as have occurred to me while writing, without study, and without coherence. I dare not be dogmatic; but I think what I have written is agreeable both to particular texts and to the general tenor of Scripture. I submit it to your judgment. – I am, &c.

Letter 26

My Lord, *July, 1777*

I owe your Lordship a quire of letters for the favour and pleasure of your late visit; and therefore I must begin and write away.

I have lately read Robertson's *History of Charles V*, which, like most other histories, I consider as a comment upon those passages of Scripture which teach us the depravity of man, the deceitfulness of the heart, the ruinous effects of sin, and the powerful, though secret rule of Divine Providence, moving, directing, controlling, the designs and actions of men, with an unerring hand, to the accomplishment of his own purposes, both of mercy and judgment. Without the clue and the light which the Word of God affords, the history of mankind, of any or every age, only presents to view a labyrinth and a chaos; a detail of wickedness and misery to make us tremble, and a confused jumble of interfering incidents, as destitute of stability, connection, or order, as the clouds which fly over our heads.

With the Scripture key, all is plain, all is instructive. Then I see, verily there is a God, who governs the earth, who pours contempt upon princes, takes the wise in their own craftiness, overrules the wrath and pride of man, to bring his own designs to pass, and restrains all that is not necessary to that end; blasting the best concerted enterprises at one time, by means apparently slight, and altogether unexpected, and at other times producing the most important events, from instruments and circumstances which are at first thought too feeble and trivial to deserve notice. I should like to see a writer of Dr Robertson's abilities give us a history upon this plan; but I think his reflections of this sort are too general, too cold, and too few. What an empty phantom do the great men of the world pursue, while they wage war with the peace of mankind, and butcher (in the course of their lives) perhaps hundreds of thousands, to maintain the shadow of authority over distant nations, whom they can reach with no other influence than that of oppression and devastation! But when we consider those who are sacrificed to their ambition, as justly suffering for their sins, then heroes and conquerors appear in their proper light, and worthy to be classed with earthquakes and pestilences, as instruments of divine vengeance. So many cares, so much pains, so many mischiefs, merely to support the idea a worm has formed of his own grandeur, is a proof that man by nature is not only depraved, but infatuated.

How awful is the case of those who live and die in such

a spirit, and who have multiplied miseries upon their fellow-creatures in order to support and feed it! Perhaps they may, upon their entrance on another state, be accosted by multitudes, to the purport of that sarcastic language in the prophet's sublime ode of triumph over the king of Babylon, (Isa. 14:5–17). But though the effects of the principle of self are more extensive and calamitous in proportion as those who are governed by it are more elevated, the principle itself is deep-rooted in every heart, and is the spring of every action, till grace infuses a new principle, and self, like Dagon, falls before the Lord of Hosts. Great and small are but relative terms; and the passions of discontent, pride, and envy, which, in the breast of a potentate, are severely felt by one-half of Europe, exert themselves with equal strength in the heart of a peasant, though for want of materials and opportunities, their operations are confined within narrow bounds. We are fallen into a state of gross idolatry, and self is the idol we worship. – I am, &c.

SIX LETTERS TO THE REV. MR S.

Letter 1

Dear Sir, *June 23, 1775*

I have met with interruptions till now, or you would have heard from me sooner. My thoughts have run much upon the subject of your last, because I perceive it has a near connection with your peace. Your integrity greatly pleases me; far be it from me to shake the principle of your conduct. Yet in the application, I think there is a possibility of carrying your exceptions too far.

From the account you gave me of your sentiments, I cannot but wonder you find it so difficult to accede to the Athanasian Creed, when it seems to me you believe and avow what that creed chiefly sets forth. The Doctrine of the Trinity, some explication of the terms being subjoined, is the Catholic Faith, without the belief of which a man cannot be saved. This damnatory clause seems to me proved by Mark 16:16: 'He that believeth shall be saved', &c. The object of faith must be truth. The doctrine of the Deity of Christ and of the Holy Spirit in union with the Father, so that they are not three Gods, but one God, is not merely a proposition expressed in words, to which our assent is required, but is absolutely necessary to be known; since without it no one truth respecting salvation can be rightly understood, no one promise duly believed, no one duty spiritually performed. I take it for granted, that this doctrine must appear irrational and absurd in the eye of reason, if by reason we mean the reason of man in his fallen state, before it is corrected and enlightened by a heavenly Teacher. No man can say Jesus is Lord, but by the Holy Spirit. I believe with you, that a man may be saved who never heard of the creed, who never read any book but the New Testament, or perhaps a single Evangelist; but he must be taught of God the things that accompany salvation, or I do not think he can be saved. The mercies of God in Christ will not save any (as I apprehend), but according to the method revealed in his Word, that is, those who are truly partakers of faith and holiness. For as the religion of the New Testament ascribes all power to God, and considers all goodness in us as the effect of his communication, we being by nature destitute of spiritual life or light; so those whom God himself is pleased to teach, will infallibly attain the knowledge of all that they are concerned to know. This teaching you are waiting for, and it shall be given you; yes, the Lord, I trust, has begun to teach you already; but if you consider yourself as a learner, and that it is possible, under the Spirit's increasing illumination, you may hereafter adopt some things which at present you cannot approve, I should think it too early as yet to prescribe to yourself rules and determinations for the government of your future life. Should the will of God appoint you a new path for service, he may, sooner than you are aware, quiet your mind, and enable you to subscribe with as full a persuasion of mind as you now object to subscription. If it depended upon me, I could be content that the creed should rest at the bottom of the sea, rather than embarrass a single person of your disposition. Nor am I a warm stickler for subscription in itself; but something of this kind seems necessary, upon the supposition of an establishment.

When I think of an inclosure, some hedge, wall, bank, ditch, &c., is of course included in my idea; for who can conceive of an inclosure without a boundary? So, in a national church, there must be, I apprehend, something marked out, the approbation or refusal of which will determine who do or do not belong to it. And for this purpose articles of some kind seem not improper. You think it would be better to have these articles in scriptural expressions. But if it be lawful to endeavour to exclude from our pulpits men who hold sentiments the most repugnant to the truth, I wish you to consider, whether this can be in any measure secured by articles in which the Scripture doctrines are not explained and stated, as well as expressed. This proposal is strenuously pleaded for by many in our day, upon views very different from yours. The Socinians, for instance, would readily subscribe a scriptural declaration of the high priesthood, atonement, and intercession of Christ (while they are allowed to put their own sense upon the terms) though the sense they maintain be utterly inconsistent with what those who are enlightened by the Holy Spirit learn from the same expressions.

I acknowledge, indeed, that the end is not answered by the present method; since there are too many like the person you mention, who would easily subscribe 900 articles rather than balk his preferment; yet the profligacy of some seems to be no just reason why the church, why any church, should not be at liberty to define the terms upon which they will accept members or teachers, or why conscientious persons should object to these terms (if they think them agreeable to the truth), merely because they are not expressed in the precise words of Scripture. If allowance may be made for human infirmity in the Liturgy, I see not why the Articles may not be entitled to the same privilege. For it seems requisite that we should be as well satisfied with the expressions we use with our lips, in frequent solemn prayer to God, as in what we subscribe with our hands. I am persuaded that the leaders of the Association at the Feathers Tavern, some of them at least, though they begin with the affair of subscription, would not (if they might have their wish) stop there, but would go on with their projected reform, till they had overturned the Liturgy also, or at least weeded from it every expression that bears testimony to the Deity of the Saviour, and the efficacious influence of the Holy Spirit. I bless God that you are far otherwise minded.

I hope, however, though you should not think yourself at liberty to repeat your subscription, the Lord will make you comfortable and useful in your present rank as a curate. Preferment is not necessary, either to our peace or usefulness. We may live and die contentedly, without the honours and emoluments which aspiring men thirst after, if he be pleased to honour us with a dispensation to preach his Gospel, and to crown our endeavours with a blessing. He that winneth souls is wise; wise in the choice of the highest end he can propose to himself in this life; wise in the improvement of the only means by which this desirable end can be attained. Wherever we cast our eyes, the bulk of the people are ignorant, immoral, careless. They live without God in the world; they are neither awed by his authority, nor affected by his goodness, nor enabled to trust to his promises, nor disposed to aim at his glory. If, perhaps, they have a serious interval, or some comparative sobriety of character, they ground their hopes upon their own doings, endeavours or purposes; and treat the inexpressible love of God revealed in Christ, and the Gospel method of salvation by faith in his name, with neglect, often with contempt. They have preachers whom, perhaps, they hear with some pleasure, because they neither alarm their consciences by insisting on the spirituality and sanction of the divine law, nor offend their pride by publishing the humiliating doctrines of that Gospel, which is the power of God through faith unto salvation. Therefore what they do speak they speak in vain; the world grows worse and worse under their instructions; infidelity and profligacy abound more and more; for God will own no other doctrine but what the apostle calls the truth as it is in Jesus; that doctrine which drives the sinner from all his vain pleas, and points out the Lord Jesus Christ as the only ground of hope, the supreme object of desire, as appointed of God to be wisdom, righteousness, sanctification and redemption, to all who believe in his name. When ministers themselves are convinced of sin, and feel the necessity of an almighty Saviour, they presently account their former gain but loss, and determine, with the apostle, to know nothing but Jesus Christ, and him crucified. In proportion as they do this, they are sure to be wondered at, laughed at, and railed at, if the providence of God and the constitution of their country secure them from severer treatment. But they have this invaluable compensation, that they no longer speak without effect. In a greater or less degree a change takes place in their auditories: the blind receive their sight, the deaf hear, the lepers are cleansed; sinners are turned from darkness to light, and from the power of Satan to God; sinful practices are forsaken; and a new course of life in the converts evidences that they have not followed cunningly devised fables, or taken up with uncertain notions; but that God has indeed quickened them by his Spirit, and given them an understanding to know him that is true. The preachers, likewise, while they attempt to teach others, are taught themselves; a blessing descends upon their studies and labours, upon their perusal of the Scripture, upon their attention to what passes within them and around them. The events of every day contribute to throw light upon the Word of God; their views of divine truth grow more enlarged, connected, and comprehensive; many difficulties which perplexed them at their first setting out, trouble them no more; the God whom they serve, and on whom they wait, reveals to them those great things, which, though plainly expressed in the letter of the Scripture, cannot be understood and realised without divine teaching (1 Cor. 2:9–15). Thus they go on from strength to strength; hard things become easy, and a divine light shines upon their paths. Opposition from men perhaps may increase; they may expect to be represented as those who turn the world upside down; the cry 'Great is Diana' will be raised against them and the gates of the temple of preferment will be seldom open to them.

It is the strain of evident sincerity which runs through your letters, that gives me a pleasing confidence the Lord is with you. A disinterested desire of knowing the truth, with a willingness to follow it through all disadvantages, is a preparation of the heart which only God can give. He has directed you to the right method, – searching the Scripture with prayer. Go on, and may his blessing attend you. You may see, from what I have written above, what is the desire of my heart for you. But I am not impatient. Follow your heavenly leader, and in his own time and manner he will make your way plain. I have travelled the way before you; I see what you yet want; I cannot impart it to you, but he can, and I trust he will. It will rejoice my soul to be any way assistant to you; but I am afraid I should not afford you much, either profit or satisfaction, by entering upon a dry defence of creeds and articles.

The truths of Scripture are not like mathematical theorems, which present exactly the same ideas to every person who understands the terms. The Word of God is compared to a mirror (2 Cor. 3:18); but it is a mirror in which the longer we look the more we see: the view will be still growing upon us; and still we shall see but in part while on this side of eternity. When our Lord pronounced Peter blessed, declaring he had learnt that which flesh and blood could not have taught him, yet Peter was at that time much in the dark. The sufferings and death of Jesus, though the only and necessary means of his salvation, were an offence to him; but he lived to glory in what he once could not bear to hear of. Peter had received grace to love the Lord Jesus, to follow him, to venture all, and to forsake all for him: these first good dispositions were of God, and they led to further advances.

So it is still. By nature, self rules in the heart; when this idol is brought low, and we are truly willing to be the Lord's, and to apply to him for strength and direction that we may serve, the good work is begun; for it is a truth that holds universally and without exception, a man can receive nothing except it be given him from heaven. The Lord first finds us when we are thinking of something else (Isa. 65:1); and then we begin to seek him in good earnest, and he has promised to be found of us. People may, by industry and natural abilities, make themselves masters of the external evidences of Christianity, and have much to say for and against different schemes and systems of sentiments; but all this while the heart remains untouched. True religion is not a science of the head, so much as an inward and heartfelt perception, which casts down imaginations, and brings every thought into a sweet and willing subjection to Christ by faith. Here the learned have no real advantage above the ignorant; both see when the eyes of the understanding are enlightened; till then both are equally blind. And the first lesson in the school of Christ is to become a little child, sitting simply at his feet, that we may be made wise unto salvation.

I was not only prevented beginning my letter so soon as I wished, but have been unusually interrupted since I began it. Often, as soon as I could well take the pen in hand, I have been called away to attend company and intervening business. Though I persuade myself, after what I have formerly said, you will put a favourable construction upon my delay, yet it has given me some pain. I set a great value upon your offer of friendship, which I trust will not be interrupted on either side, by the freedom with which we mutually express our difference of sentiments when we are constrained to differ. You please me with entrusting me with the first rough draught of your thoughts; and you may easily perceive, by my manner of writing, that I place equal confidence in your candour. I shall be glad to exchange letters as often as it suits us, without constraint, ceremony, or apology; and may he who is always present with our hearts make our correspondence useful. I pray God to be your sun and shield, your light and strength, to guide you with his eye, to comfort you with his gracious presence in your own soul, and to make you a happy instrument of comforting many. – I am, &c.

Letter 2

My Dear Friend, *July 14, 1775*

I gladly adopt your address, and can assure you that the interchange of every letter unites my heart more closely to you. I am glad to find that your views of articles and creeds are not likely to hinder you from going forward in your present situation; and if, without contracting your usefulness, they only prove a bar to your preferment, I am sure it will be no grief of mind to you at the hour of death, or the day of judgment, that you were enabled to follow the dictates of conscience, in opposition to all the pleas of custom or interest. Since, therefore, I have no desire of shaking your resolves, may we not drop this subject entirely? For indeed, I act but an awkward part in it, being by no means myself an admirer of articles and creeds, nor disposed to be a warm advocate for church power. The propriety of our national establishment, or of any other, is what I have not much to do with; I found it as it is, nor have I influence to alter it were I willing. The question in which I was concerned was simply: Whether I could submit to it, as conscientiously to take a designation to the ministry under it? I thought I could; I accordingly did, and I am thankful that I never have seen cause to repent it.

You seem gently to charge me with a want of candour in what I observed or apprehended concerning the gentlemen of the Feathers Tavern. If I mistake not (for I retain no copies of my letters) I expressed myself with a double restriction, by first saying, – the leaders of that society; and then adding, – or some of them at least. I apprehend your candour will hardly lead you to suppose, that there are none amongst them who would pull down the whole fabric (that is, I mean so far as it crosses the Socinian scheme) if it was left to their choice. I apprehend I may, without the least breach of candour, suppose that the exceptions which Mr Lindsay has made to the Liturgy are not peculiar to himself. It seems plain in his case, and from his own writings, that the mere removal of subscriptions, which is the immediate and ostensible object of the clerical petition, could not have satisfied him; and it is past a doubt with me, that there are others of the clergy like-minded with him. Indeed I could wish to be thought candid by you: though I confess I am not a friend to that lukewarmness and indifference for truth, which bears the name of candour among many in the present day. I desire to maintain a spirit of candour and benevolence to all men, to wish them well, to do them every good office in my power, and to commend what appears to me commendable in a Socinian, as readily as in a Calvinist. I must judge of principles by the Word of God, and of the tree by its fruit. I meddle with no man's final state; because I know that he who is exalted to give repentance and remission of sins, can do it whenever, and to whomsoever he is pleased. Yet I firmly believe, and I make no scruple of proclaiming it, that swearers, drunkards, adulterers, continuing such, cannot inherit the kingdom of God: and I look with no less compassion upon some persons, whose characters in common life may be respectable, when I see them unhappily blinded by their own wisdom: and while they account themselves, and are accounted by many others, master-builders in Zion, rejecting the only foundation upon which a sinner's hope can be safely built.

I am far from thinking the Socinians all hypocrites, but

I think they are all in a most dangerous error; nor do their principles exhibit to my view a whit more of the genuine fruits of Christianity than Deism itself. You say: 'If they be sincere, and fail not for want of diligence in searching, I cannot help thinking that God will not condemn them for an inevitable defect in their understandings.' Indeed, my friend, I have such a low opinion of man in his depraved state, that I believe no one has real sincerity in religious matters till God bestows it: and when he makes a person sincere in his desires after truth, he will assuredly guide him to the possession of it in due time, as our Lord speaks (John 6:44,45). To suppose that any persons can sincerely seek the way of salvation, and yet miss it through an inevitable defect of their understandings, would contradict the plain promises of the Gospel, such as (Matt. 7:7,8; John 7:16,17); but to suppose that nothing is necessary to be known, which some persons who profess sincerity cannot receive, would be in effect to make the Scripture a nose of wax, and open a wide door for scepticism. I am not a judge of the heart; but I may be sure, that whoever makes the foundation stone a rock of offence, cannot be sincere in his inquiries. He may study the Scripture accurately, but he brings his own preconceived sentiments with him, and instead of submitting them to the touchstone of truth, he makes them a rule by which he interprets. That they who lean to their own understandings should stumble and miscarry, I cannot wonder; for the same God who has promised to fill the hungry with good things, has threatened to send the rich empty away (Matt. 11:25). It is not through defect of understanding, but a want of simplicity and humility, that so many stumble like the blind at noonday, and can see nothing of those great truths which are written in the Gospel as with a sunbeam.

You wish me to explain myself concerning the doctrine of the Trinity. I will try; yet I know I cannot, any farther than as he who taught me shall be pleased to bear witness in your heart to what I say. My first principle in religion is what the Scripture teaches me of the utter depravity of human nature, in connection with the spirituality and sanction of the law of God. I believe we are by nature sinners; by practice universally transgressors; that we are dead in trespasses and sin; and that the bent of our natural spirit is enmity against the holiness, government, and grace of God. Upon this ground, I see, feel, and acknowledge the necessity of such a salvation as the Gospel proposes, which, at the same time that it precludes boasting, and stains the pride of all human glory, affords encouragement to those who may be thought, or who may think themselves, the weakest or the vilest of mankind. I believe, that whatever notions a person may take up from education or system, no one ever did, or ever will, feel himself and own himself to be such a lost, miserable, hateful sinner, unless he be powerfully and supernaturally convinced by the Spirit of God. There is, when God pleases, a certain light thrown into the soul, which differs not merely in degree, but in kind, from anything that can be effected, or produced by moral persuasion or argument. But (to take in another of your queries) the Holy Spirit teaches or reveals no new truths, either of doctrine or precept, but only enables us to understand what is already revealed in the Scripture. Here a change takes place, the person that was spiritually blind begins to see. The sinner's character, as described in the Word of God, he finds to be a description of himself; that he is afar off, a stranger, a rebel; that he has hitherto lived in vain. Now he begins to see the necessity of an atonement, an advocate, a shepherd, a comforter; he can no more trust to his own wisdom, strength, and goodness; but, accounting all his former gain but loss, for the excellency of the knowledge of Christ, he renounces every other refuge, and ventures his all upon the person, work, and promise of the Redeemer. In this way, I say, he will find the doctrine of the Trinity not only a proposition, but a principle; that is, from his own wants and situation he will have an abiding conviction, that the Son and Holy Spirit are God, and must be possessed for the attributes and powers of Deity, to support the offices the Scriptures assign them, and to deserve the confidence and worship the Scriptures require to be placed in them, and paid to them. Without this awakened state of mind, a divine reputed orthodox will blunder wretchedly even in defending his own opinions. I have seen laboured defences of the Trinity, which have given me not much more satisfaction than I should probably receive from a dissertation upon the rainbow composed by a man blind from his birth. In effect the knowledge of God cannot be attained by studious discussion on our part; it must be by a revelation on his part (Matt. 11:27; 16:17); a revelation not objectively of new truth, but subjectively of new light in us. Then he that runs may read. Perhaps you may not quite understand my meaning, or not accede to my sentiment at present; I have little doubt, however, but the time is coming when you will. I believe the Lord God has given you that sincerity which he never disappoints.

Far be it from me to arrogate infallibility to myself, or to any writer or preacher: yet, blessed be God, I am not left to float up and down on the uncertain tide of opinion, in those points wherein the peace of my soul is nearly concerned. I know, yes I infallibly know, whom I have believed. I am under no more doubt about the way of salvation than of the way to London. I cannot be deceived, because the Word of God cannot deceive me. It is impossible, however, for me to give you or any person full satisfaction concerning my evidence, because it is of an experimental nature (Rev. 2:17). In general, it arises from the views I have received of the power, compassion, and grace of Jesus, and a consciousness that I, from a conviction of my sin and misery, have fled to him for refuge, entrusted and devoted myself and my all to him. Since my mind has been enlightened, everything within me, and everything around me, confirms and explains to me what I read in Scripture; and though I have reason enough to distrust my own judgment every hour, yet I have no reason to question the great essentials, which the Lord himself hath taught me.

Besides a long letter, I send you a great book. A part of it (for I do not ask you to read the whole) may perhaps explain my meaning better than I have leisure to do myself. I set a high value upon this book of Mr Halyburton's; so that unless I could replace it with another, I know not if I would part with it for its weight in gold. The first and longest treatise is, in my judgment, a masterpiece; but I would chiefly wish you to peruse the Essay concerning Faith, towards the close of the book. I need not beg you to read it carefully, and to read it all. The importance of the subject, its immediate connection with your inquiries, and the accuracy of the reasoning, will render the motive of my request unnecessary. I cannot style him a very elegant writer; and being a Scotsman, he abounds with the Scottish idiom. But you will prefer truth to ornament. I long to hear your opinion of it. It seems to me so adapted to some things that have passed between us as if written on purpose.

The Inquiry concerning Regeneration and Justification, which stands last in the book, I do not desire nor even wish you to read; but if you should, and then think that you have read a speculation more curious than useful, I shall not contradict you. I think it must appear to you in that light; but it was bound up with the rest, and therefore could not stay behind; but I hope the Essay on Faith will please you.

I take great pleasure in your correspondence, still more in the thought of your friendship, which I hope to cultivate to the utmost, and to approve myself sincerely and affectionately yours.

Letter 3

My Dear Friend, *August 11, 1775*

Next week I go to London, where I purpose (if nothing unforeseen prevents) to stay a month. Many things, which must necessarily be attended to before my departure, abridge me of that leisure which I could wish to employ in answering your last. However, I will spare you what I can. I thank you for yours. Your objections neither displease nor weary me. While truth is the object of your inquiry, the more freedom you use with me the better. Nor do they surprise me; for I have formerly made the like objections myself. I have stood upon your ground, and I continue to hope you will one day stand upon mine. As I have told you more than once, I do not mean to dictate to you, but, in the simplicity of friendship, I will give you my thoughts from time to time upon the points you propose, and leave the event to the divine blessing.

I am glad you do not account the Socinians master-builders. However, they esteem themselves so, and are so esteemed, not only by a few (as you think) but by many. I fear Socinianism spreads rapidly amongst us, and bids fair to be the prevailing scheme in this land, especially with those who profess to be the thinking part. The term Arminian, as at present applied, is very indiscriminate, and takes in a great variety of persons and sentiments, amongst whom, I believe, there are many who hold the fundamental truths of the Gospel, and live a life of faith in the Son of God. I am far from supposing that God will guide every sincere person exactly to adopt all my sentiments. But there are some sentiments which I believe essential to the very state and character of a true Christian. And these make him a Christian, not merely by being his acknowledged sentiments, but by a certain peculiar manner in which he possesses them. There is a certain important change that takes place in the heart, by the operation of the Spirit of God, before the soundest and most orthodox sentiments can have their proper influence upon us. This work, or change, the Scripture describes by various names, each of which is designed to teach us the marvellous effects it produces, and the almighty power by which it is produced. It is sometimes called a new birth (John 3:3); sometimes causing the light to shine out of darkness (2 Cor. 4:6); sometimes the opening the eyes of the blind, (Acts 26:18); sometimes the raising the dead to life (Eph. 2:5). Till a person has experienced this change, he will be at a loss to form a right conception of it; but it means not being proselyted to an opinion, but receiving a principle of divine life and light in the soul. And till this is received, the things of God, the truths of the Gospel, cannot be rightly discerned or understood, by the utmost powers of fallen man, who, with all his wisdom, reason, and talents, is still but what the apostle calls the natural man, till the power of God visits his heart (1 Cor. 2:14). This work is sometimes wrought suddenly, as in the case of Lydia (Acts 16:14); at other times very gradually. A person who before was a stranger even to the form of godliness, or at best content with a mere form, finds new thoughts arising in his mind, feels some concern about his sins, some desire to please God, some suspicions that all is not right. He examines his views of religion, hopes the best of them, and yet cannot rest satisfied in them. Today, perhaps, he thinks himself fixed; tomorrow he will be all uncertainty. He inquires of others, weighs, measures, considers, meets with sentiments which he had not attended to, thinks them plausible; but is presently shocked with objections, or supposed consequences, which he finds himself unable to remove. As he goes on in his inquiry, his difficulties increase.

New doubts arise in his mind; even the Scriptures perplex him. He would sound the depths of truth by the plummet of his reason, but he finds his line is too short. Yet even now the man is under a guidance which will at length lead him right. The importance of the subject takes up his thoughts, and takes off the relish he once had for the things of the world. He reads, he prays, he strives, he resolves; sometimes inward embarrassments and outward temptations bring him to his wits' end. He almost wishes to stand where he is, and inquire no more; but he cannot stop. At length he begins to feel the inward depravity which he had before owned as an opinion; a sense of sin and guilt cut him out new work. Here reasoning will stand him in no stead. This is a painful change of mind; but it prepares the way for a blessing. It silences some objections better than a thousand arguments, it cuts the comb of his own wisdom and attainments, it makes him weary of working for life, and teaches him, in God's due time, the meaning of that text: 'To him that worketh not, but believeth in him who justifieth the ungodly, his faith is counted for righteousness.' Then he learns, that scriptural faith is a very different thing from a rational assent to the Gospel – that it is the immediate gift of God (Eph. 2:8); the operation of God (Col. 2:12); that Christ is not only the object, but the author and finisher of faith (Heb. 12:2); and that faith is not so properly a part of that obedience we owe to God, as an inestimable benefit we receive from him, for Christ's sake (Phil. 1:29), which is the medium of our justification (Rom. 5:1) and the principle by which we are united to Christ (as the branch to the vine John 17:21). I am well aware of the pains taken to put a different sense upon these and other seemingly mysterious passages of Scripture; but thus far we speak that which we know, and testify that which we have seen. I have described a path in which I have known many led, and in which I have walked myself.

The Gospel, my dear sir, is a salvation appointed for those who are ready to perish, and is not designed to put them in a way to save themselves by their own works. It speaks to us as condemned already, and calls upon us to believe in a crucified Saviour, that we may receive redemption through his blood, even the forgiveness of our sins. And the Spirit of God, by the Gospel, first convinces us of unbelief, sin, and misery; and then, by revealing the things of Jesus to our minds, enables us, as helpless sinners, to come to Christ, to receive him, to behold him, or, in other words, to believe in him, and expect pardon, life, and grace from him; renouncing every hope and aim in which we once rested, 'and accounting all things loss and dung for the excellency of the knowledge of Christ' (John 6:35; Isa. 45:22; with John 6:40; Col. 2:6). In some of Omicron's letters you will find my thoughts more at large upon these subjects than I have now time to write them. For a farther illustration, I refer you to the manuscript sent herewith. The first part, written in short-hand, does not so immediately concern our present point as the second, which you may read without a key. It relates a matter of indisputable fact, concerning a person with whom (as you will perceive) I was well acquainted. You may depend upon the truth of every tittle. I intrust it to you in the confidence of friendship, and beg that it may not go out of your hands, and that when you have perused it, you would return it, sealed up, by a safe conveyance to my house. You will see in it the sentiments of a man of great learning, sound reasoning, an amiable and irreproachable character, and how little he accounted of all these advantages, when the Lord was pleased to enlighten his mind.

Though we have not exactly the same view of human depravity, yet as we both agree to take our measure of it from the Word of God, I trust we shall not always differ about it. Adam was created in the image of God, in righteousness and true holiness (Eph. 4:24). This moral image, I believe was totally lost by sin. In that sense he died the day, the moment, he ate the forbidden fruit. God was no longer his joy and delight; he was averse from the thoughts of his presence, and would (if possible) have hid himself from him. His natural powers, though doubtless impaired, were not destroyed. Man by nature is still capable of great things. His understanding, reason, memory, imagination, etc., sufficiently proclaim that the hand that made him is divine. He is, as Milton says of Beelzebub, majestic though in ruins. He can reason, invent, and by application attain a considerable knowledge in natural things. The exertions of human genius, as specified in the characters of some philosophers, poets, orators, etc., are wonderful. But man cannot know, love, trust, or serve his Maker, unless he be renewed in the spirit of his mind. God has preserved in him likewise some feelings of benevolence, pity – some sense of natural justice and truth, etc., without which there could be no society; but these, I apprehend, are little more than instincts, by which the world is kept in some small degree of order; but being under the direction of pride and self, do not deserve the name of virtue and goodness; because the exercise of them does not spring from a principle of love to God, nor is directed to his glory, or regulated by the rule of his Word, till a principle of grace is superadded. You think, I will not say, 'that God, judicially, in punishment of one man's sin, added these corruptions to all his posterity'. Let us suppose that the punishment annexed to eating the forbidden fruit had been the loss of Adam's rational powers, and that he should be degraded to the state and capacity of a brute. In this condition, had he begotten children after the fall in his own likeness, his nature being previously changed they must have been of course brutes like himself; for he could not convey to them those original powers which he had lost. Will this illustrate my meaning? Sin did not deprive him of rationality, but of spirituality. His nature became earthly, sensual, yes devilish; and this fallen nature, this carnal mind, which is enmity against God, which is not subject to his law, neither indeed can be (Rom. 8:7), we universally derive from him. Look upon children; they presently show themselves averse from good, but have an overriding propensity to evil. This they can learn even without a master; but ten thousand instructors and instructions cannot instil good into them, so as to teach them to love their Creator, unless a divine power co-operates. Just as it is with the earth, which produces weeds spontaneously; but if you only see a cabbage or an apple-tree, you are sure it was planted or sown there, and did not spring from the soil. I know many hard questions may be started upon this subject; but the Lord in due time will clear his own cause, and vindicate his own ways. I leave all difficulties with him. It is sufficient for me that Scripture asserts, and experience proves, that it is thus in fact (Rom. 3:9-21; Job 14:4). Thus we have not only forfeited our happiness by transgression, but are, by our depravity, incapable of it, and have no more desire or taste for such a state as the Scripture describes heaven to be, than a man born deaf can have for a concert of music. And therefore our Lord declares that except a man be born again he not only shall not, but cannot see the kingdom of God. Hence a two fold necessity of a Saviour – his blood for the pardon of our sins – his life, spirit, and grace to quicken our souls, and form us anew for himself, that we may feel his love, and show forth his praise.

St Paul, before his conversion, was not sincere, in the sense I hope you to be: he thought himself in the right, without doubt, as many have done when they killed God's servants (John 16:2). He was blindly and obstinately zealous: I think he did not enter into the merits of the cause, or inquire into facts with that attention which sincerity would have put him upon. You think that his sincerity and zeal were the very things that made him a chosen instrument; he himself speaks of them as the very things that made him peculiarly unworthy of that honour (1 Cor. 15:9); and he tells us that he was set forth as a pattern of the Lord's long-suffering and mercy, that the very chief of sinners might be encouraged (1 Tim. 1:15,16). Had he been sincerely desirous to know whether Jesus was the Messiah, there was enough in his character, doctrines, miracles, and the prophecies concerning him, to have cleared up the point; but he took it for granted he was right in his opinion, and hurried blindly on in his complete opposition to them. Such a kind of sincerity is common enough. People believe themselves right, and therefore treat others with scorn or rage; appeal to the Scriptures, but first lay down their own preconceived sentiments for truths, and then examine what Scriptures they can find to countenance them. Surely a person's thinking himself right, will not give a sanction to all that he does under that persuasion.

Ignorance and obstinacy are in themselves sinful, and no plea of sincerity will exempt from the danger of being under their influence (Isa. 27:11; Luke 6:39). It appears to me, that though you will not follow any man implicitly, you are desirous of discovering your mistakes, supposing you are mistaken in any point of importance. You read and examine the Word of God, not to find arms wherewith to defend your sentiments at all events, but to know whether they are defensible or not. You pray for God's light and teaching, and in this search, you are willing to risk what men are commonly much afraid of hazarding – character, interest, preferment, favour, etc. A sincerity of this kind I too seldom meet with; when I do, I account it a token for good, and am ready to say so: 'No man can do this, except God be with him.' However, sincerity is not conversion; but I believe it is always a forerunner of it.

I would not be uncharitable and censorious, hasty and peremptory in judging my fellow-creatures. But if I acknowledge the Word of God, I cannot avoid forming my judgment upon it. It is true, I cannot look into people's hearts; but hearts and principles are delineated to my hand in the Scripture. I read, that no murderer has eternal life in him; I read, likewise, 'If any man love not the Lord Jesus Christ, let him be anathema;' and therefore I conclude, that there are speculative errors, as heinous in their guilt, as destructive in their effects, as murder; and that the most moral regular man, as to social life, if he loves not the Lord Jesus Christ, is, in the sight of God the Judge of all, as displeasing as a murderer. It has pleased God, for the peace and support of society, to put a black mark upon those sins which affect the peace and welfare of our neighbour, such as adultery and murder. But undoubtedly the sins committed immediately against himself, must be more heinous than any which offend our fellow-creatures. The second commandment (Matt. 22:39) is like the first; but it depends upon it, and is therefore inferior to it. Men ordinarily judge otherwise. To live regardless of God and the Gospel, is looked upon as a peccadillo, in comparison with offences against society. But sooner or later it will appear otherwise to all. A parcel of robbers may pique themselves upon the justice, honour, and truth they observe towards one another; but because they set up a petty interest, which is inconsistent with the public good, they are deservedly accounted villains, and treated as such, notwithstanding their petty morality among themselves. Now, such a company of robbers bears a much greater proportion to a whole nation, than a nation, or all the nations of the earth, bears to the great God. Our dependence upon him is absolute, our obligations to him infinite. In vain shall men plead their moral discharge of relative duties to each other, if they fail in the unspeakably greater relation under which they stand to God: and therefore, when I see people living without God in the world, as all do till they are converted, I cannot but judge them in a dangerous state – not because I take pleasure in censuring, or think myself authorised to pass sentence upon my fellow-creature, but because the Scripture decides expressly on the case, and I am bound to take my sentiments from thence.

The jailer was certainly a Christian when baptised, as you observe. He trembled; he cried out, 'What must I do to be saved?' Paul did not bid him amend his life, but believe in the Lord Jesus. He believed and rejoiced. But the Lord blessed the apostle's words, to produce in him that saving faith, which filled him with joy and peace. It was, as I observed before, something more than an assent to the proposition that Jesus is the Christ; a resting in him for forgiveness and acceptance, and a cleaving to him in love. No other faith will purify the heart, work by love, and overcome the world.

I need not have pleaded want of leisure as an excuse for a short letter, for I have written a long one. I feel myself much interested in your concerns; – and your unexpected frank application to me (though you well know the light in which I appear to some people) I consider as a providential call, which binds me to your service. I hope our correspondence will be productive of happy effects, and that we shall both one day rejoice in it. – I am, &c.

Letter 4

My Dear Friend, *October 28, 1775*

You complain that I have hitherto disappointed your expectations. If you have preserved my first papers, I believe you will find that I apprised you this might probably be the event, and certainly must, unless it should please God to make what I should write a means of giving you the same views with myself. I only proposed, as a witness, to bear a simple testimony to what I had seen and known. So far as you believed me sincere and unwilling to impose upon you, I thought you might admit there was perhaps some weight in what I advanced, though for the present you could not see things in the same light. And if you allowed a possibility, that my changing the sentiments which I once held in common with yourself, might be upon sufficient grounds, you would, as I trust you do, wait upon the Great Teacher for his instruction; otherwise I did not expect to convince you, nor do I yet, only I am glad to put myself in his hands as an instrument. You quite misunderstood what I spoke of the light and influence of the Spirit of God. He reveals to me no new truths, but has only shown me the meaning of his own written Word; nor is this light a particular revelation, it is common to all who are born again. And thus though you and I cannot fully agree about it, yet I almost daily meet with persons from the east, west, north, and south, whom, though I never saw them before, I find we understand each other at once. This (as you beg me be explicit) is the one thing which I think you at present lack. And I limited my expression to 'one thing', because it is our Lord's expression, and because that 'one thing' includes many.

As I said before, I cannot give it you; but the Lord can; and from the desire he has raised in your heart, I have a warm hope that he will. You place the whole stress of your inquiries upon reason; I am far from discarding reason, when it is enlightened and sanctified; but spiritual things must be spiritually discerned, and can be received and discerned no other way; for to our natural reason they are foolishness (1 Cor. 2:14,15; Matt. 11:25). This certain something I can no more describe to those who have not experienced it, than I could describe the taste of a pineapple to a person who had never seen one. But scriptural proofs might be adduced in abundance, yet not so as to give a solid conviction of it, till we actually experience it. Thus it was with my friend, – whose case I sent you. When God gave him the key (as he expressed it), then the Scriptures were unlocked. His wishing himself a Deist some time before, was not from any libertine exceptions he made to the precepts of the Gospel, by endeavouring to understand the doctrines by dint of reason, though reason in him was as strong and penetrating as in most men I ever met with. Upon your present plan, how can I hope to satisfy you, though even St Paul asserts it, that the carnal mind is enmity against God! You will readily agree with me to the proposition as it stands in St Paul's word, but I think will not so readily assent to what I have no more doubt than of my own existence, is the sense of it: – that the heart of man, of any man, every man, however apparently amiable in his outward conduct, however benevolent to his fellow-creatures, however abundant and zealous in his devotions, is by nature enmity against God: not indeed against the idea he himself forms of God, but against the character which God has revealed of himself in the Scripture. Man is an enemy to the justice, sovereignty, and law of God, and to the one method of salvation he has appointed in the Gospel by faith only; by such a faith, as it is no more in his power to contribute to the production of in himself, than he can contribute to raising the dead, or making a world. Whatever is of the flesh is flesh, and can rise no higher than its principle; but the Lord could convince you of this by a glance or thought.

But I must break off, for want both of room and time. Let me remind you of our agreement, to use and to allow the greatest freedom, and not to be offended with what is meant well on either side. Something in your last letter made me apprehensive you were a little displeased with me. He that knows my heart, knows that I wish you well as my own soul.

Letter 5

My Dear Friend, *November 17, 1775*

You may have observed, I have several times waived speaking about predestination or election, not that I am ashamed of the doctrine; because if it be indeed absurd, shocking, and unjust, the blame will not deservedly fall upon me, for I did not invent it, but upon the Scriptures, where I am sure it is laid down in as plain terms, as that God created the heavens and the earth. I own I cannot but wonder, that persons professing any reverence for the Bible should so openly and strongly declare their abhorrence of what the Bible so expressly teaches, namely, that there is a discrimination of persons by the grace and good pleasure of God, where by nature there is no difference; and that all things respecting the salvation of these persons is infallibly secured by a divine predestination.

I do not offer this as a rational doctrine (though it be highly so to me), but it is scriptural, or else the Scripture is a mere nose of wax, and without a determinate meaning. What ingenuity is needful to interpret many passages in a sense more favourable to our natural prejudices against God's sovereignty! (See Matt. 11:25,26, and 13:10–17; Mark 13:20–22; John 17; John 10:26; Rom. 8:28–30, and 9:13–24, and 11:7; Eph. 1:4,5; 1 Pet. 1:2.) Were I fond of disputing, as I am not, I think I could put a close reasoner hard to it, to maintain the truth of Scripture prophecies, or the belief of a particular providence, unless he would admit a divine predestination of causes and events as the ground of his arguments. However, as I said, I have chosen to waive the point; because, however true and necessary in itself, the knowledge and comprehension of it is not necessary to the being of a true Christian, though I can hardly conceive he can be an established consistent believer without it. This doctrine is not the turning point between you and me; the nature of justification, and the method of a sinner's acceptance with God, are of much more immediate importance; and therefore, if I am to speak plainly, I must say, that I look upon your present sentiments, attainments, and advances, as you describe them, to constitute that kind of gain the apostle speaks of, and concerning which I hope you will one day be of his mind, and be glad to account it all loss, that you may win Christ, and be found in him, 'not having your own righteousness, which is of the law, but the righteousness which is of God by faith' (Phil. 3:4,7–10); for as you tell me, you never remember a time when you were not conscious, before God, of great unworthiness, and intervals of earnest endeavours to serve him, though not with the same success, yet something in the same way as at present: this is but saying in other words, you never remember a time when old things passed away, and all things became new; and yet the apostle insists much upon this (2 Cor. 4:6, and 5:17). The convictions of natural conscience, and those which are wrought in the heart by the Holy Spirit, are different, not only in degree, but in kind, – the light of a glow-worm and of the sun do not more essentially differ. The former are partial and superficial, leave us in possession of a supposed power of our own, are pacified by some appearances of an outward change, and make us no further sensible of the necessity of a Saviour, than to make our doings and duties (if I may so express myself) full weight, which, perhaps, might otherwise be a little deficient when brought to the balances of the sanctuary. But truly spiritual convictions give us far other views of sin; they lead us to a deep and awful consideration of the root, our total absolute depravity, and our utter apostasy from God, by which we are incapable of doing good, as a dead man is, of performing the functions of life. They lead us to the rule and standard, the strict, holy, inflexible law of God, which reaches to the thoughts and intents of the heart; requires perfect, universal, persevering obedience; denounces a curse upon every failure (Gal. 3:10), and affords neither place nor strength for repentance. Thus they sweep away every hope and refuge we had before, and fix upon us a sense of guilt and condemnation, from which there is no relief, till we can look to Jesus, as the wounded Israelites did to the brazen serpent; which was not to give efficacy to medicines and plasters of their own application, but to heal them completely of itself by looking at it (John 3:14,15, and 6:40; Isa. 43:22).

You wish me to explain my distinction between faith and rational assent; and though I know no two things in the world more clearly distinct in themselves, or more expressly distinguished in Scripture, yet I fear I may not easily make it appear to you. You allow faith, in your sense, to be the gift of God; but in my sense, it is likewise wrought by the operation of God (Col. 2:12; Eph. 1:19) – that same energy of the power of his strength, by which the dead body of Jesus was raised from the dead: can these strong expressions intend no more than a rational assent, such as we give to a proposition in Euclid? I believe fallen reason is, of itself, utterly incapable even of assenting to the great truths of revelation; it may assent to the terms in which they are proposed, but it must put its own interpretation upon them, or it would despise them. The natural man can neither receive nor discern the things of God; and if anyone would be wise, the apostle's first advice to him is: 'Let him become a fool, that he may be wise; for the wisdom of the world is foolishness with God.'

Indeed, when the heart is changed, and the mind enlightened, then reason is sanctified, and, if I may so say, baptised, renounces its curious disquisitions, and is content humbly to tread in the path of revelation. This is one difference; assent may be the act of our natural reason; faith is the effect of immediate almighty power. Another difference is, faith is always efficacious, 'it worketh by love'; whereas assent is often given where it has little or no influence upon the conduct. Thus for instance, everyone will assent to this truth: All men are mortal. Yet the greatest part of mankind, though they readily assent to the proposition, – and it would be highly irrational to do otherwise, – yet live as they might do if the reverse were true. But they who have divine faith, feel, as well as say, they are pilgrims and sojourners upon the earth. Again, faith gives peace of conscience, access to God, and a sure evidence and substance of things not seen (Rom. 5:1,2; Heb. 11:1); whereas a calm dispassionate reasoner may be compelled to assent to the external arguments in favour of Christianity, and yet remain a total stranger to that communion with God, that spirit of adoption, that foretaste of glory, which is the privilege and portion of believers. So, likewise, faith overcomes the world, which rational assent will not do. Witness the lives and tempers of thousands who yet would be affronted if their assent to the Gospel should be questioned. To sum up all in a word: 'He that believes shall be saved.' But surely many who give a rational assent to the Gospel live and die in those sins which exclude from the kingdom of God (Gal. 5:19–21). Faith is the effect of a principle of new life implanted in the soul, that was before dead in trespasses and sins: and it qualifies not only for obeying the Saviour's precepts, but chiefly and primarily for receiving from and rejoicing in his fulness, admiring his love, his work, his person, his glory, his advocacy. It makes Christ precious, enthrones him in the heart, presents him as the most delightful object to our meditations; as our wisdom, righteousness, sanctification, and strength; our root, head, life, shepherd, and husband. These are all scriptural expressions and images, setting forth, so far as words can declare, what Jesus is in himself and to his believing people. But how cold is the comment which rational assent puts upon very many passages, wherein the apostle Paul endeavours (but in vain) to express the fulness of his heart upon this subject. A most valued friend of mine, a clergyman now living, had for many years given a rational assent to the Gospel. He laboured with much earnestness upon your plan, was very exemplary in his whole conduct, preached almost incessantly (two or three times every day in the week for years), having a parish in the remote parts of Yorkshire, of great extent, and containing five or six different hamlets at some distance from each other. He succeeded, likewise, with his people, so far as to break them off from outward irregularities; and was mentioned in a letter to the Society for Propagating the Gospel (which I have seen in print) as the most perfect example of a parish priest which this nation, or perhaps this age, has produced. Thus he went on for many years, teaching his people what he knew – for he could teach them no more. He lived in such retirement and recess that he was unacquainted with the persons and principles of any who are now branded as enthusiasts and Methodists. One day, reading Ephesians 3 in his Greek Testament, his thoughts were stopped by the Word in verse 8. He was struck, and led to think with himself to this purpose: 'The apostle, when speaking of the love and riches of Christ, uses remarkable expressions; he speaks of heights, depths, and lengths, and breadths, and unsearchables, where I seem to find everything plain, easy, and rational. He finds mysteries where I can perceive none. Surely, though I use the words, Gospel, faith and grace with him, my ideas of them must be different from his.' This led him to a close examination of all the epistles, and, by the blessing of God, brought on a total change in his views and preaching. He no longer set his people to keep a law of faith, to trust in their sincerity and endeavours, upon some general hope that Christ would help them out where they came short; but he preached Christ himself, as the end of the law for righteousness to everyone that believeth. He felt himself, and laboured to convince others, that there is no hope for a sinner, but merely in the blood of Jesus, and no possibility of his doing any works acceptable to God, till he himself be first made accepted in the Beloved. Nor did he labour in vain. Now his preaching effected not only an outward reformation, but a real change of heart in very many of his hearers. The Word was received, as Paul expresses it, not with a rational assent only, but with demonstration and power in the Holy Spirit, and in much assurance; and their endeavours to observe the Gospel precepts were abundantly more extensive, uniform, and successful, when they were brought to say, with the apostle, 'I am crucified with Christ: nevertheless I live, yet not I, but Christ liveth in me; and the life I live in the flesh, I live by faith in the Son of God.'

Such a change of views and sentiments I pray God my friend may experience. These things may appear uncouth to you at present, as they have done to many, who now bless God for showing them what their reason could never have taught them. My divinity is unfashionable enough at present, but it was not so always; you will find few books written from the era of the Reformation till a little before Laud's time, that set forth any other. There were few pulpits till after the Restoration from which any other was heard. A lamentable change has indeed since taken place; but God has not left himself without witnesses. You think, though I disclaim infallibility, I arrogate too much in speaking with so much certainty. I am fallible indeed; but I am sure of the main points of doctrine I hold. I am not in the least doubt, whether salvation be of faith or of works; whether faith be of our own power or of God's operation; whether Christ's obedience, or our own, be the just ground of our hope; whether a man can truly call Jesus Lord, but by the teaching of the Holy Spirit. I have no more hesitation about these points than I should have, were I asked whether it was God or man who created the heavens and the earth. Besides, as I have more than once observed, your sentiments were once my own; so that I, who have travelled both roads, may have perhaps some stronger reasons to determine me which is the right, than you can who have only travelled one.

Your two sheets may lead me to write as many quires, if I do not check myself. I now come to the two queries you propose, the solution of which you think will clearly mark the difference of our sentiments. The substance of them is, first, Whether I think any sinner ever perished in his sins (to whom the Gospel has been preached,) because God refused to supply him with such a proportion of his assistance as was absolutely necessary to his believing and repenting, or without his having previously rejected the incitements of his Holy Spirit? A full answer to this would require a sheet. But briefly, I believe, that all mankind being corrupt and guilty before God; he might, without impeachment to his justice, have left them all to perish, as we are assured he did the fallen angels. But he has pleased to show mercy, and mercy must be free. If the sinner has any claim to it, so far it is justice, not mercy. He who is to be our Judge, assures us, that few find the gate that leadeth to life, while many throng the road to destruction. Your question seems to imply, that you think God either did make salvation equally open to all, or that it would have been more becoming his goodness to have done so.

But he is the potter, we are the clay: his ways and thoughts are above ours, as the heavens are higher than the earth. The Judge of all the earth will do right. He has appointed a day, when he will manifest, to the conviction of all, that he has done right. Till then, I hold it best to take things upon his word, and not too harshly determine what it becomes Jehovah to do. Instead of saying what I think, let it suffice to remind you of what St Paul thought (Rom. 9:15–21). But farther, I say, that unless mercy were afforded to those who are saved, in a way peculiar to themselves, and what is not afforded to those who perish, I believe no one soul could be saved. For I believe fallen man, universally considered as such, is as incapable of doing the least thing towards his salvation, till preceded by the grace of God (as our article speaks), as a dead body is of restoring itself to life. Whatever difference takes place between men in this respect is of Grace – this is, of God, undeserved. Yes, his first approaches to our hearts are undesired too; for, till he seeks us, we can not, we will not, seek him. It is the day of his power, and not before, his people are made willing. But I believe where the Gospel is preached, they who do perish, do wilfully resist the light, and choose and cleave to darkness, and stifle the convictions which the truths of God, when his true Gospel is indeed preached, will, in one degree or other, force upon their minds. The cares of this world, the deceitfulness of riches, the love of other things, the violence of sinful appetites, their prejudices, pride, and self-righteousness, either prevent the reception, or choke the growth of the good seed: thus their own sin and obstinacy is the proper cause of their destruction; they will not come to Christ that they may have life. At the same time, it is true that they cannot, unless they are supernaturally drawn of God (John 5:40; 6;44). They will not, and they cannot come. Both are equally true, and they are consistent. For a man's 'cannot' is not a natural but a moral inability: not an impossibility in the nature of things, as it is for me to walk upon the water, or to fly in the air; but such an inability, as, instead of extenuating, does exceedingly enhance and aggravate his guilt. He is so blinded by Satan, so alienated from God by nature and wicked works, so given up to sin, so averse from that way of salvation, which is contrary to his pride and natural wisdom, that he will not embrace it or seek after it; and therefore he cannot, till the grace of God powerfully enlightens his mind, and overcomes his obstacles. But this brings me to your second query.

Secondly, do I think that God, in the ordinary course of his providence, grants this assistance in an irresistible manner, or affects faith and conversion without the sinner's own hearty consent and concurrence? I rather choose to term grace invincible than irresistible. For it is too often resisted even by those who believe; but, because it is invincible, it triumphs over all resistance when he is pleased to bestow it. For the rest, I believe no sinner is converted without his own hearty will and concurrence. But he is not willing till he is made so. Why does he at all refuse? Because he is insensible of his state; because he knows not the evil of sin, the strictness of the law, the majesty of God whom he has offended, nor the total apostasy of his heart; because he is blind to eternity, and ignorant of the excellency of Christ; because he is comparatively whole, and sees not his need of this great Physician; because he relies upon his own wisdom, power, and supposed righteousness. Now in this state of things, when God comes with a purpose of mercy, he begins by convincing the person of sin, judgment, and righteousness, and causes him to feel and know that he is a lost, condemned, helpless creature, and then reveals to him the necessity, sufficiency, and willingness of Christ to save them that are ready to perish, without money or price, without doings or deservings. Then he sees faith to be very different from a rational assent, finds that nothing but the power of good can produce a well-grounded hope in the heart of a convinced sinner; therefore looks to Jesus, who is the author and finisher of faith, to enable him to believe. For this he waits on what we call the means of grace; he prays, he reads the Word, he thirsts for God, as the hart pants for the water brooks; and though perhaps for a while he is distressed with many doubts and fears, he is encouraged to wait on, because Jesus has said: 'Him that cometh unto me, I will in no wise cast out.' The obstinacy of the will remains while the understanding is dark, and ceases when that is enlightened. Suppose a man walking in the dark, where there are pits and precipices of which he is not aware: You are sensible of his danger, and call after him; but he thinks he knows better than you, refuses your advice, and is perhaps angry with you for your importunity. He sees no danger, therefore will not be persuaded there is any; but if you go with a light, get before him, and show him plainly, that if he takes another step he falls beyond the power of recovery; – then he will stop of his own accord, blame himself for not heeding you before, and be ready to comply with your farther directions. In either case man's will acts with equal freedom; the difference of his conduct arises from conviction. Something like this is the case of our spiritual concerns. Sinners are called and warned by the Word; but they are wise in their own eyes, and take but little notice till the Lord gives them light, which he is not bound to give to any, and therefore cannot be bound to give to all. They who have it have reason to be thankful, and subscribe to the apostle's words: 'By grace are ye saved, through faith; and that not of yourselves, it is the gift of God.'

Unless it should please God to make what I offer satisfactory, I well know beforehand what objections and answers will occur to you; for these points have been often debated; and, after a course of twenty-seven years, in which religion has been the chief object of my thoughts and inquiries, I am not entirely a stranger to what can be offered on either side. What I write, I write simply and in love; beseeching him, who alone can set a seal to his own truth, to guide you and bless you. This letter has been more than a week in hand; I have been called from it I suppose ten times, frequently in the middle of a paragraph or a line. My leisure, which before was small, is now reduced almost to nothing. But I am desirous to keep up my correspondence with you, because I feel an affectionate interest in you, and because it pleased God to put it into your heart to apply to me. You cannot think how your first letter struck me; it was so unexpected, and seemed so improbable that you should open your mind to me, I immediately conceived a hope that it would prove for good. Nor am I yet discouraged.

I recommend you to the blessing and care of the great Shepherd; and remain, &c.

Letter 6

My Dear Friend, *December 8, 1775*

The carnal mind is enmity. An enemy may be reconciled; but enmity itself is incurable. This carnal mind, natural man, old man, flesh, – for the expressions are all equivalent, and denote and include the heart of man as he is by nature – may be crucified, must be mortified, but cannot be sanctified. All that is good or gracious is the effect of a new creation, a supernatural principle, wrought in the heart by the Gospel of Christ, and the agency of his Spirit; and till that is effected, the highest attainment, the finest qualifications in man, however they may exalt him in his own eyes, or recommend him to the notice of his fellow worms, are but abomination in the sight of God (Luke 16:15). The Gospel is calculated and designed to stain the price of human glory. It is provided, not for the wise and the righteous, for those who think they have good dispositions and good works to plead, but for the guilty, the helpless, the wretched, for those who are ready to perish; it fills the hungry with good things, but it sends the rich empty away (see Rev. 3:17,18).

True faith, my dear Sir, unites the soul to Christ, and thereby gives access to God, and fills it with a peace passing understanding, a hope, a joy unspeakable and full of glory; teaches us that we are weak in ourselves, but enables us to be strong in the Lord, and in the power of his might. To those who thus believe Christ is precious, their beloved; they hear and know his voice; the very sound of his name gladdens their hearts, and he manifests himself to them as he does not to the world. Thus the Scriptures speak, – thus the first Christians experienced; and this is precisely the language which, in our days, is despised as enthusiasm and folly. For it is now as it was then, though these things are revealed to babes, and they are as sure of them as that they see the noon-day sun, they are hidden from the wise and prudent, till the Lord makes them willing to renounce their own wisdom, and to become fools, that they may be truly wise (1 Cor. 1:18,19; 8:2). Attention to the education of children is an undoubted duty; and it is a mercy when it so far succeeds as to preserve them from gross wickedness; but it will not change the heart. They who receive Christ are born, not of blood, nor of the will of the flesh, nor of the will of man, but of God (John 1:13).

If a man professes to love the Lord Jesus, I am willing to believe him, if he does not give me proof to the contrary; but I am sure, at the same time, no one can love him in the scriptural sense who does not know the need and the worth of a Saviour; in other words, who is not brought, as a ruined helpless sinner, to live upon him for wisdom, righteousness, sanctification and redemption. They who love him thus will speak highly of him, and acknowledge that he is their all in all. And they who thus love him, and speak of him, will get little thanks for their pains in such a world as this; 'all that live godly in Christ Jesus must suffer persecution, – the world that hated him will hate them.' And though it is possible by his grace to put to silence, in some measure, the ignorance of foolish men; and though his providence can protect his people, so that not a hair of their heads can be hurt without his permission; yet the world will show their teeth, even if they are not suffered to bite. The apostles were accounted babblers. I need not point out to you the force of these expressions. We are no better than the apostles; nor have we reason to expect much better treatment, so far as we walk in their steps. On the other hand, there is a sober decent way of speaking of God, and goodness, and benevolence, and sobriety, which the world will bear well enough; – nay, we may say a little about Jesus Christ, as ready to make up the deficiencies of our honest and good endeavours, and this will not displease them. But, if we preach him as the only foundation, lay open the horrid evils of the human heart, tell our hearers that they are dead in trespasses and sins, and have no better ground of hope in themselves than the vilest malefactors, in order to exalt the glory of Jesus, as saving those who are saved wholly and freely for his own name's sake; if we tell the virtuous and decent, as well as the profligate, that unless they are born again, and made partakers of living faith, and count all things loss for the excellency of the knowledge of Christ, they cannot be saved: this the world cannot bear. We shall be called knaves or fools, uncharitable bigots, and twenty hard names. If you have met with nothing like this, I wish it may lead you to suspect whether you have yet received the right key to the doctrines of Christ; for, depend upon it, the offence of the cross is not ceased.

At present it remains with you whether our correspondence continues or not, as this is the third letter I have written since I heard from you, and therefore must be the last till I do. I should think what remains might be better settled viva voce; for which purpose I shall be glad to see you, or ready to wait on you when leisure will permit, and when I know it will be agreeable: but if (as life and all its affairs are precarious) we should never meet in this world, I pray God we may meet at the right hand of Jesus, in the great day when he shall come to gather up his jewels, and to judge the world. There is an endless diversity of opinions in matters of religion; which of them are right and safe, and will lead to eternal glory. I am still in a manner lost amidst more engagements than I have time to comply with; but I feel and know that I am, &c.

FIVE LETTERS TO MR B.

Letter 1

My Dear Sir, *May 19, 1775*

I hope you will find the Lord present at all times, and in all places. When it is so, we are at home everywhere; when it is otherwise, home is a prison, and abroad a wilderness. I know what I ought to desire, and what I do desire. I point him out to others as the all in all; I esteem him as such in my own judgment; but, alas, my experience abounds with complaints. He is my sun; but clouds, and sometimes walls, intercept him from my view. He is my strength; yet I am prone to lean upon reeds. He is my friend; but on my part there is such coldness and ingratitude, as no other friend could bear. But still he is gracious, and shames me with his repeated multiplied goodness. O for a warmer heart, a more simple independence, a more active zeal, a more sensible deliverance from the effects of this body of sin and death! He helps me in my endeavours to keep the vineyards of others; but alas, my own does not seem to flourish as some do around me. However, though I cannot say I labour more abundantly than they all, I have reason to say with thankfulness: 'By the grace of God I am what I am.' My poor story would soon be much worse, did not he support, restrain, and watch over me every minute. Let me entreat your praises and prayers on the behalf of me and mine; and may the Lord bless you and yours with an increase in every good. – I am, &c.

Letter 2

My Dear Sir, *September 2, 1776*

The young woman I spoke of is still living, and not much weaker than when I left her. The Lord was pleased to relieve her on Tuesday evening, and she was comfortable the remainder of the week. But yesterday her conflicts returned, and she was in great distress. The enemy, who always fights against the peace of the Lord's children, finds great advantage against them when their spirits are weakened and worn down by long illness, and is often permitted to assault them. The reasons are hidden from us, but they are doubtless worthy of his wisdom and love, and they terminate in victory, to the praise of his glorious grace, which is more signally manifested by his leading them safely through fire and water than if their path was always smooth. He is sovereign in his dispensations, and appoints some of his people to trials and exercises, to which others, perhaps, are strangers all their days. Believers are soldiers. All soldiers, by their profession, are engaged to fight if called upon; but who shall be called to sustain the hottest service, and be most frequently exposed upon the field of battle, depends upon the will of the general or king. Some of our soldiers are now upon hard service in America, while others are stationed around the palace, see the king's face daily, and have no dangers or hardships to encounter. These, however, are just as likely to be called on for active service as the others; but, if not called upon, they may enjoy with thankfulness the easier post assigned them. Thus, the Captain of our salvation allots to his soldiers such stations as he thinks proper – he has a right to employ whom he will, and where he will. Some are comparatively at ease, – they are not exposed to the fiercest onsets, but live near his presence; others are, pressed above measure, beyond strength, so that they despair even of life, – yet they are supported, and in the end made more than conquerors through him who hath loved them. Long observation convinces me, that the temptations which some endure are not chastisements brought upon them by unfaithfulness, or for anything remarkably wrong in their spirit or walk; I often rather consider that, in his warfare, as in worldly wars, the post of danger and difficulty is the post of honour, and as such, assigned to those whom he has favoured with a peculiar measure of his grace. This young woman, in particular, was always, from her first awakening, remarkably humble and spiritual, and possessed a broken and contrite spirit. I never saw her in a wrong spirit, or heard her speak an unadvised word; yet I believe it is impossible to express the agonies she has endured. The effect of them is visible. Her animal frame was unable to sustain the burden. I believe these agonies were the immediate cause of that illness which is now bringing her down to the grave. I doubt not but these cases depend in a great measure upon constitution; but then the temperament of our bodies depends upon his pleasure; for if the very hairs of our head are numbered, it is impossible that those circumstances of our frame which, by the near connection between body and soul, have a powerful influence upon the state of our minds, can escape his notice. He could cure such bodily disorders which affect the peace of his people in a moment; yet he does not, though he loves them. There must be wise reasons why he does not; and though we know them not now, we shall know them hereafter. Possibly some suffer for the instruction of the rest, that we may learn to be more thankful to him for the peace we enjoy, and to be more humbly dependent upon him for the continuance of it. The Lord's way is in the deep; and his path in the great waters, untraceable by our feeble reasonings; but faith brings in a good report. We need not doubt but he does all things well, and in due time we shall see it. In the meanwhile, he checks our vain inquiries, and calls upon us to be still, and know that he is God.

I brought home with me a thankful sense of the kindness and friendship I am favoured with from you and all yours. I account this connection one of the great comforts of my life; and I hope it has been, and will be, not only pleasant but profitable to me. Though I am but a poor scholar, I hope I am not unwilling to learn; and the Lord, in his merciful providence, appoints me many teachers. There is little praise due to us, if we either communicate or receive benefit in our fellowship with our fellow-disciples. In both we are but instruments under the influence of a higher hand. Were Christians to meet together without their Lord, they would either trifle or quarrel their time away. But as he has said: 'Where two or three are met, there am I in the midst of them.' We may well be glad of opportunities of coming together. And though, for my own part, I am so poor an improver of such seasons that the recollection of them, when past, is generally accompanied with shame and regret, yet he is gracious and merciful, and seldom leaves me to complain that they were wholly in vain. – I am, &c.

Letter 3

My Dear Sir, *July 22, 1777*

The complaints you make of what passes within, encourage me in what I feel myself. Indeed, if those whom I have reason to believe are more spiritual and humble than I am, did not give some testimony that they find their hearts made of the same materials as mine is, I should be sometimes hard put to it to believe that I have any part or lot in the matter, or any real knowledge of the life of faith. But this concurrent testimony of many witnesses confirms me in what I think the Scripture plainly teaches, – that the soil of human nature, though many spots are certainly better weeded, planted, and cultivated than others, is universally bad. It is so bad that it cannot be worse, and of itself is only capable of producing noxious weeds, and nourishing venomous creatures. We often see the effects of culture, skill, and expense will make a garden where all was desert before. When Jesus, the good husbandman, incloses a soil, and separates it from the waste of the world, to make it a residence for himself, a change presently takes place; it is infinitely more cheering and fruitful than those of the material sun. But its natural propensity to produce weeds still continues, and one half of his dispensations may be compared to a company of weeders, whom he sends forth into his garden to pluck up all which he has not planted with his own hand, and which, if left to grow, would quickly overpower the rest. But, alas, the ground is so impregnated with evil seeds, and they shoot in such quick succession, that if this weeding work were not constantly repeated, all former labour would be lost. Hence arises the necessity of daily crosses and disappointments, daily changes of frame, and such multiplied convictions, that we are nothing, and can do nothing of ourselves; all are needful, and barely sufficient to prevent our hearts from being overrun with pride, self-dependence, and security. – Yours, &c.

Letter 4

My Dear Sir, *November 6, 1777*

You say you are more disposed to cry, Lord have mercy on me, than, hallelujah. Why not both together? When the treble is praise, and heart-humiliation for the bass, the melody is pleasant, and the harmony is good. However, if not both together, we must have them alternately;

not all singing, not all sighing, but an interchange and balance, that we may be neither lifted too high nor cast down too low, – which would be the case if we were very comfortable or very sorrowful for a long time. But though we change, the Saviour changes not. All our concerns are in his hands, and therefore safe. His path is in the deep waters, his thoughts and methods of conduct are as high above ours as the heavens are high above the earth; and he often takes a course for accomplishing his purpose directly contrary to what our narrow views would prescribe. He wounds in order to heal, kills that he may make alive, casts down when he designs to raise, brings a death upon our feelings, wishes and prospects, when he is about to give us the desire of our hearts.

These things he does to prove us; but he himself knows, and has determined beforehand, what he will do. The proof indeed usually turns out to our shame. Impatience and unbelief show their heads, and prompt us to suppose this and the other thing, yet perhaps all things are against us, to question whether he be with us and for us, or not. But it issues, likewise, in the praise of his goodness, when we find that, despite all our unkind complaints and suspicions, he is still working wonderfully for us, causing light to shine out of darkness, and doing us good in spite of ourselves. – I am, &c.

Letter 5

To Mr B. junior

Dear Sir, *August 24, 1774*

The lowness of your voice, and a blameable absence of mind on my part, prevented me from understanding what you said when you took your leave of me; nor did I just at that instant recollect that you were so soon going away. I could not otherwise have parted with you, without a particular expression of my warmest wishes for your welfare, and commending you with an emotion which my heart always feels for you, to our God, and the Word of his grace. Permit me, therefore, by writing to assure you, so far as I can answer for myself, that the request you were pleased to make for my remembrance will not be forgotten by me.

You are going abroad; you will carry with you, I doubt not, the best advice, strengthened by the authority and affection of parents whom you greatly love and greatly reverence. This may seem to make anything a stranger can offer unnecessary, if not impertinent; yet, confiding in your candour, and in your good opinion of my intention, I shall venture to let my pen run on a little longer, not only my wishes, but my hopes are strong on your behalf. Perhaps there is hardly a young man in the kingdom, born to a fortune, who is setting out in life upon equal advantages with yourself. How many, at your years, who have been brought up in affluence, are unprincipled, uninstructed, and have already entered upon a course of dissipation and folly in which it is impossible that they themselves can find satisfaction, and which (unless they are reclaimed from it by an almighty arm) will infallibly preclude them from usefulness or esteem! In contrast to this, your early years have been successfully employed in the pursuit of knowledge, and your education formed under the most animating and endearing influence; and the Lord has furnished you with every natural ability of body and mind, which may qualify you to serve him in that situation of life which his providence has allotted you.

What may I then further hope from these beginnings, especially, as it is easy to observe, that he has given you an amiable and promising disposition of spirit, and has not only preserved you from being hurried down the stream of a giddy world, but enabled you to account the tender restraint under which you have been educated, not a yoke, but a privilege? I sympathise with you at what you will feel when you are first separated from your happy family. But the Lord God, who is the sun and shield of those who fear him, will be always near you. His favour is the one thing needful, which no human teaching can communicate.

Were I most intimate with you, I could have asked the question, and perhaps received the satisfaction to know, that you have already begun to consider him in this light; that you feel a vanity in science, an emptiness in creatures, and find that you have desires, which only he who gave them can satisfy. I trust it either is or will be thus. As to learning, though it is useful when we know how to make a right use of it, yet considered as in our own power, and to those who trust to it, without seeking a superior guidance, it is usually the source of perplexity, strife, scepticism, and infidelity. It is indeed like a sword in a madman's hands, which gives him the more opportunity of hurting himself and others. As to what the world calls pleasure, there is so little in it, that even the philosophers of old, or many of them, though they had little of value to substitute in its room, could despise it. You will perhaps meet with some, who will talk another language, who will pretend to be too wise to submit to the Bible, and too happy in worldly things, to expect or desire any other happiness. However, I trust you have seen enough to enable you to treat such persons with the pity, and such pretensions with the contempt they deserve.

Should we set our concerns with an eternal world aside for a moment, it would be easy to demonstrate that religion is necessary, in order to make the most of this life, and to enjoy temporal good with the highest relish. In such a world as this, where we are every moment liable to so many unforeseen and unavoidable contingencies, a man without religion may be compared to a ship in a storm, without either rudder, anchor or pilot. But then, the religion which only deserves the name, must come from above; it must be suited to the state and wants of a sinner, it must be capable of comforting the heart, it must take away the sting and dread of death, and fix our confidence upon one who is always able to help us. Such is the religion of Jesus, such are its effects, and such are the criteria whereby we are to judge the various forms and schemes under which it is proposed to us. I am only reminding you of what you know, and what you have known to be verified by living and dying examples. This happiness, my dear Sir, is open to you – to all who seek. He is enthroned in heaven, but prayer will bring him down to the heart. Indeed he is always with us; and if we feel one desire towards him, we may accept it as a token that he gave it us to encourage us to ask for more.

May he be your guide and guard, be with you at all times, and in all places, and bring you back to your father's house in peace. Should I live to see that day, you have few friends whose congratulations would be warmer or more sincere than mine; and if, when you are settled and at leisure, you will afford me a letter, it will be both a pleasure and a favour to me, dear Sir, – Yours, &c.

THREE LETTERS TO MISS M.

Letter 1

My Dear Miss M., *November 11, 1775*

Our late visit to ——— was very pleasant for me; if anything that passed was of service to you, we know to whom the thanks are due; for we can neither communicate nor receive anything but so far as he is pleased to enable us. One reason why he often disappoints us is, that we may learn to depend on him alone. The Lord's comforts are not, however, the proper ground of our hope; a good hope springs from such a sense of our wants, and such a persuasion of his power and grace, as engages the heart to venture, upon the warrant of his promises, to trust in him for salvation. In a sense, we are often hindering him by our impatience and unbelief; but, strictly speaking, when he really begins the good work, and gives us a desire which will be satisfied with nothing short of himself, he will not be hindered from carrying it on. Had it depended upon myself, upon my wisdom or faithfulness, I should have hindered him and ruined myself long ago. How often have I grieved and resisted his Spirit! But hereby I have learned more of his patience and tenderness than I could otherwise have known. He knows our frame, and what effects our evil nature will have; he sees us from first to last. A thousand evils arise in our hearts, a thousand wrong actions in our conduct, which, as they do arise, are new to ourselves, and perhaps at some times we were ready to think we were capable of such things; but none of them are new to him to whom past, present and future are the same. The foresight of them did not prevent his calling us by his grace. Though he knew we were vile, and should prove ungrateful and unfaithful, yet he would be found of us; he would knock at the door of our hearts, and gain himself an entrance. Nor shall they prevent his accomplishing his gracious purpose. It is our part to be abased before him, and quietly to hope and wait for his salvation in the use of his appointed means. The power, success, and blessing are wholly from himself. To make us more sensible of this, he often withdraws from our perceptions: and as, in the absence of the sun, the wild beasts of the forest roam abroad: so, when Jesus hides himself, we presently perceive what is in our hearts, and what a poor progress we can make without him; when he returns, his light chases the evils away, and we are well again.

It is your great and singular mercy, my dear Miss, that he has taught you to seek him so early in life. You are entered in the way of salvation, but you must not expect all at once. The work of grace is compared to the corn, and to a building; the growth of the one, and the carrying forward of the other, are gradual. In a building, for instance, if it be large, there is much to be done in preparing and laying the foundation, before the walls appear above ground; much is going on within, when the work does not seem perhaps to advance without; and when it is considerably forward, yet being encumbered with scaffolds and rubbish, a bystander sees it at a great disadvantage, and can form but an imperfect judgment of it. But all this while the architect himself, even from the laying of the first stone, conceives of it according to the plan and design he has formed; he prepares and adjusts the materials, disposing each in its proper time and place and views it, in idea, as already finished. In due season it is completed, but not in a day. The top-stone is fixed, and then the scaffolds and rubbish being removed, it appears to others as he intended it should be. Men indeed often plan what, for want of skill or ability, or from unforeseen disappointments, they are unable to execute. But nothing can disappoint the heavenly Builder; nor will he ever be reproached with forsaking the work of his own hands, or beginning that which he could not or would not accomplish (Phil. 1:6). Let us therefore be thankful for beginnings, and patiently wait the event. His enemies strive to retard the work, as they did when the Jews, by his order, set about rebuilding the temple. Yet it was finished in defiance of them all. – Believe me to be, &c.

Letter 2

My Dear Miss M., *April 29, 1776*

I thank you for your last; and I rejoice in the Lord's goodness to you. To be drawn by love, exempted from those distressing terrors and temptations which some are beset with; to be favoured with the ordinances and means of grace, and connected with those, and with those only, who are disposed and qualified to assist and encourage you in seeking the Saviour; these are peculiar privileges, which all concur in your case: he loves you, he deals gently with you, he provides well for you, and accompanies every outward privilege with his special blessing; and I trust he will lead you on from strength to strength, and show you still greater things than you have yet seen. They whom he teaches are always increasing in knowledge both of themselves and of him. The heart is deep, and, like Ezekiel's vision, presents so many chambers of imagery, one within another, that it requires time to get a considerable acquaintance with it, and we shall never know it thoroughly. It is now more than twenty-eight years since the Lord began to open mine to my own view; and from that time to this, almost every day has shown me something which till then was unobserved; and the farther I go, the more I seem convinced that I have entered but a little way. A person who travels in some parts of Derbyshire, may easily be satisfied that the country is cavernous; but how large, how deep, how numerous the caverns may be, which are hidden from us by the surface of the ground, and what is contained in them, are questions which our keenest inquiries cannot fully answer. Thus I judge of the heart, that it is very deep and dark, and full of evil; but as to particulars, I know not one of a thousand.

And if our own hearts are beyond our comprehension, how much more incomprehensible is the heart of Jesus! If sin abounds in us, grace and love superabound in him: his ways and thoughts are higher than ours, as the heavens are higher than the earth; his love has a height, and depth, and length, and breadth that passeth all knowledge; and his riches of grace are unsearchable riches (Eph. 3:8, 18–19). All that we have received, or can receive from him, or know of him in this light, compared with what he is in himself, or what he has for us, is but as the drop in a bucket compared with the ocean, or a single ray of light in comparison with the sun. The waters of the sanctuary flow to us at first almost upon a level, ankle deep, so graciously does the Lord condescend to our weakness; but they rise as we advance, and constrain us to cry out with the apostle, O the depth! We find before us, as Dr Watts beautifully expresses it:

> A sea of love and grace unknown,
> Without a bottom or a shore.

O the excellency of the knowledge of Christ! It will be growing upon us through time, yes, I believe through eternity. What an astonishing and what a cheering thought, that this high and lofty One should unite himself to our nature, that so, in a way worthy of his adorable perfections, he might, by his Spirit, unite us to himself! Could such a thought have arisen in our hearts, without the warrant of his Word (but it is a thought which no created mind was capable of conceiving till he revealed it) it would have been presumption and blasphemy; but now he has made it known, it is the foundation of our hope, and an inexhaustible spring of life and joy. Well may we say: 'Lord, what is man, that thou shouldst thus visit him?' – I am, &c.

Letter 3

My Dear Miss M., *September 3, 1776*

We saw no danger upon the road homeward; but my judgment tells me we are always upon the brink of danger, though we see it not; and that, without the immediate protection and care of him who preserveth the stars in their courses, there could be no travelling safely a few miles, nor even sitting in safety by the fireside. But with him we are safe in all places and circumstances, till our race is done, and his gracious purposes concerning us, in the present life, are completely answered; – then he will call us home, that we may see his face, and be with him for ever, and then it will not much signify what messenger he shall be pleased to send for us.

While he took care of us abroad, he watched over our concerns at home likewise; so that we found all well upon our return, and met with nothing to grieve us. Many go out and return home no more, and many find distressing things have happened in their absence; but we have to set up our Ebenezer, and to say, 'Hitherto he has helped us.' 'Assist me to praise him.' The Lord is leading you in the good old way, in which you may perceive the footsteps of his flock who have gone before you. They had in their day the same difficulties, fears, and complaints as we have, and through mercy we partake of the same consolation which supported and refreshed them; and the promises which they trusted and found faithful, are equally sure to us. It is still true, that they who believe shall never be confounded. If left to ourselves, we should have built upon sand; but he has provided and revealed a sure foundation, removed our natural prejudices against it; and now, though rains and floods and storms assault our building, it cannot fall, for it is founded upon a rock. The suspicions and fears which arise in an awakened mind, proceed, in a good measure, from remaining unbelief; but not wholly so; for there is a jealousy and diffidence of ourselves, a wariness, owing to a sense of the deceitfulness of our hearts, which is a grace and a gift of the Lord. Some people who have much zeal, but are destitute of this jealous fear, may be compared to a ship that spreads a great deal of sail, but is not properly ballasted, and is therefore in danger of being blown over whenever a storm comes. A sincere person has many reasons for distrusting his own judgment; is sensible of the vast importance of the case, and afraid of too hastily concluding in his own favour, and therefore not easily satisfied. However, this fear, though useful, especially to young beginners, is not comfortable; and they who simply wait upon Jesus are gradually freed from it, as their knowledge of him and their experience of his goodness increases. He has a time for settling and establishing them in himself, and his time is best. We are hasty, and would be satisfied at once, but his word is: 'Tarry thou the Lord's leisure.' The work of grace is not like Jonah's gourd, which sprang up and flourished in a night, and as quickly withered, but rather like the oak, which, from a little acorn and a tender plant, advances with an almost imperceptible growth from year to year, till it becomes a broad, spreading, and deep-rooted tree, and then it stands for ages. The Christian oak shall grow and flourish for ever. When I see anyone, soon after they appear to be awakened, making a speedy profession of great joy, before they have a due acquaintance with their own hearts, I am in pain for them. I am not sorry to hear them afterwards complain that their joys are gone, and they are almost at their wits end; for without some such check, to make them feel their weakness and dependence, I seldom find them to turn out well; either their fervour abates without seeming reason, till they become quite cold, and sink into the world again (of which I have seen many instances), or if they do not give up all, their walk is uneven, and their spirit has not the savour of brokenness and true humility, which is a chief ornament of our holy profession. If they do not feel the plague of their hearts at first, they find it out afterwards, and too often manifest it to others. Therefore, though I know the Spirit of the Lord is free, and will not be confined to our rules, and there may be excepted cases; yet, in general, I believe the old proverb, 'Soft and fair goes far', will hold good in Christian experience. Let us be thankful for the beginnings of grace, and wait upon our Saviour patiently for the increase. And as we have chosen him for our physician, let us commit ourselves to his management, and not prescribe to him what he shall prescribe for us. He knows us, and he loves us better than we do ourselves, and will do all things well.

You say: 'It never came with power and life to my soul, that he died for me.' If you mean, you never had any extraordinary sudden manifestation, something like a vision or a voice from heaven, confirming it to you, I can say the same. But I know he died for sinners; I know I am a sinner; I know he invites them that are ready to perish; I am such a one; I know, upon his own invitation, I have committed myself to him; and I know, by the effects, that he has been with me hitherto, otherwise I should have been an apostate long ago; and therefore I know that he died for me; for had he been pleased to kill me (as he justly might have done,) he would not have shown me such things as these.

> If I must perish, would the Lord
> Have taught my heart to love his word?
> Would he have giv'n me eyes to see
> My danger and my remedy?
> Reveal'd his name, and bid me pray,
> Had he resolv'd to say me nay?

I know that I am a child, because he teaches me to say – Abba, Father. I know that I am his, because he has enabled me to choose him for mine; for such a choice and desire never could have taken place in my heart, if he had not placed it there himself. By nature I was too blind to know him, too proud to trust him, too obstinate to serve him, too base-minded to love him. The enmity I was filled with against his government, righteousness, and grace, was too strong to be subdued by any power but his own. The love I bear him is but a faint and feeble spark, but it is an emanation from himself: he kindled it, and he keeps it alive; and because it is his work, I trust many waters shall not quench it.

I have only room to assure you, that I am, &c.

THREE LETTERS TO THE REV. MR R.

Letter 1

My Dear Sir, *April 15, 1776*

I often rejoice on your behalf. Your call out of the world was a singular instance of the power of grace. And when I consider the difficulties and snares of your situation, and that you have been kept in the middle path, preserved from undue compliances on the one hand, and unnecessary singularities on the other, I cannot doubt but the Lord has hitherto helped and guided you. Indeed, you have need of his guidance. At your years, and with your expectations in life, your health firm, and your natural spirits lively, you are exposed to many snares: yet if the Lord keeps you sensible of your danger, and dependent upon him, you will walk safely. Your security, success, and comfort, depend upon him; and in the way of means, chiefly upon your being preserved in an humble sense of your own weakness. It is written: 'Fear not, I am with thee.' It is written again: 'Blessed is the man who feareth always.' There is a perfect harmony in those seemingly different texts. May the wisdom that cometh from above teach you and me to keep them both united in our view. If the Lord be with us, we have no reason to fear. His eye is upon us, his arm over us, his ear open to our prayer; his grace sufficient, his promise unchangeable. Under his protection, though the path of duty should lie through fire and water, we may cheerfully and confidently pursue it. On the other hand, our hearts are so deceitful, fallible, and frail, our spiritual enemies so subtle, watchful, and powerful, and they derive so many advantages from the occasions of every day, in which we are unavoidably and unexpectedly concerned; there is so much combustible within, and so many temptations arising from without, capable of setting all in a flame, that we cannot be too jealous of ourselves and our circumstances. When we can say, in the Psalmist's spirit, 'Hold thou me up', we may warrantably draw his conclusion, 'and I shall be safe'; but the moment we lean to our own understanding, we are in imminent danger of falling. The enemy who wars against our souls is a consummate master in his way, clever in his strategies, and equally skilful in carrying on his assaults by stealth or by storm. He studies us, if I may so say, all round, to discover our weak sides, and he is able to change his appearance, and can appear as a sly serpent, a roaring lion, or an angel of light, as best suits his purpose. It is a great mercy to be in some measure acquainted with his devices, and aware of them. They who wait humbly upon the Lord, and consult carefully his Word and come before the throne of grace, are made wiser than their enemy, and enabled to escape and withstand his wiles. I know you will not expect me to apologise for them. I have a double warrant; the love I bear you, and the Lord's command (Heb. 3:13). Use the same freedom with me; I need it, and hope to be thankful for it, and accept it as one of the best proofs of friendship.

The Lord bless and keep you. Pray for us, and believe me to be sincerely yours.

LETTER 2

My Dear Friend, *December 21, 1776*

Your letter brought me tidings of joy, and then furnished me with materials for a bonfire upon the occasion. It was an act of passive obedience to burn it, but I did obey. I congratulate you upon the happy issue to which the Lord has brought your affairs. I see that his good Spirit and good providence have been and are with you. I doubt not but your union with Miss ——— will be a mutual blessing, and, on your part, heightened by being connected with such a family. I could enlarge upon this head, if my letter likewise was to be burnt as soon as you have read it. I look upon the friendship the Lord has given me there, as one of my prime privileges; and I hope I shall always be thankful that it proved a means of introducing you to it.

I congratulate you, likewise, upon your accession to ———, not because it is a good living, in a genteel neighbourhood, and a fine country; but because I believe the Lord sends you there for fulfilling the desires he has given you, of being useful to souls. Church preferment, in any other view, is dreadful; and I would as soon congratulate a man upon seeing a millstone tied about his neck, to sink him into the depths of the sea, as upon his obtaining what is called a good living, except I thought him determined to spend and be spent in the cause of the gospel. A parish is an awful millstone indeed to those who see nothing valuable in the flock but the fleece. But the Lord has impressed your heart with a sense of the glory and importance of this truth, and the worth of souls, and animated your zeal by the most powerful motive, the knowledge of his constraining love. Your case is extraordinary. Perhaps, when you review in your mind the circle of your former acquaintance, you may say, with Job's servant 'I only am escaped alive.' The rest are either removed into an eternal state, or are still hurrying down the stream of dissipation, and living without God in the world. Yet there was a time when there seemed no more probability on your side than on theirs, that you should obtain mercy, and be called to the honour of preaching the glorious Gospel. You are setting out with every possible advantage – in early life, with a cheerful flow of spirits, affluent circumstances, and now, to crown it all, the Lord gives you the very choice of your heart in a partner; one who, besides deserving and meeting your affection, will, I am persuaded, be a real help-meet to you in your spiritual walk. How much is here to be thankful for!

I trust the Lord has given you, and will maintain in you a right spirit, so as not to rest in his gifts, but to hold them in connection with the love and favour of the giver. It is a low time with us, when the greatest amount of earthly blessings can seem to satisfy us without a real communion with him. His grace is sufficient for you; but undoubtedly such a scene of prosperity as seems to lie before you, is full of snares, and calls for a double effort of watchfulness and prayer. Your situation will fix many eyes upon you, and Satan will doubtless watch you, and examine every corner of the hedge around you, to see if he can find a gap by which to enter. We have but few rich gospel ministers; but it is too evident that he has found a way to damp the zeal and hurt the spirits of some of those few, who for a time acted nobly, and seemed to walk out of the reach of the allurements of the world. I am not jealous of you; I feel a comfortable persuasion that the Lord has taken a fast hold of your heart, and given you a fast hold of his almighty arm. Yet I believe you will not be displeased with me for dropping a hint of this kind, and at this time.

You have heard of the trial with which the Lord has been pleased to visit us: it still continues, though considerably alleviated. It is tempered with many mercies, and I hope he disposes us in a measure to submission. I trust it will be for good. My dear friend, you are now coming into my school, where you will learn, as occasions offer, to feel more in the person of another than in your own. But be not discouraged; the Lord only afflicts for our good. It is necessary that our sharpest trials should sometimes spring from our dearest comforts, else we should be in danger of forgetting ourselves, and setting up our rest here. In such a world, and with such hearts as we have, we shall often need something to prevent our cleaving to the dust, to quicken us to prayer, and to make us feel that our dependence for one hour's peace is upon the Lord alone. I am ready to think I have known as much of the good and happiness which this world can afford, as most people who live in it. I never saw the person with whom I wished to exchange places. And for many years past I have thought my trials have been light and few, compared with what many, or most of the Lord's people have endured. And yet, though in the main possessed of my own wishes, when I look back upon the twenty-seven years past, I am ready to style them, with Jacob, few and evil; and to give the sum total of their contents, in Solomon's words – all is vanity. If I take these years to pieces, I see a great part of them was filled up with sins and sorrows. The pleasures too are gone, and have no more real existence than the baseless fabric of a dream. The shadows of the evening will soon begin to come over us; and if our lives are prolonged, a thousand pains and infirmities, from which the Lord has in a remarkable measure exempted us hitherto, will probably overtake us; and at last we must feel the parting pang. Sin has so envenomed the soil of this earth, that no flowers will grow upon it. But we are hasting to a better world, and bright unclouded skies, where our sun will go down no more, and all tears shall be wiped from our eyes. – I am, &c.

Letter 3

My Dear Friend, *September 27, 1777*

Mr ——— called on us Thursday evening, and from that hour my thoughts, when awake, have seldom been absent from ———. Few people are better qualified to feel for you, yourself and the family excepted; perhaps there is no person living more nearly interested in what concerns Mrs ——— than myself. I could not therefore, at such a time as this, refrain from writing; and glad should I be, if the Lord may help me to drop a suitable word, and accompany it with a blessing to you in the reading.

I am glad to be assured (though I expected no less) that Mrs. ——— happily feels herself safe in the Lord's hand, and under the care of the good Shepherd and Saviour, to whom she has often committed herself; and finds him faithful to his promise, giving her strength in her soul according to her day, and enabling her quietly to submit to his holy, wise, and gracious will. And it is my prayer, that he may strengthen you likewise, and reveal his own all-sufficiency so clearly and powerfully to your heart, that you may not be afraid of any event, but cheerfully rely upon him, to be all that to you, in every circumstance and change, which his promise warrants you to expect.

I am willing to hope that this is but a short season of anxiety, appointed for the exercise of your faith and patience, and to give you, in his good time, a signal proof of his power and goodness in answering prayer. He sometimes brings us into such a situation, that the help of creatures is utterly unavailing, that we may afterwards be more clearly sensible of his interposition. Then we experimentally learn the vanity of all things here below, and are brought to a more immediate and absolute dependence upon the Lord himself. We have need of having these lessons frequently inculcated upon us; but when his end has been achieved, how often, after he has caused grief, does he show his great compassion and save us from our fears by an outstretched arm, and such a seasonable and almost unexpected relief, as constrains us to cry out, 'What has God wrought? and who is a God like unto thee?' Such, I hope, will be the issue of your present trial; and that he who gave her to you at first, will restore her to you again. I see you in the furnace; but the Lord is sitting by it as a refiner of silver, to moderate the fire, and manage the process, so that you shall lose nothing but dross, and be brought forth as refined gold, to praise his name. Apparent difficulties, however great, are nothing to him. If he speaks, it is done; for to God the Lord belong the issues from death. Should his pleasure be otherwise, and should he call your dear partner to a state of glory before you, still I know he is able to support you. What he does, however painful to the flesh, must be right because he does it. Having bought us with his blood, and saved our souls from hell, he has every kind of right to dispose of us and ours as he pleases; and this we are sure of, he will not lay so much upon us as he freely endured for us; and he can make us amends for all we suffer, and for all we lose, by the light of his countenance. A few years will set all to rights; and they who love him and are beloved of him, though they may suffer as others, shall not sorrow as others, for the Lord will be with them here, and he will soon have them with him: there all tears shall be wiped from their eyes.

Perhaps I know as well how to calculate the pain of such a separation, as anyone who has not actually experienced it. Many a time the desire of my eyes has been threatened, many a time my heart has been brought low; but, from what I have known at such seasons, I have reason to hope, that had it been his pleasure to bring upon me the thing that I feared, his everlasting arm would have upheld me from sinking under the stroke. As ministers, we are called to comfort the Lord's afflicted people, and to tell them the knowledge of his love is a cordial able to keep the soul alive under the sharpest trials. We must not wonder that he sometimes puts us in a way of showing that we do not deal with unfelt truths, but that we find for ourselves that solid consolation in the Gospel which we encourage others to expect from it. You have now such an occasion of glorifying the Lord; I pray he may enable you to improve it, and that all around you may see that he is with you, and that his good Word is the support and anchor of your soul. Then I am sure, if it, upon the whole, is best for you, he will give you the desire of your heart, and you shall yet live to praise him together. – I am, &c.

ONE LETTER TO THE REV. MR P.

Dear Sir, *January 11, 1777*

We all need, and at the seasons the Lord sees best, we all receive, chastisement. I hope you likewise have reason to praise him, for supporting, sanctifying, and delivering mercy. The coward flesh presently sinks under the rod, but faith need not fear it, for it is in the hand of one who loves us better than we do ourselves, and who knows our frame, that we are but dust, and therefore will not suffer us to be overdone and overwhelmed.

I feel as a friend should feel for Mr B. were I able, I would soon send him health. If the Lord, who is able to remove his illness in a minute, permits it to continue, we may be sure, upon the whole, it will be better for him. It is, however, very lawful to pray that his health may be restored, and his usefulness prolonged. I beg you to give my love to him, and tell him that my heart bears him an affectionate remembrance; and I know the God whom he serves will make every dispensation supportable and profitable to him.

If, as you observe, the Song of Solomon describes the experience of his church, it shows the dark as well as the bright side. No one part of it is the experience of every individual at any particular time. Some are in his banqueting-house, others upon their beds. Some sit under his banner, supported by his arm; while others have a faint perception of him at a distance, with many a hill and mountain between. In one thing, however, they all agree, that he is the leading object of their desires, and that they have had such a discovery of his person, work, and love, as makes him precious to their hearts. Their judgment of him is always the same, but their sensibility varies. The love they bear him, though rooted and grounded in their hearts, is not always equally in exercise, nor can it be so. We are like trees, which, though alive, cannot put forth their leaves and fruit without the influence of the sun. They are alive in winter as well as in summer; but how different is their appearance in these different seasons! Were we always alike, could we always believe, love, and rejoice, we should think the power inherent, and our own; but it is more for the Lord's glory, and more suited to form us to a temper becoming the Gospel, that we should be made deeply sensible of our own inability and dependence, than that we should be always in a lively frame. I am persuaded a broken and a contrite spirit, a conviction of our vileness and nothingness, connected with an acceptance of Jesus as revealed in the Gospel, is the highest attainment we can reach in this life. Sensible comforts are desirable, and we must be sadly declined when they do not appear so to us; but I believe there may be a real exercise of faith and growth in grace, when our sensible feelings are faint and low. A soul may be in as thriving a state when thirsting, seeking, and mourning after the Lord, as when actually rejoicing in him – as much in earnest when fighting in the valley, as when singing upon the mount. Dark seasons afford the surest and strongest manifestations of the power of faith. To hold fast the word of promise, to maintain a hatred of sin, to go on stedfastly in the path of duty, in defiance both of the frowns and smiles of the world, when we have but little comfort, is a more certain evidence of grace, than a thousand things which we may do or forbear when our spirits are warm and lively. I have seen many who have been upon the whole but uneven walkers, though at times they have seemed to enjoy, at least have talked of great comforts. I have seen others for the most part complain of much darkness and coldness, who have been remarkably humble, tender, and exemplary in their spirit and conduct. Surely were I to choose my lot, it should be with the latter. – I am, &c.

THREE LETTERS TO MRS G.

Letter 1

Madam, *June 20, 1776*

It would be both unkind and ungrateful in me, to avail myself of any plea of business, for delaying the acknowledgment I owe you for your acceptable favour from —— ——, which though dated the 6th instant, I did not receive till the 10th.

Could I have known in time that you were at Mr —— —'s, I should have endeavoured to have called upon you while there; and very glad should I have been to have seen you with us. But they who fear the Lord may be sure, that whatever is not practicable is not necessary. He could have overruled every difficulty in your way, had he seen it expedient; but he is pleased to show you, that you depend not upon me, but upon himself; and that, notwithstanding your connections may exclude you from some advantages in point of outward means, he who has begun a good work in you, is able to carry it on, in defiance of all seeming hindrances, and make all things (even those which have the most unfavourable appearances) work together for your good.

A sure effect of his grace, is a desire and longing for gospel ordinances; and when they are afforded, they cannot be neglected without loss. But the Lord sees many souls who are dear to him, and whom he is training up in a growing meetness for his kingdom, who are by his providence so situated, that it is not in their power to attend upon Gospel preaching; and perhaps they have seldom either Christian minister or Christian friend to assist or comfort them. Such a situation is a state of trial; but Jesus is all-sufficient, and he is always near. They cannot be debarred from his word of grace, which is everywhere at hand, nor from his throne of grace; for they who feel their need of him, and whose hearts are drawn towards him, are always at the foot of it. Every room in the house, yes, every spot they stand on, fields, lanes, and hedge-rows, all is holy ground to them; for the Lord is there. The chief difference between us and the disciples when our Saviour was upon earth, is in this. They then walked by sight, and we are called to walk by faith. They could see him with their bodily eyes, we cannot; but he said before he left them: 'It is expedient for you that I go away.' How could this be, unless that spiritual communion which he promised to maintain with his people after his ascension, were preferable to that fellowship he allowed them whilst he was visibly with them? But we are sure it is preferable, and they who had tried both were well satisfied he had made good his promise; so that though they had known him after the flesh, they were content not to know him so any more. Yes, Madam, though we cannot see him, he sees us, he is nearer to us than we are to ourselves. In a natural state, we have very dark, and indeed dishonourable thoughts of God; we conceive of him as at a distance. But when the heart is awakened, we begin to make Jacob's reflection: 'Surely the Lord is in this place, and I knew it not.' And when we receive faith, we begin to know that this ever-present God is in Christ; that the government of heaven and earth, the dispensations of the kingdom of nature, providence, and grace, are in the hands of Jesus; that it is he with whom we have to do, who once suffered agony and death for our redemption, and whose compassion and tenderness are the same; now he reigns over all and is to be blessed for ever, as when he conversed amongst men in the days of his humiliation. Thus God is made known to us by the Gospel, in the endearing views of a Saviour, a Shepherd, a Husband, a Friend; and a way of access is opened for us through the veil, that is, the human nature of our Redeemer, to enter, with humble confidence, into the holiest of all, and to repose all our cares and concerns upon the strength of that everlasting arm which upholds heaven and earth, and upon that infinite love which submitted to the shame, pain, and death of the cross, to redeem sinners from wrath and misery.

Though there is a height, a breadth, a length, and a depth, in this mystery of redeeming love, exceeding the comprehension of all finite minds, yet the great and leading principles which are necessary for the support and comfort of our souls, may be summed up in a very few words. Such a summary we are favoured with in Titus 2:11-14, where the whole of salvation, all that is needful to be known, experienced, practised, and hoped for, is comprised within the compass of four verses. If many books, much study, and great discernment were necessary in order to be happy, what must the poor and simple do? Yet for them especially is the Gospel designed; and few but such as these attain the knowledge and comfort of it. The Bible is a sealed book till the heart is awakened, and then he that runs may read. The propositions are few; I am a sinner, therefore I need a Saviour, one who is able and willing to save to the uttermost: such a one is Jesus; he is all that I want, wisdom, righteousness, sanctification, and redemption. But will he receive me? Can I answer a previous question? Am I willing to receive him? If so, and if his word may be taken, if he meant what he said, I may be sure of a welcome. He knew, long before, the doubts, fears, and suspicions which would arise in my mind when I should come to know what I am, what I have done, and what I have deserved; and therefore he declared, before he left the earth: 'Him that cometh to me I will in no wise cast out.' I have no money or price in my hand, no worthiness to recommend me; and I need none, for he saveth freely, for his own name's sake. I have only to be thankful for what he has already shown me, and to wait upon him for more. It is my part to commit myself to him as the physician of sin-sick souls, not to prescribe to him how he shall treat me. To begin, carry on, and perfect the cure, is his part.

The doubts and fears you speak of, are, in a greater or less degree, the common experience of all the Lord's people, at least for a time. Whilst any unbelief remains in the heart and Satan is permitted to tempt, we shall feel these things. In themselves they are groundless and evil; yet the Lord permits and overrules them for good. They tend to make us know more of the plague of our own hearts, and feel more keenly the need of a Saviour, and make his rest (when we attain it) doubly sweet and sure. And they likewise qualify us for pitying and comforting others. Fear not; only believe, wait, and pray. Expect not all at once. A Christian is not of hasty growth, like a mushroom, but rather like the oak the progress of which is hardly perceptible, but in time becomes a great deep-rooted tree. If my writings have been useful to you, may the Lord have the praise. To administer any comfort to his children is the greatest honour and pleasure I can receive in this life. I cannot promise to be a very punctual correspondent, having many engagements; but I hope to do all in my power to show myself, Madam, yours, &c.

Letter 2

Madam, *August 20, 1776*

Though, in general, I think myself tolerably punctual when I can answer a letter in six or seven weeks after receipt, yet I feel some pain for not having acknowledged yours sooner. A case like that which you have favoured me with an account of, deserved an immediate attention, and when I read it, I proposed writing within a post or two, and I can hardly allow any plea of business to be sufficient excuse for delaying it so long; but our times are in the Lord's hands: may he now enable me to send you what may prove a word in season.

Your exercises have been by no means singular, though they may appear so to yourself; because, in your retired situation, you have not (as you observe) had much opportunity of knowing the experience of other Christians; nor has the guilt with which your mind has been so greatly burdened, been properly your own. It was a temptation forced upon you by the enemy, and he shall answer for it. Undoubtedly it is a mournful proof of the depravity of our nature, that there is that within us which renders us so easily open to his suggestions; a proof of our extreme weakness, that after the clearest and most satisfying evidences of the truth, we hold fast our confidence, if the Lord permits Satan to sift and shake us. But I can assure you these changes are not uncommon. I have known people, who, after walking with God comfortably in the main for forty years, have been at their wits' end from such assaults as you mention, and been brought to doubt, not only of the reality of their own hopes, but of the very foundation upon which their hopes were built. Had you remained, as it seems you once were, attached to the vanities of a dissipated life, or could you have been content with a form of godliness, destitute of the power, it is probable you would have remained a stranger to these troubles. Satan would have employed his arts in a different and less perceptible way, to have soothed you into a false peace, and prevented any thought or suspicion of danger from arising in your mind. But when he could no longer detain you in his bondage, or seduce you back again into the world, then, of course, he would change his method, and declare open war against you. A specimen of his power and malice you have experienced; and the

Lord whom you loved, because he first loved you, permitted it not to gratify Satan, but for your benefit – to humble and prove you, to show you what is in your heart, and to do you good in the issue. These things, for the present, are not joyous but grievous; yet in the end they yield the peaceable fruits of righteousness. In the meantime his eye is upon you; he has appointed bounds both to the degree and the duration of the trial; and he does and will afford you such supports, that you shall not be tried beyond what you are enabled to bear. I doubt not but your conflicts and sorrows will in due time terminate in praise and victory, and be sanctified to your fuller establishment in the truth.

I greatly rejoice in the Lord's goodness to your dying parent. How wisely timed, and how exactly suited, was that affecting dispensation, to break the force of those suggestions with which the enemy was aiming to overwhelm your spirit! He could not stand against such an illustrious demonstrative attestation, that the doctrines you had embraced were not cunningly devised fables. He could proceed no farther in that way; but he is fruitful in resources. His next attempt, of course, was to fix guilt upon your conscience, as if you had yourself formed and willingly entertained those thoughts, which, indeed, you suffered with extreme reluctance and pain. Here, likewise, I find he succeeded for a time; but he who broke the former snare, will deliver you from this likewise.

The dark and dishonourable thoughts about God, which I hinted at as belonging to a natural state, are very different from the thoughts of your heart concerning him. You do not conceive of him as a hard master, or think you could be more happy in the breach than in the observance of his precepts. You do not prefer the world to his favour, or think you can please him, and make amends for your sins, by an obedience of your own. These, and such as these, are the thoughts of the natural heart – the very reverse of yours. One thought, however,

I confess you have indulged, which is no less dishonourable to the Lord than uncomfortable to yourself. You say: 'I dare not believe that God will not impute to me as sin, the admission of thoughts which my soul ever abhorred, and to which my will never consented.' Nay, you fear lest they should not only be imputed but unpardonable. But how can this be possible? Indeed I will not call it your thought, it is your temptation. You tell me you have children. Then you will easily feel a plain illustration, which just now occurs to me. Let me suppose a case which has sometimes happened: a child, three or four years of age we will say, while playing incautiously at a little distance from home, should suddenly be seized and carried away by a gipsy. Poor thing, how terrified, how distressed must it be! Methinks I hear it crying. The sight and violence of the stranger, the recollection of its dear parents, the loss of its pleasing home, the dread and uncertainty of what is yet to befall it. Is it not a wonder that it does not die in agonies? But see, help is at hand! The gipsy is pursued, and the child recovered. Now, my dear Madam, permit me to ask you, if this were your child, how would you receive it? Perhaps, when the first transports of your joy for its safety would permit you, you might gently chide it for leaving your door. But would you disinherit it? Would you disown it? Would you deliver it up again to the gipsy with your own hands, because it had suffered a violence which it could not withstand, which it abhorred, and to which its will never consented? And yet what is the tenderness of a mother, of ten thousand mothers, to that which our compassionate Saviour bears to every poor soul that has been enabled to flee to him for salvation! Let us be far from charging that to him, of which we think we are utterly incapable ourselves. Take courage, Madam; resist the devil and he will flee from you. If he were to tempt you to anything criminal, you would start at the thought, and renounce it with abhorrence. Do the same when he tempts you to question the Lord's compassion and goodness. But there he imposes upon us with a show of humility, and persuades us that we do well to oppose our unworthiness as sufficient exception to the many express promises of the Word. It is said the blood of Jesus cleanseth from all sin; that all manner of sin shall be forgiven for his sake; that whoever cometh he will in no wise cast out; and that he is able to save to the uttermost. Believe his word, and Satan shall be found a liar. If the child had deliberately gone away with the gipsy, had preferred that wretched way of life, had refused to return, though frequently and tenderly invited home; perhaps a parent's love might, in time, be too weak to plead for the pardon of such continued obstinacy. But, indeed, in this manner we have all dealt with the Lord; and yet whenever we are willing to return, he is willing to receive us with open arms, and without an upbraiding word (Luke 15:20–22). Though our sins have been deep dyed like scarlet and crimson, enormous as mountains, and countless as the sands, the sum total is, sin has abounded; but where sin has abounded, grace has much more abounded. After all, I know the Lord keeps the key of comfort in his own hands, yet he has commanded us to attempt comforting one another. I should rejoice to be his instrument of administering comfort to you. I shall hope to hear from you soon; and that you will then be able to inform me he has restored to you the joys of his salvation. But if not yet, wait for him, and you shall not wait in vain. – I am, &c.

Letter 3

My Dear Madam, *June, 1777*

Temptations may be compared to the wind, which, when it has ceased raging from one point, after a short calm, frequently renews its violence from another quarter. The

Lord silenced Satan's former assaults against you, but he is permitted to try you again another way. Be of good courage, Madam; wait upon the Lord, and the present storm shall likewise subside in good time. You have an infallible pilot, and are embarked in a boat against which the winds and waves cannot prevail. You may be tossed about, and think yourself in apparent jeopardy; but sink you shall not, except the promises and faithfulness of God can fail. Upon an attentive consideration of your complaint, it seems to me to amount only to this, that though the Lord has done great things for you, he has not yet brought you to a state of dependence on himself, nor released you from that impossibility, which all his people feel, of doing anything without him. And is this indeed a matter of complaint? Is it not every way better, more for his glory, and more suited to keep us mindful of our obligations to him, and in the event more for our safety, that we should be reduced to a happy necessity of receiving daily out of his fulness (as the Israelites received the manna), than to be set up with something of a stock of wisdom, power, and goodness of our own? Adam was thus furnished at the beginning with strength to stand; yet, he quickly fell and lost all. We who are by nature sinners, are not left to so hazardous an experiment. He has himself engaged to keep us, and treasured up all fulness of grace for our support, in a Head who cannot fail. Our gracious Saviour will communicate all needful supplies to his members, yet in such a manner that they shall feel their need and weakness, and have nothing to boast of from first to last, but his wisdom, compassion, and care. We are in no worse off than the apostle Paul, who, though eminent and exemplary in the Christian life, found, and freely confessed, that he had no sufficiency in himself to think a good thought. Nor did he wish it otherwise; he even gloried in his infirmities, that the power of Christ might rest upon him. Unbelief and a thousand evils are still in our hearts: though their reign and dominion is at an end, they are not slain nor eradicated; their effects will be felt more or less sensibly, as the Lord is pleased more or less to afford or abate his gracious influence. When they are kept down, we are no better in ourselves, for they are not kept down by us; but we are very prone to think better of ourselves at such a time, and therefore he is pleased to permit us at seasons to feel a difference, that we may never forget how weak and how vile we are. We cannot absolutely conquer these evils, but it becomes us to be humbled for them; and we are to fight, and strive, and pray against them. Our great duty is to be at his footstool, and to cry to him who has promised to perform all things for us. Why are we called soldiers, but because we are called to a warfare? And how could we fight, if there were no enemies to resist? The Lord's soldiers are not merely for show, to make an empty parade in a uniform, and to brandish their arms when none but friends and spectators are around them. No, we must stand upon the field of battle; we must face the fiery darts; we must wrestle (which is the closest and most arduous kind of fighting) with our foes; nor can we well expect wholly to escape wounds; but the leaves of the tree of life are provided for their healing. The Captain of our Salvation is at hand, and leads us on with an assurance, which might make even a coward bold – that in the end we shall be more than conquerors through him who has loved us.

I am ready to think, that some of the sentiments in your letters are not properly yours, such as you yourself have derived from the Scriptures, but rather borrowed from authors or preachers, whose judgment your humility has led you to prefer to your own. At least, I am sure the Scripture does not authorise the conclusion which distresses you, that if you were a child of God you should not feel such changes and oppositions. Were I to define a Christian, or rather to describe him at large, I know no text I would choose sooner, as a ground for the subject, than Galatians 5:17. A Christian has noble aims, which distinguish him from the bulk of mankind. His leading principles, motives, and desires, are all supernatural and divine. Could he do as he would, there is not a spirit before the throne who should excel him in holiness, love, and obedience. He would tread in the very footsteps of his Saviour, fill up every moment in his service, and employ every breath in his praise. This he would do, but alas, he cannot. Against this desire of the spirit, there is a contrary desire and working of a corrupt nature, which meets him at every turn. He has a beautiful copy set before him; he is enamoured with it, and though he does not expect to equal it, he writes carefully after it, and longs to attain to the nearest possible imitation. But indwelling sin and Satan continually jog his hand, and spoil his strokes. You cannot, Madam, form a right judgment of yourself, except you make due allowance for those things which are not peculiar to yourself, but common to all who have spiritual perception, and are indeed the inseparable appendages of this mortal state. If it were not so, why should the most spiritual and gracious people be so ready to confess themselves vile and worthless? One eminent branch of our holiness, is a sense of shame and humiliation for those evils which are only known to ourselves, and to him who searches our hearts. I will venture to assure you that though you will possess a more stable peace, in proportion as the Lord enables you to live more simply upon the blood, righteousness, and grace of the Mediator, you will never grow into a better opinion of yourself than you have at present. The nearer you are brought to him, the quicker sense you will have of your continual need of him, and thereby your admiration of his power, love, and compassion, will increase likewise from year to year.

I would observe, further, that our spiritual exercises are not a little influenced by our constitutional temperament. As you are only known as a correspondent, I can but conjecture about you upon this head. If your frame is delicate, and your nervous system very sensible and tender, I should probably ascribe some of your apprehensions to this cause. It is an abstruse subject, and I will not enter into it; but according to the observations I have made, persons of this habit seem to live more upon the confines of the visible world, if I may so speak, and to be more likely to suffer from it than others. That complaint, which, for want of a better name, we call lowness of spirits, may probably afford the enemy some peculiar advantages and occasions of distressing you. The mind then perceives objects as through a tinctured medium, which gives them a dark and discouraging appearance; and I believe Satan has more influence than we are aware of in managing the glass. And when this is not the case at all times, it may be occasionally, from sickness or other circumstances. You tell me that you have lately been ill, which, together with your present situation, and the prospect of your approaching hour, may probably have such an effect as I have hinted. You may be charging yourself with guilt, for what springs from indisposition, in which you are merely passive, and which may be no more properly sinful, than the headache, or any of the thousand natural shocks the flesh is prone to. The enemy can take no advantage but as the Lord permits him; and he will permit him none but what he designs to overrule for your greater advantage in the end. He delights in your prosperity; and you should not be in heaviness for an hour, were there not a reason for it. Notwithstanding your fears, I have a good hope that he who you say has helped you in six troubles, will appear for you in the seventh, and you will not die, but live, and declare the works of the Lord, and come forth to testify to his praise, that he has turned your mourning into joy. – I am, &c.

TWO LETTERS TO MISS F.

Letter 1

Dear Madam, *October 3, 1778*

You would have me tell you what are the best means to be used by a young person, to prevent the world, with all its opening and ensnaring scenes, from drawing the heart away from God. It is an important question: but I apprehend your own heart will tell you, that you are already possessed of all the information concerning it which you can well expect from me. I could only attempt to answer it from the Bible, which lies open to you likewise. If your heart is like mine, it must confess, that when it turns aside from God, it is seldom through ignorance of the proper means or motives which should have kept us near him, but rather from an evil principle within, which prevails against our better judgment, and renders us unfaithful to light already received.

I could offer you rules and advice in abundance; for I find it comparatively easy to preach to others. But if you should farther ask me, how you shall effectually reduce them to practice? I feel that I am so deficient, and so much at a loss in this matter myself, that I know not well what to say to you. Yet something must be said.

In the first place, then, I would observe, that though it be our bounden duty, and the highest privilege we can propose to ourselves, to have our hearts kept close to the Lord, yet we must not expect it absolutely or perfectly, much less all at once: we shall keep close to him, in proportion as we are convinced of the infinite disparity between him and the things which would presume to stand in competition with him, and the folly as well as ingratitude, of departing from him. But these points are only to be learned by experience, and by smarting under a series of painful disappointments in our expectations from creatures. Our judgments may be quickly satisfied that his favour is better than life, while yet it is in the power of a mere trifle to turn us aside. The Lord permits us to feel our weakness, for though we are ready in words to confess that we are weak, we do not so properly know it, till that secret is brought to the trial, and fails us. To be humble, and like a little child, afraid of taking a step alone, and so conscious of snares and dangers around us, as to cry to him continually to hold us up that we may be safe, is the sure, the infallible, the only secret of walking closely with him.

But how shall we attain this humble frame of spirit? It must be, as I said, from a real and sensible conviction of our weakness and vileness, which we cannot learn (at least I have not been able to learn it) merely from books or preachers. The providence of God concurs with his Holy Spirit in his merciful design of making us acquainted with ourselves. It is indeed a great mercy to be preserved from such declensions as might fall under the notice of our fellow-creatures; but when they can observe nothing of consequence to object to in us, things may be far from right with us in the sight of him who judges not only actions, but the thoughts and first motions of the heart. And indeed could we for a season so cleave to God as to find little or nothing in ourselves to be ashamed of, we are such poor creatures, that we should presently grow vain and self-sufficient, and expose ourselves to the greatest danger of falling.

There are, however, means to be observed on our part; and though you know them, I will repeat the principal, because you desire it of me. The first is prayer; and here, above all things, we should pray for humility. It may be called both the guard of all other graces, and the soil in which they grow. The second is attention to the Scripture. Your question is directly answered in Psalm 119:9. The precepts are our rule and delight, the promises our strength and encouragement; the good recorded of the saints is proposed for our encouragement; their miscarriages are as landmarks set up to warn us of the rocks and shoals which lie in the way of our passage. The study of the whole scheme of gospel salvation, respecting the person, life, doctrine, death and glory of our Redeemer, is appointed to form our souls to a spiritual and divine taste; and so far as this prevails and grows in us, the trifles that would draw us from the Lord will lose their influence, and appear, divested of the glare with which they strike the senses, mere vanity and nothing. The third main means is consideration or recollection; a careful regard to those temptations and snares, to which, from our tempers, situations, or connections, we are more immediately exposed, and by which we have been formerly hindered. It may be well in the morning, before we leave our chambers, to forecast, as far as we are able, the probable circumstances of the day before us. Yet the observance of this, as well as of every rule that can be offered, may dwindle into a mere form. However, I trust the Lord, who has given you a desire to live to him, will be your guard and teacher. No one teaches like him. – I am, &c.

Letter 2

Dear Madam, *March – 1779*

Our experiences pretty much tally; they may be drawn out into sheets and quires, but the sum total may be comprised in a short sentence: 'Our life is a warfare.' For our encouragement the apostle calls it a good warfare. We are engaged in a good cause, fight under a good Captain, the victory is sure beforehand, and the prize is a crown, – a crown of life. Such considerations might make even a coward bold. But then we must be content to fight: and, considering the nature, number, situation, and subtlety of our enemies, we may expect sometimes to receive a wound; but there is a medicinal tree, the leaves of which are always at hand to heal us. We cannot be too attentive to the evil which is always working in us, or to the stratagems which are employed against us; yet our attention should not be wholly confined to these things. We are to look upwards likewise to him who is our head, our life, our strength. One glance of Jesus will convey more effectual assistance than pouring upon our own hearts for a month. The one is to be done, but the other should upon no account be omitted. It was not by counting their wounds, but by beholding the brazen serpent, the Lord's instituted means of cure, that the Israelites were healed. That was an emblem of our instruction. One great cause of our frequent conflicts is, that we have a secret desire to be rich, and it is the Lord's design to make us poor. We want to gain an ability of doing something; and he suits his dispensations, to convince us that we can do nothing. We want a stock in ourselves, and he would have us absolutely dependent upon him. So far as we are content to be weak, that his power may be magnified in us, so far we shall make our enemies know that we are strong, though we ourselves shall never be directly sensible that we are so; only by comparing what we are, with the opposition we stand against, we may come to a comfortable conclusion, that the Lord worketh mightily in us (Ps. 41:11).

If our views are simple, and our desires towards the Lord, it may be useful to consider some of your faults and my faults as the fault of that depraved nature, which is common to us with all the Lord's people, and which made Paul groan as feelingly and as heartily as we can do. But this consideration, though true and scriptural, can only be safely applied when the mind is sincerely and in good earnest devoted to the Lord. There are too many unsound and half professors, who eagerly catch at it, as an excuse for those evils they are unwilling to part with. But I trust I may safely recommend it to you. This evil nature, this indwelling sin, is a living principle, an active, powerful cause; and a cause that is active will necessarily produce an effect. Sin is the same thing in believers as in the unregenerate; they have, indeed, a contrary principle of grace, which counteracts and resists it, which can prevent its outbreakings, but will not suppress its risings. As grace resists sin, so sin resists grace (Gal. 5:17). The proper tendency of each is mutually weakened on both sides; and, between the two, the poor believer, however blameless and exemplary in the sight of men, appears in his own view the most inconsistent character under the sun. He can hardly think it is so with others, and judging them by what he sees, and by what he himself feels, he esteems others better than himself. This proves him to be right; for it is the will of God concerning him (Phil. 2:3). This is the warfare. But it shall not always be so, – grace shall prevail. The evil nature is already enervated, and before long it shall die the death. Jesus will make us more than conquerors. – I am, &c.

ONE LETTER TO MRS ———

My Dear Madam, *December, 1776*

I have often preached to others of the benefit of affliction; but my own path for many years has been so smooth, and my trials comparatively so light and few, that I have seemed to myself to speak by rote upon a subject of which I had not a proper feeling. Yet the many exercises of my poor afflicted people, and the sympathy the Lord has given me with them in their troubles, has made this is a frequent and favourite topic of my ministry among them. The advantages of afflictions, when the Lord is pleased to employ them for the good of his people, are many and great. Permit me to mention a few of them; and the Lord grant that we may all find those blessed ends answered to ourselves, by the trials he is pleased to appoint us.

Afflictions quicken us to prayer. It is a pity it should be so; but experience testifies, that a long course of ease and prosperity, without painful changes, has an unhappy tendency to make us cold and formal in our secret worship; but troubles rouse our spirits, and constrain us to call upon the Lord in good earnest, when we feel a need of that help which we only can have from him.

They are useful, and in a degree necessary, to keep alive in us the conviction of the vanity and unsatisfying nature of the present world, and all its enjoyments; to remind us that this is not our rest, and to call our thoughts upwards, where our true treasure is, and where our conversation ought to be. When things go as we want them to our hearts are too prone to say, It is good to be here. It is probable, that had Moses, when he came to invite Israel to Canaan, found them in prosperity, as in the days of Joseph, they would have been very unwilling to remove; but their previous afflictions made his message welcome. Thus the Lord, by pain, sickness, and disappointments, by breaking our cisterns, and withering our gourds, weakens our attachment to this world, and makes the thought of quitting it more familiar and more desirable.

A child of God cannot but greatly desire a more enlarged and experimental acquaintance with his holy Word; and this attainment is greatly promoted by our trials. The far greater part of the promises in Scripture are made and suited to a state of affliction; and though we may believe they are true, we cannot so well know their sweetness, power, and suitableness, unless we ourselves are in a state to which they refer. The Lord says: 'Call upon me in the day of trouble, and I will deliver.' Now, till the day of trouble comes, such a promise is like a city of refuge to an Israelite, who not having slain a man, was in no danger of the avenger of blood. He had a privilege near him, of which he knew not the use and value, because he was not in need of it. But some can say, I not only believe this promise upon the authority of the speaker, but I can set my seal to it; I have been in trouble; I took this course for relief, and I was not disappointed. The Lord verily heard and delivered me. Thus afflictions likewise give occasion of our knowing and noticing more of the Lord's wisdom, power, and goodness, in supporting and relieving, than we should otherwise have known.

I have not time to take another sheet; must therefore contract my homily. Afflictions evidence to ourselves, and manifest to others, the reality of grace. And when we suffer as Christians, exercise some measure of that patience and submission, and receive some measure of these supports and supplies, which the Gospel requires and promises to believers, we are more confirmed that we have not taken up with mere notions; and others may be convinced, that we do not follow cunningly devised fables. They likewise strengthen by exercise our graces: as our limbs and natural powers would be feeble if not called to daily exertion, so the graces of the Spirit would languish, if something was not provided to draw them out and use them. And, to say no more, they are honourable, as they advance our conformity to Jesus our Lord, who was a man of sorrows for our sake. Methinks, if we might go to heaven without suffering, we should be unwilling to desire it. Why should we ever wish to go by any other path than that which he has consecrated and endeared by his own example? The sufferings of God's people are not penal; there is no wrath in them; the cup he puts in their hands is very different from that which he drank for their sakes, and is only medicinal to promote their chief good. Here I must stop; but the subject is fruitful, and might be pursued through a quire of paper. – I am, &c.

ONE LETTER TO MRS T.

My Dear Madam, *March 12, 1774*

My heart is full, yet I must restrain it. Many thoughts which crowd on my mind, and would have vent were I writing to another person, would to you be unseasonable. I write not to remind you of what you have lost, but of what you have, which you cannot lose. May the Lord put a word in my heart that may be acceptable; and may his good Spirit accompany the perusal, and enable you to say with the apostle, that as sufferings abound, consolations also abound by Jesus Christ. Indeed I can sympathise with you. I remember, too, the delicacy of your frame, and the tenderness of your natural spirits; so that were you not interested in the exceeding great and precious promises of the Gospel, I should be ready to fear you must sink under your trial; but I have some faint conceptions of the all-sufficiency and faithfulness of the Lord, and may address you in the king's words to Daniel: 'Thy God, whom thou servest continually, he will deliver thee.' Motives for resignation to his will abound in his Word; but it is an additional and crowning mercy that he has promised to apply and enforce them in time of need. He has said: 'My grace shall be sufficient for thee;' and, 'as thy day is, so shall thy strength be.' This I trust you have already experienced. The Lord is so rich and so good that he can easily compensate his children for whatever his wisdom sees fit to deprive them of. If he gives them a lively sense of what he has delivered them from, and prepared for them, or of what he himself submitted to endure for their sakes, they find at once light springing up out of darkness, hard things become easy, and bitter sweet. I remember reading about a good man in the last century who, when his beloved and only son lay ill, was for some time greatly anxious about the event. One morning he stayed longer than usual in his closet; while he was there his son died. When he came out, his family were afraid to tell him; but, like David, he perceived it by their looks; and when upon inquiry they said it was so, he received the news with a composure that surprised them. But he soon explained the reason, by telling them that for such discoveries of the Lord's goodness as he had been favoured with that morning, he could be content to lose a son every day. Yes, Madam, though every stream must fail, the fountain is still full and still flowing. All the comfort you ever received in your dear friend was from the Lord, who is abundantly able to comfort you still; and he is gone but a little before you. May your faith anticipate the joyful and glorious meeting you will have in a better world. Then your worship and converse together will be to your great advantage, will be perfect and will have no end. Then all tears shall be wiped away, and every cloud removed; and then you will see that all your concerns here below (the late afflicting dispensation not excepted,) were appointed and adjusted by infinite wisdom and infinite love.

The Lord, who knows our frame, does not expect or require that we should aim at a stoical indifference under his visitations. He allows that afflictions are at present not joyous, but grievous; yes, he was pleased when upon earth to weep with his mourning friends, when Lazarus died. But he has graciously provided for the prevention of that anguish and bitterness of sorrow, which is, upon such occasions, the portion of such as live without God in the world; and has engaged that all shall work together for good, and yield the peaceable fruits of righteousness. May he bless you with a sweet serenity of spirit, and a cheerful hope of the glory that shall shortly be revealed.

I intimated that I would not trouble you with my own sense and share of this loss. If you remember the great kindness I always received from Mr T. and yourself, as often as opportunity afforded, and if you will believe me possessed of any sensibility or gratitude, you will conclude that my concern is not small. I feel likewise for the public. Will it be a consolation to you, Madam, to know that you do not mourn alone? A character so exemplary as a friend, a counsellor, a Christian, and a minister, will be long and deeply regretted; and many will join with me in praying that you, who are most nearly interested, may be signally supported, and feel the propriety of Mrs Rowe's acknowledgement,

> Thou dost but take the dying lamp away,
> To bless me with thine own unclouded day.

We join in most affectionate respects and condolence. May the Lord bless you and keep you, lift up the light of his countenance upon you, and give you peace. – I am, &c.

ONE LETTER TO MR ———

Dear Sir, *March 7, 1765*

Your favour of the 19th February came to my hand yesterday. I have read it with attention, and very willingly sit down to offer you my thoughts. Your case reminds me of my own: my first desires towards the ministry were attended with great uncertainties and difficulties, and the perplexity of my own mind was heightened by the various and opposite judgments of my friends. The advice I have to offer is the result of painful experience and for this reason, perhaps, may not be unacceptable to you. I pray our gracious Lord to make it useful.

I was long distressed, as you are, about what was or was not a proper call to the ministry; it now seems to me an easy point to solve, but perhaps will not be so to you, till the Lord shall make it clear to yourself in your own case. I have not room to say so much as I could: in brief, I think it principally includes three things:

1. A warm and earnest desire to be employed in this service. I apprehend, the man who is once moved by the Spirit of God to this work, will prefer it, if attainable, to thousands of gold and silver; so that though he is at times intimidated by a sense of its importance and difficulty, compared with his own great insufficiency (for it is to be presumed a call of this sort, if indeed from God, will be accompanied with humility and self-

abasement), yet he cannot give it up. I hold it a good rule to inquire about this point, whether the desire to preach is most fervent in our most lively and spiritual frames, and when we are most laid in the dust before the Lord. If so, it is a good sign. But if, as is sometimes the case, a person is very earnest to be a preacher to others, when he finds but little hungerings and thirstings after grace in his own soul, it is then to be feared his zeal springs rather from a selfish principle than from the Spirit of God.

2. Besides this affectionate desire and readiness to preach, there must in due season appear some competent sufficiency as to gifts, knowledge, and utterance. Surely, if the Lord sends a man to teach others, he will furnish him with the means. I believe many have intended well in setting up for preachers, who yet went beyond or before their call in so doing. The main difference between a minister and a private Christian seems to consist in these ministerial gifts, which are imparted to him, not for his own sake, but for the edification of others. But then I say, these are to appear in due season; they are not to be expected instantaneously, but gradually, in the use of proper means; they are necessary for the discharge of the ministry, but not necessary as prerequisites to warrant our desires after it. In your case, you are young, and have time before you; therefore I think you need not as yet perplex yourself with inquiring if you have these gifts already: it is sufficient if your desire is fixed, and you are willing, in the way of prayer and diligence, to wait upon the Lord for them: as yet you need them not.

3. That which finally evidences a proper call, is a correspondent opening in providence, by a gradual train of circumstances, pointing out the means, the time, the place of actually entering upon the work, – and till this

occurs, you must not expect to be always clear from hesitation in your own mind. The principal caution on this head is, not to be too hasty in catching at first appearances. If it be the Lord's will to bring you into his ministry, he has already appointed your place and service; and though you know it not at present, you shall at a proper time. If you had the talents of an angel, you could do no good with them till his hour is come, and till he leads you to the people whom he has determined to bless by your means. It is very difficult to restrain ourselves within the bounds of prudence here; when our zeal is warm, a sense of the love of Christ upon our hearts, and a tender compassion for poor sinners, is ready to prompt us to break out too soon, – but he that believeth shall not make haste. I was about five years under this constraint: sometimes I thought I must preach, though it was in the streets. I listened to everything that seemed plausible, and to many things that were not so. But the Lord graciously, and as it were insensibly, hedged up my way with thorns; otherwise, if I had been left to my own spirit, I should have put it quite out of my power to have been brought into such a sphere of usefulness as he in his good time has been pleased to lead me to: and I can now see clearly, that at the time I would first have gone out, though my intention was, I hope, good in the main, yet I overrated myself, and had not that spiritual judgment and experience which are requisite for so great a service. I wish you therefore to take time; and if you have a desire to enter into the Established Church, endeavour to keep your zeal within moderate bounds, and avoid everything that might unnecessarily clog your admission with difficulties. I would not have you hide your profession, or be backward to speak for God; but avoid what looks like preaching, and be content with being a learner in the school of Christ for some years. The delay will not be lost in time; you will be so much the more acquainted with the Gospel, with your own heart, and with human nature, – the last is a necessary branch of a minister's knowledge, and can only be acquired by comparing what passes within us, and around us, with what we read in the Word of God.

I am glad to find you have a distaste both for Arminian and Antinomian doctrines; but let not the mistakes of others sit too heavy upon you. Be thankful for the grace that has made you to differ; be ready to give a reason for the hope that is in you with meekness and fear; but beware of engaging in disputes, without evident necessity, and some probable hopes of usefulness. They tend to eat out the life and savour of religion, and to make the soul lean and dry. Where God has begun a real work of grace, incidental mistakes will be lessened by time and experience; where he has not, it is of little signification what sentiments people hold, or whether they call themselves Arminians or Calvinists.

I agree with you, it is time enough for you to think of Oxford yet; and that if your purpose is fixed, and all circumstances render it prudent and proper to devote yourself to the ministry, you will do well to spend a year or two in private studies. It would be further helpful, in this view, to place yourself where there is Gospel preaching, and a lively people. If your favourable opinion of this place should induce you to come here, I shall be very ready to give you every assistance in my power. As I have trod exactly the path you seem to be setting out in, I might so far perhaps be more serviceable than those who are, in other respects, much better qualified to assist you. I doubt not but in this, and every other step, you will entreat the Lord's direction; and I hope you will not forget to pray for, Sir, your affectionate friend, &c.

TWO LETTERS TO THE REV. MR ———

Letter 1

Dear Sir, *June 29, 1757*

I endeavour to be mindful of you in my prayers, that you may find both satisfaction and success, and that the Lord himself may be your light, to discover to you every part of your duty. I would earnestly press you and myself to be followers of those who have been followers of Christ; to aim at a life of self-denial; to renounce self-will, and to guard against self-wisdom. The less we have to do with the world the better; and, even in conversing with our brethren, we have been, and unless we watch and pray shall often be ensnared. Time is precious, and opportunities once gone are gone for ever. Even by reading, and what we call studying, we may be comparatively losers. The shorter way is to be closely waiting upon God in humble, secret, fervent prayer. The treasures of wisdom and knowledge are in his hands; and he gives bountifully, without upbraiding. On the other hand, whatever we may undertake with a sincere desire to promote his glory, we may comfortably pursue: nothing is trivial that is done for him. In this view, I would have you, at proper intervals, pursue your studies, especially at those times when you are unfit for better work. Pray for me that I may be enabled to break through the snares of vanity that lie in my way; that I may be crucified with Christ, and live a hidden life by faith in him who loved me and gave himself for me. – Adieu.

Letter 2

Dear Sir, *August 31, 1757*

I wish you much of that spirit which was in the apostle, which made him content to become all things to all men, that he might gain some. I am persuaded that love and humility are the highest attainments in the school of Christ, and the brightest evidences that he is indeed our master. If any should seem inclined to treat you with less regard, because you are, or have been, a Methodist teacher, you will find forbearance, meekness, and long-suffering, the most prevailing means to conquer their prejudices. Our Lord has not only taught us to expect persecution from the world, though this alone is a trial too hard for flesh and blood; but we must look for what is much more grievous to a renewed mind, to be in some respects slighted, censured, and misunderstood, even by our Christian brethren, and that perhaps in cases where we are really striving to promote the glory of God, and the good of souls, and cannot, without the reproach of our consciences, alter our conduct, however glad we should be to have their approbation. Therefore we are required, not only to resist the world, the flesh, and the devil, but likewise to bear one another's burdens: which plainly intimates there will be something to be borne with on all hands; and happy indeed is he that is not offended. You may observe what unjust reports and surmises were received, even at Jerusalem, concerning the apostle Paul; and it seems he was condemned unheard, and that by many thousands too, Acts 21:20,21; but we do not find he was at all ruffled, or that he sought to retort anything upon them, though doubtless, had he been so disposed, he might have found something to have charged them with in his turn; but he calmly and willingly complied with everything in his power to soften and convince them. Let us be followers of this pattern, so far as he was a follower of Christ; for even Christ pleased not himself. How did he bear with the mistakes, weakness, intemperate zeal, and imprudent proposals of his disciples while on earth; and how does he bear with the same things from you and me, and every one of his followers now? And do we, can we, think much to bear with each other for his sake? Have we all a full remission of ten thousand talents, which we owed him, and were utterly unable to pay, and do we wrangle amongst ourselves for a few pence? God forbid!

If you should be numbered among the regular Independents, I advise you not to offend any of them by unnecessary singularities. I wish you not to part with any truth, or with anything really expedient; but if the omitting anything of an indifferent nature will obviate prejudices, and increase in mutual confidence, why should not so easy a sacrifice be made? Above all, my dear friend, let us keep close to the Lord in prayer: he giveth wisdom that is profitable to direct; he is the Wonderful Counsellor; there is no teacher like him. Why do the living seek assistance from the dead? Why do we weary our friends and ourselves, in running up and down, and turning over books for advice? If we shut our eyes upon the world and worldly things, and raise our thoughts upwards in humility and silence, should we not often hear the secret voice of the spirit of God whispering to our hearts, and pointing out to us the way of truth and peace? Have we not often gone astray, and hurt either ourselves or our brethren, for want of attending to this divine instruction? Have we not sometimes mocked God, by pretending to ask direction from him, when we had fixed our determination beforehand? It is a great blessing to know that we are sincere; and next to this, to be convinced of our insincerity, and to pray against it. – I am, &c.

ONE LETTER TO THE REV. MR B.

Very Dear Sir, *November 2, 1765*

Your letter of the 4th ult. gave me great pleasure. I thank you for the particular account you have favoured me with. I rejoice with you, sympathise with you, and find my heart opened to correspond with unreserved freedom. May the Lord direct our pens and help us to help each other. The work you are engaged in is great, and your difficulties many; but faithful is he that hath called you, who also will do it. The weapons which he has now put into your hands are not carnal, but mighty through God to the pulling down of strongholds. Men may fight, but they shall not prevail against us, if we are but enabled to put our cause simply in the Lord's hands, and keep steadily on in the path of duty. He will plead our cause, and fight our battles; he will pardon our mistakes, and teach us to do better. My experience as a minister is but small, having been but eighteen months in the vineyard; but for about twelve years I have been favoured with an increasing acquaintance among the people of God, of various ranks and denominations, which, together with the painful exercises of my own heart, gave me opportunity of making observations which were of great use to me when I entered upon the work myself: and even since, I have found the Lord graciously supplying new insights and new strength, as new occurrences arise. So I trust I will be with you. I endeavour to avail myself of the examples, advice, and sentiments of my brethren, yet at the same time to guard against calling any man master. This title belongs exclusively to Christ. The best are but men; the wisest may be mistaken; and that which may be right in another might be wrong in me, through a difference of circumstances. The Spirit of God distributes variously, both in gifts and dispensations: and I would no more be tied to act strictly by others' rules, than to walk in shoes of the same size. My shoes must fit my own feet.

I endeavour to guard against extremes: our nature is prone to them: and we are liable likewise, when we have found the inconvenience of one extreme, to revert insensibly (sometimes to fly suddenly) to the other. I pray to be led in the midst of the path. I am what they call a Calvinist; yet there are flights, niceties, and hard sayings, to be found among some of that system, which I do not choose to imitate. I dislike those sentiments against which you have borne your testimony in the note at the end of your preface; but having known many precious souls in that party, I have been taught, that the kingdom of God is not in names and sentiments, but in righteousness, faith, love, peace, and joy in the Holy Ghost. I should, however, upon some occasions, oppose those tenets, if they had any prevalence in my neighbourhood: but they have not; and in general, I believe, the surest way to refute or prevent error, is to preach the truth. I am glad to find you are aware of that spirit of enthusiasm which has so often broken loose and blemished hopeful beginnings, and that the foundation you build upon is solid and scriptural: this will, I hope, save you much trouble, and prevent many offences. Let us endeavour to make our people acquainted with the Scripture, and to impress them with a high sense of its authority, excellence, and sufficiency. Satan seldom remarkably imposes on ministers or people, except where the Word of God is too little consulted or regarded. Another point in which I aim at a medium is in what is called prudence. There is certainly such a thing as Christian prudence, and a remarkable deficiency of it is highly inconvenient. But caution too often degenerates into cowardice; and if the fear of man, under the name of prudence, gets within our guard, like a chilling frost, it nips everything in the bud. Those who trust the Lord, and act openly with an honest freedom and consistence, I observe he generally bears them out, smooths their way, and makes their enemies their friends, or at least restrains their rage. If we trust to him, he will stand by us; if we regard men, he will leave us to make the best we can of them.

I have set down hastily what occurred to my pen, not to dictate to you, but to tell you how I have been led, and because some expressions in your letter seemed to imply that you would not be displeased with me for so doing. As to books, I think there is a medium here likewise. I have read too much in time past; yet I do not wholly join with some of our brethren, who would restrain us entirely to the Word of God. Undoubtedly this is the fountain; here we should dwell; but a moderate and judicious perusal of other authors may have its use; and I am glad to be beholden to such helps, either to explain what I do not understand, or to confirm me in what I do. Of the writings of the last age afford an immense variety.

But, above all, may we, dear Sirs, live and feed upon the precious promises (John 14:16, 17-26, and 16:13-15). There is no teacher like Jesus, who by his Holy Spirit reveals himself in his Word to the understanding and affections of his children. When we thus behold his glory in the Gospel, we are changed into the same image. Then our hearts melt, our eyes flow, our stammering tongues are unloosed. That this may be your increasing experience, is the prayer of, dear Sir, – Yours, &c.

SEVEN LETTERS TO ———

Letter 1

March 18, 1767

I can truly say, that I bear you upon my heart and in my prayers. I have rejoiced to see the beginning of a good and gracious work in you; and I have confidence in the Lord Jesus, that he will carry it on and complete it, and that you will be amongst the number of those who shall sing redeeming love to eternity: therefore fear none of the things appointed for you to suffer by the way, but gird up the loins of your mind, and hope to the end. Be not impatient, but wait humbly upon the Lord. You have one hard lesson to learn, – that is, the evil of your own heart: you know something of it, but it is needful that you should know more; for the more we know of ourselves, the more we shall prize and love Jesus and his salvation. I hope what you find in yourself by daily experience, will humble you, but not discourage you, – humble you it should, and I believe it does. Are you not amazed sometimes that you should have so much as a hope, that, poor and needy as you are, the Lord thinketh of you? But let not all you feel discourage you; for if our Physician is almighty, our disease cannot be desperate; and if he casts none out that come to him, why should you fear? Our sins are many, but his mercies are more, our sins are great, but his righteousness is greater; we are weak, but he is powerful. Most of our complaints are due to unbelief, and the remainder are of a legal spirit; and these evils are not removed in a day. Wait on the Lord, and he will enable you to see more and more of the power and grace of our High Priest. The more you know him, the better you will trust him; the more you trust him, the better you will love him; the more you love him, the better you will serve him. This is God's way: you are not called to buy, but to beg; not to be strong in yourself, but in the grace that is in Christ Jesus. He is teaching you these things, and I trust he will teach you to the end. Remember the growth of a believer is not like a mushroom, but like an oak, which increases slowly indeed, but surely. Many suns, showers, and frosts, pass upon it before it comes to perfection; and in winter, when it seems dead, it is gathering strength at the root. Be humble, watchful, and diligent in the means, and endeavour to look through all, and fix your eye upon Jesus, and all shall be well. I commend you to the care of the good Shepherd, and remain, for his sake, yours, &c.

Letter 2

May 31, 1769

I was sorry I did not write as you expected, but I hope it will do now. Indeed I have not forgotten you: you are often in my thoughts, and seldom omitted in my prayers. I hope the Lord will make what you see and hear while abroad profitable to you, to increase your knowledge, to strengthen your faith, and to make you from henceforth well satisfied with your situation. If I am not mistaken, you will understand that, though there are some desirable things to be met with in London, preferable to any other place, yet, upon the whole, a quiet situation in the country, under one state ministry, and in connection with one people, has the advantage. It is pleasant now and then to have opportunity of hearing a variety of preachers, but the best and greatest of them are no more than instruments: some can please the ear better than others, but none can reach the heart any further than the Lord is pleased to open it. This he showed you upon your first going up, and I doubt not but your disappointment did you more good than if you had heard with all the pleasure you expected.

The Lord was pleased to visit me with a slight illness in my late journey. I was far from well on the Tuesday, but supposed it owing to the fatigue of riding, and the heat of the weather; but the next day I was taken with a shivering, which was followed by a fever. I was then near sixty miles from home. The Lord gave me much peace in my soul, and I was enabled to hope he would bring me safe home, in which I was not disappointed; and though I had the fever most part of the way, my journey was not unpleasant. He likewise strengthened me to preach twice on Sunday; and at night I found myself well, only very weary, and I have continued well ever since. I have reason to speak much of his goodness, and to kiss the rod, for it was sweetened with abundant mercies. I thought that, had it been his pleasure, I should have continued sick at Oxford, or even have died there, I had no objection. Though I had not that joy and sensible comfort which some are favoured with, yet I was quite free from pain, fear, and care, and felt myself sweetly composed to his will, whatever it might be. Thus he fulfils his promise in making our strength equal to our day; and every new trial gives us a new proof about how happy it is to be enabled to put our trust in him.

I hope, in the midst of all your engagements, you find a little time to read his good Word, and to wait at his mercy-seat. It is good for us to draw nigh to him. It is an honour that he permits us to pray; and we shall surely find he is a prayer-hearing God. Endeavour to be diligent in the means; yet watch and strive against a legal spirit, which is always aiming to represent him as a hard master, watching, as it were, to take advantage of us. But it is far otherwise, – his name is Love; he looks upon us with compassion: he knows our frame, and remembers that we are but dust; and when our infirmities prevail, he does not bid us to be despondent, but reminds us that we have an Advocate with the Father, who is able to pity, to pardon and to save to the uttermost. Think of the names and relations he bears. Does he not call himself a Saviour, a Shepherd, a Friend, and a Husband? Has he not made known unto us his love, his blood, his righteousness, his promises, his power, and his grace, and all for our encouragement? Away, then, with all doubting, unbelieving thoughts: they will not only distress your heart, but weaken your hands. Take it for granted, upon the warrant of his Word, that you are his, and he is yours; that he has loved you with an everlasting love, and therefore in loving-kindness has drawn you to himself; that he will surely accomplish that which he has begun, and that nothing which can be named or thought of shall ever be able to separate you from him. This persuasion will give you strength for the battle; this is the shield which will quench the fiery darts of Satan; this is the helmet which the enemy cannot pierce. Whereas, if we go forth doubting and fearing, and are afraid to trust any further than we can feel, we are weak as water, and easily overcome. Be strong, therefore, not in yourself, but in the grace that is in Christ Jesus. Pray for me, and believe me to be, yours, &c.

Letter 3

March 14

I think you would hardly expect me to write if you knew how I am forced to live at London. However, I would have you believe I am as willing to write to you as you are to receive my letters. As a proof, I try to send you a few lines now, though I am writing to you and talking to Mrs ——— both at once! and this is the only season I can have to change a few words with her. She is a woman of a sorrowful spirit; she talks and weeps. I believe she would think herself happy to be situated as you are, notwithstanding the many advantages she has in London. I see daily, and I hope you have likewise learnt, that places and outward circumstances cannot of themselves either hinder or help us in walking with God. So far as he is pleased to be with us, and to teach us by his Spirit, wherever we are we shall get forward; and if he does not bless us and water us every moment, the more we have of our wishes and wills, the more uneasy we shall make ourselves.

One thing is needful; an humble, dependent spirit, to renounce our own wills, and give up ourselves to his disposal without a reserve. This is the path of peace; and it is the path of safety: for he has said, the meek he will teach his way, and those who yield up themselves to him he will guide with his eye. I hope you will fight and pray against every rising of a murmuring spirit, and be thankful for the great things which he has already done for you. It is good to be humbled for sin, but not to be discouraged; for though we are poor creatures, Jesus is a complete Saviour; and we bring more honour to God, by believing on his name, and trusting his word of promise, than we could do by a thousand outward works.

I pray the Lord to shine upon your soul, and to fill you with all joy and peace in believing. Remember to pray for us, that we may be brought home to you in peace. – I am, &c.

Letter 4

London, August 19, 1775

You see I am mindful of my promise, and glad should I be to write something that the Lord may be pleased to make a word in season. I went yesterday into the pulpit very dry and heartless. I seemed to have fixed upon a text, but when it came to the pinch, it was so shut up that I could not preach from it. I had hardly a minute to choose, and therefore was forced to snatch at that which came first upon my mind, which proved to be 2 Timothy 1:12. Thus I set off at a venture, having no resource but in the Lord's mercy and faithfulness; and, indeed, what other can we wish for? Presently my subject opened; and I know not when I have been favoured with more liberty. Why do I tell you this? Only as an instance of his goodness, to encourage you to put your strength in him, and not to be afraid, even when you feel your own weakness and insufficiency most keenly. We are never more safe, never have more reason to expect the Lord's help, than when we are most sensible that we can do nothing without him. This was the lesson Paul learnt, to rejoice in his own poverty and emptiness, that the power of Christ might rest upon him. Could Paul have done anything, Jesus would not have had the honour of doing everything. This way of being saved entirely by grace, from first to last, is contrary to our natural wills; it mortifies self, leaving it nothing to boast of, and through the remains of an unbelieving, legal spirit, it often seems discouraging. When we think ourselves so utterly helpless and worthless, we are too ready to fear that the Lord will therefore reject us; whereas, in truth, such a poverty of spirit is the best mark we can have of an interest in his promises and care.

How often have I longed to be an instrument of establishing you in the peace and hope of the Gospel! I have but one way of attempting it, by telling you over and over of the power and grace of Jesus. You want nothing to make you happy, but to have the eyes of your understanding more fixed upon the Redeemer, and more enlightened by the Holy Spirit to behold his glory. O, he is a suitable Saviour! He has power, authority, and compassion, to save to the uttermost. He has given his word of promise to engage our confidence, and he is able and faithful to make good the expectations and desires he has raised in us. Put your trust in him: believe (as we say) through thick and thin, in defiance of all objections from within and without. For this, Abraham is recommended as a pattern to us. He overlooked all difficulties; he ventured and hoped even against hope, in a case which to all appearances was desperate, because he knew that he who had promised was also able to perform.

Your sister is much upon my mind. Her illness grieves me; were it in my power, I would quickly remove it. The Lord can, and I hope will, when he has answered the end for which he sent it. I trust he has brought her to us for good, and that she is chastised by him that she may not be condemned with the world. I hope, though she says little, she lifts up her heart to him for a blessing. I wish you may be enabled to leave her and yourself, and all your concerns, in his hands. He has a sovereign right to do with us as he pleases, and if we consider what we are, surely we shall confess we have no reason to complain; and to those who seek him, his sovereignty is exercised in a way of grace. All shall work together for good; everything is needful that he sends; nothing can be needful that he withholds. Be content to bear the cross; others have borne it before you. You have need of patience; and if you ask, the Lord will give it; but there can be no settled peace till our will is in a measure subdued. Hide yourself under the shadow of his wings; rely upon his care and power; look upon him as a physician who has graciously undertaken to heal your soul from the worst sickness of all – sin. Yield to his prescriptions, and fight against every thought that would represent it as desirable to be permitted to choose for yourself. When you cannot see your way, be satisfied that he is your leader. When your spirit is overwhelmed within you, he knows your path; he will not leave you to sink. He has appointed seasons of refreshment, and you shall find he does not forget you. Above all, keep close to the throne of grace. If we seem to get no good by attempting to draw near him, we may be sure we shall get none by keeping away from him. – I am, &c.

Letter 5

I promised you another letter, and now for the performance. If I had said, if may be, or perhaps I will, you will be in suspense; but if I promise, then you expect that I will not disappoint you, unless something should render it impossible for me to make my word good. I thank you for your good opinion of me, and for thinking I mean what I say: and I pray that you may be enabled more and more to honour the Lord, by believing his promise; for he is not like a man that should fail or change, or be prevented by anything unforeseen from doing what he has said. And yet we find it easier to trust to worms than to the God of truth. Is it not so with you? And I can assure you it is often so with me. But here is the mercy, that his ways are above ours, as the heavens are higher than the earth. Though we are foolish and unbelieving, he remains faithful; he will not deny himself. I recommend to you especially that promise of God, which is so comprehensive that it takes in all our concerns – I mean, that all things shall work together for good. How hard is it to believe, that not only those things which are grievous to the flesh, but even those things which draw forth our corruptions, and reveal to us what is in our hearts, and fill us with guilt and shame, should work for our good! Yet the Lord has said it. All your pains and trials, all that befalls you in your own person, or that affects you upon the account of others, shall in the end prove to your advantage. And your peace does not depend upon any change of circumstances which may appear desirable, but in having your will bowed to the Lord's will, and made willing to submit all to his disposal and management. Pray for this, and wait patiently for him, and he will do it. Be not surprised to find yourself poor, helpless, and vile: all whom he favours and teaches will find themselves so. The more grace increases, the more we shall seek to abase ourselves in our own eyes; and this will make the Saviour and his salvation more precious to us. He takes his own wise methods to humble you, and to prove you, and I am sure he will do you good in the end. – I am, &c.

Letter 6

September 16, 1775

When you receive this, I hope it will give you pleasure to think that if the Lord be pleased to favour us with health, we shall all meet again in a few days. I have met with much kindness in London, and many comforts and mercies; however, I shall be glad to return home. There my heart lives, let my body be where it will. I long to see all my dear people, and I shall be glad to see you. I steal a little time to write another line or two, more to satisfy you than for anything special that I have to say. I thank you for your letter. I do not doubt that the Lord is bringing you forward, and that you have a good reason to say to your soul: 'Why art thou cast down and disquieted? Hope thou in

God; for I shall yet praise him.' An evil heart, an evil temper, and the many crosses we meet with in passing through an evil world, will cause us many troubles; but the Lord has provided a balm for every wound, a cordial for every care; the fruit of all is to take away sin, and the end of all will be eternal life in glory. Think of these words; put them in the balance of the sanctuary, and then throw all your trials into the opposite scale, and you will find there is no comparison between them. Say then: 'Though he slay me, I will trust him'; for when he has fully tried me, I shall come forth like gold. You would have liked to have been with me last Wednesday. I preached at Westminster Bridewell. It is a prison and house of correction. The bulk of my congregation were housebreakers, highwaymen, pickpockets, and poor unhappy women, such as infest the streets of this city, sunk in sin, and lost to shame. I had a hundred or more of these before me. I preached from 1 Timothy 1:15, and began by telling them my own story which gained their attention more than I expected. I spoke to them for nearly an hour and a half. I shed many tears myself, and saw some of them shed tears as well. Ah, had you seen their present condition, and could you hear the history of some of them, it would make you sing: 'O to grace how great a debtor!' By nature they were no worse than the most sober and modest people. And there was doubtless a time when many of them little thought what they should live to do and suffer. I might have been, like them, in chains, and one of them have come to preach to me, had the Lord so pleased. – I am, &c.

Letter 7

October 10, 1777

I am just come from seeing A ——— N ———. The

people told me she is much better than she was, but she is far from being well. She was brought to me into a parlour, which saved me the painful task of going to inquire and seek for her among the patients. My spirits always sink when I am within those mournful walls, and I think no money could prevail on me to spend an hour there every day. Yet surely no sight upon earth is more suited to teach one thankfulness and resignation. Surely I have reason, in my worst times, to be thankful that I am out of Hell, out of Bedlam, out of Newgate. If my eyes were as bad as yours, and my back worse, still I hope I should set a great value upon his mercy, that my senses are preserved. I hope you will think so too. The Lord afflicts us at times; but it is always a thousand times less than we deserve, and much less than many of our fellow-creatures are suffering around us. Let us therefore pray for grace to be humble, thankful, and patient.

A year ago today I was under Mr W———'s knife. There is another cause for thankfulness, that the Lord inclined me to submit to the operation, and brought me happily through it. In short, I have so many reasons for thankfulness, that I cannot count them. I may truly say they are more in number than the hairs of my head. And yet, alas, how cold,insensible, and ungrateful I am. I could make as many complaints as you; but I find that it is no good to complain, except to him who is able to help me. It is better for you and me to be admiring the compassion and fulness of grace that is in our Saviour, than to dwell upon our own poverty and vileness. He is able to help and save to the uttermost; there I desire to cast anchor, and wish you to do so likewise. Hope in God, for you shall yet praise him. – I am, &c.

ONE LETTER TO MR C.

Dear Sir, *January 16, 1775*

The death of a near relative called me from home in December, and a fortnight's absence threw me so far behind-hand in my course, that I deferred acknowledging your letter much longer than I intended. I now thank you for it. I can sympathise with you in your troubles; yet knowing the nature of our calling, that. by an unalterable appointment, the way to the kingdom lies through many tribulations, I ought to rejoice rather than otherwise, that to you it is given, not only to believe, but also to suffer. If you escaped these things, whereof all the Lord's children are partakers, might you not question your adoption into his family? How could the power of grace be manifest, either to you, in you, or by you, without afflictions? How could the corruptions and devastations of the heart be checked without a cross? How could you acquire a tenderness and skill in speaking to those who are weary, without a taste of such trials as they also meet with? You could only be a hearsay witness to the truth, power, and sweetness of the precious promises, unless you have been in such a situation as to need them, and to find their suitableness and sufficiency. The Lord has given you a good desire to serve him in the Gospel, and he is now training you for that service. Many things, yes, the most important things, belonging to the Gospel ministry, are not to be learned from books and study, but by painful experience.

You must expect a variety of exercise; but two things he has promised you, – that you shall not be tried above what he will enable you to bear, and that all shall work together for your good. We read somewhere of a conceited orator, who declaimed upon the management of war in the presence of Hannibal, and of the contempt with which Hannibal treated his performance. He deserved it; for how should a man who had never seen a field of battle be a competent judge on such a subject? Just so, were we to acquire no other knowledge of the Christian warfare than what we could derive from cool and undisturbed study, instead of coming forth as able ministers of the New Testament, and competently acquainted with the devices, the deep-laid counsels and stratagems of Satan, we should prove but mere declaimers. But the Lord will take better care of those whom he loves and designs to honour. He will try, and permit them to be tried in various ways, – he will make them feel much in themselves, that they may know how to feel much for others.

And as this previous discipline is necessary to enable us to take the field in a public capacity with courage, wisdom, and success, that we may lead and animate others in the fight, it is equally necessary, for our own sakes, that we may obtain and preserve the grace of humility, which I perceive he has taught you to set a high value upon. Indeed, we cannot value it too highly; for we can be neither comfortable, safe, nor habitually useful, without it. The root of pride lies deep in our fallen nature, and where the Lord has given natural and acquired abilities, it would grow apace, if he did not mercifully watch over us, and suit his dispensations to keep it down. Therefore I trust he will make you willing to endure hardships, as a good soldier of Jesus Christ. May he enable you to behold him with faith holding out the prize, and saying to you: 'Fear none of these things that thou shalt suffer: be thou faithful unto death, and I will give thee a crown of life.'

We sail upon a turbulent and tumultuous sea; but we

are embarked on a good boat, and in a good cause, and we have an infallible and almighty pilot, who has the winds and weather at his command, and can silence the storm into a calm with a word whenever he pleases. We may be persecuted, but we shall not be forsaken; we may be cast down, but we cannot be destroyed. Many will strongly oppose us trying to knock us over, but the Lord will be our stay.

I am sorry to find you are quite alone at Cambridge, for I hoped there would be a succession of serious students to supply the place of those who are transplanted to shine as lights in the world. Yet you are not alone, for the Lord is with you, the best counsellor and the best friend. There is a strange backwardness in us (at least in me) fully to improve that gracious intimacy to which he invites us. Alas, that we so easily wander from the fountain of life to hew out cisterns for ourselves, and that we seem more attached to a few drops of his grace in our fellow-creatures, than to the fulness of grace that is in himself. I think nothing gives me a more striking sense of my depravity than my perverseness and folly in this respect; yet he bears with me, and does me good continually.

THREE LETTERS TO MRS H.

Letter 1

Long and often I have thought of writing to you: now the time has come. May the Lord help me to send a word in season! I know not how it may be with you, but he does, and to him I look to direct my thoughts accordingly. I suppose you are still in the school of the cross, learning the happy art of extracting real good out of seeming evil, and to grow tall by stooping. The flesh is a sad dunce in this school; but grace makes the spirit willing to learn by suffering; yes, it cares not what it endures, so sin may be mortified, and a conformity to the image of Jesus be increased. Surely when we see the most and the best of the Lord's children so often in heaviness, and when we consider how much he loves them, and what he has done and prepared for them, we may take it for granted that there is a reason for their sufferings. For it would be well within his power, and not a thousandth part of what his love intends to do for them, should he make their whole life here, from the hour of their conversion to their death, a continued course of satisfaction and comfort, without anything to distress them from within and without. But were it so, should we not miss many advantages? In the first place, we should not be able to say: 'As he was, so are we in this world.' I think a believer would be ashamed to be so utterly unlike his Lord. What, the Master always a man of sorrows and acquainted with grief, and the servant always happy and full of comfort! Jesus despised, reproached, neglected, opposed, and betrayed, and his people admired and caressed; he living in the want of all things, and they filled with abundance; he sweating blood for anguish, and they strangers to distress; how unsuitable would these things be!

How much better to be called to the honour of filling up the measure of his sufferings! A cup of suffering was put into his hand on our account, and his love engaged him to drink it for us. The wrath which it contained he drank wholly himself, but he left us a little affliction to taste, that we might pledge him, and remember how he loved us, and how much more he endured for us than he will ever call us to endure for him. Again, how could we, without sufferings, manifest the nature and truth of Gospel grace? What place should we then have for patience, submission, meekness, forbearance, and a readiness to forgive, if we had nothing to try us either from the hand of the Lord, or from the hand of men. A Christian without trials would be like a mill without wind or water: the contrivance and design of the wheel-work inside would be unnoticed and unknown, without something to put it in motion from outside. Nor would our graces grow, unless they were called out to exercise; the difficulties we meet with not only prove but strengthen the graces of the Spirit. If a person was always to sit still, without making use of legs or arms, he would probably wholly lose the power of moving his limbs eventually; but by walking and working he becomes strong and active. So, in a long course of ease, the powers of the new man would certainly languish; the soul would grow soft, indolent, cowardly, and faint; and therefore the Lord appoints his children such dispensations as make them strive and struggle, and pant: they must press through a crowd, swim against a stream, endure hardships, run, wrestle, and fight, and their strength grows as they use it.

By these things, likewise, they are made more willing to

leave the present world, to which we are prone to cleave too closely in our hearts when our path is smooth. Had Israel enjoyed their former peace and prosperity in Egypt when Moses came to invite them to Canaan, I think they would hardly have listened to him. But the Lord suffered them to be brought into great trouble and bondage, and then the news of deliverance was more welcome; yet still they were but half willing, and they carried a love for the flesh-pots of Egypt with them into the wilderness. We are like them; though we say this world is vain and sinful, we are too fond of it; and though we hope for true happiness only in heaven, we are often well content to stay longer here. But the Lord sends afflictions one after another to quicken our desires, and to convince us that this cannot be our rest. Sometimes, if you drive a bird from one branch of a tree, he will hop to another a little higher, and from there to a third; but if you continue to disturb him, he will at last take wing and fly right away. Thus we, when forced from one creature comfort, perch upon another, and so on; but the Lord mercifully follows us with trials, and will not let us rest upon any; by degree our desires take a nobler flight, and can be satisfied with nothing short of himself; and we say: 'To depart and be with Jesus is best of all.'

I trust you find the name and grace of Jesus more and more precious to you; his promises more sweet, and your hope in them more abiding; your sense of your own weakness and unworthiness daily increasing: your persuasion of his all-sufficiency to guide, support, and comfort you, more confirmed. You owe your growth in these respects in a great measure to his blessing upon those afflictions which he has prepared for you, and sanctified to you. May you praise him for all that is past, and trust him for all that is to come. – I am, &c.

Letter 2

Though I have the pleasure in hearing about you, and sending a remembrance from time to time, I am willing, by this opportunity, to direct a few lines to you, as a more express testimony of my sincere regard.

I think your experience is generally of the fearful, doubting type. Such souls, however, the Lord has given particular charge to his ministers to comfort. He knows our infirmities, and what temptations mean, and, as a good Shepherd, he expresses a peculiar care and tenderness for the weak of the flock. But how must I attempt your comfort? Surely not by strengthening a mistake, to which we are all too liable, by leading you to look into your own heart for (what you will never find there) something in yourself whereon to ground your hopes, if not wholly, yet at least in part. Rather let me endeavour to lead you out of yourself; let me invite you to look unto Jesus. Should we look for light in our own eyes, or in the sun? Is it indwelling sin that distresses you? Then I can tell you (though you know it) that Jesus died for sin and sinners. I can tell you, that his blood and righteousness are of infinite value; that his arm is almighty, and his compassions infinite; yes, you yourself read his promises every day, and why should you doubt that they will be fulfilled? If you say you do not question their truth, or that they are true for many people, but that you can hardly believe they belong to you; I would ask what evidence you would require? A voice or an angel from heaven you do not expect. Consider, if many of the promises are not expressly directed to those to whom they belong. When you read your name on the superscription of this letter, you make no scruple in opening it: why, then, do you hesitate at embracing the promises of the Gospel, where you read they are addressed to those who mourn, who hunger and thirst after righteousness, who are poor in spirit, and cannot but be sensible that a gracious God has begun to work these dispositions in your heart? If you say that though you do at times mourn and hunger but that you are afraid you do not do it enough, or in the right way; consider, that this sort of reasoning is very far from the spirit and language of the Gospel. For it is grounded on a secret supposition, that in the forgiveness of sin God has a respect to something more than the atonement and mediation of Jesus; namely, to some previous good qualifications in a sinner's heart, which are to share with the blood of Christ in the honour of salvation. The enemy deceives us in this matter the more easily, because a propensity to the covenant of works is a part of our natural depravity. Depend upon it, you never will have a suitable and sufficient sense of the evil of sin, and of your share in it, so long as you have any sin remaining in you. We must see Jesus as he is, before our apprehensions of any spiritual truth will be complete. But if we know that we must perish without Christ, and that he is able to save to the uttermost, we know enough to warrant us to cast our souls upon him, and we dishonour him by fearing that when we do so he will disappoint our hope. But if you are still perplexed about the high points of election I would advise you to leave the disposal of others to the great Judge; and as to yourself, I think I need not say much to persuade you, that if ever you are saved at all, it must be in a way of free and absolute grace. Leave disputes to others; wait upon the Lord, and he will teach you all things, in such degree and time as he sees best. Perhaps you have suffered for taking things too much on trust from men. Cease from man, whose breath is in his nostrils. One is your master, even Christ. Study and pray over the Bible; and you may take it as a sure rule, that whatever sentiment makes any part of the Word of God unwelcome to you is justly to be suspected. Aim at a cheerful spirit. The more you trust God, the better you will serve him. While you indulge unbelief and suspicion, you weaken your own hands, and discourage others. Be thankful for what he has shown you, and wait upon him for more; you shall find he has not said: 'Seek ye my face in vain.' I heartily commend you to his grace and care, and am, &c.

Letter 3

At length, and without farther apology for my silence, I sit down to ask you how you fare. Afflictions, I hear, have been your lot; and if I had not heard so, I should have taken it for granted; for I believe the Lord loves you; and as many as he loves he chastens. I think you can say, afflictions have been good for you, and I doubt not but you have found strength according to your day; so that though you may have been sharply tried, you have not been overpowered. For the Lord has engaged his faithfulness for this to all his children, that he will support them in all their trials; so that the fire shall not consume them, nor the floods drown them (Isa. 43:2).

If you can say thus much, cannot you go a little further, and add, in the apostle's words: 'None of these things move me, neither count I my life dear. I rather glory in my infirmities, that the power of Christ may rest upon me; yes, doubtless, I count all things loss and of no regard, for the excellency of the knowledge of Christ Jesus my Lord; for when I am weak, then I am strong.' I think I hear you say: 'God, who comforteth those who are cast down, has comforted my soul; and as my troubles have abounded, my consolations in Christ have abounded also. He has delivered, he does deliver, and in him I trust that he will yet deliver me.' Surely you can set your seal to these words. The Lord help you, then, to live more and more a life of faith, to feed upon the promises, and to rejoice in the assurance that all things are yours, and shall surely work for your good.

If I guess right at what passes in your heart, the name of Jesus is precious to you; and this is a sure token of salvation, and that of God. You could not have loved him, if he had not loved you first. He spoke to you, and said: 'Seek my face', before your heart cried to him: 'Thy face, O Lord, will I seek.' But you complain: 'Alas! I love him so little.' That very complaint proves that you love him a great deal; for if you loved him but a little, you would think you loved him enough. A mother loves her child a great deal, yet does not complain for not loving it more; no, perhaps, she hardly thinks it possible. But such an infinite object is Jesus, that those who love him better than parents or child, or any earthly relation or comfort, will still think they hardly love him at all; because they see such a vast discrepancy between the utmost they can give him, and what in himself he deserves from them. But I can give you good advice and good news: love him as well as you can now, and before long you shall love him better. O, when you see him as he is, then I am sure you will love him indeed! If you want to love him better now while you are here, I believe I can tell you the secret how this is to be attained: 'Trust him. The more you trust him the better you will love him.' If you ask farther: 'What should I do to trust him?' I answer: 'Try him: the more you make trial of him, the more your trust in him will be strengthened. Venture upon his promises; carry them to him, and see if he will not be as good as his word.' But, alas, Satan and unbelief work the contrary way. We are unwilling to try him, and therefore unable to trust him; and what wonder, then, that our love is faint, for who can love uncertainties?

If you are in some measure thankful for what you have

received, and hungering and thirsting for more, you are in the frame I would wish for myself; and I desire to praise the Lord on your behalf. Pray for us. We join in love to you. – I am, &c.

ONE LETTER TO MISS P.

August 17, 1776

It is indeed natural for us to wish and to plan, and it is merciful in the Lord to disappoint our plans, and to cross our wishes. For we cannot be safe, much less happy, but in proportion as we are weaned from our own wills, and made simply desirous of being directed by his guidance. This trust (when we are enlightened by his Word) is sufficiently familiar to the judgment; but we seldom learn to put it into practice, without being trained a while in the school of disappointment. The schemes we form look so plausible and convenient, that when they are broken we are ready to say, What a pity! We try again, and with no better success; we are grieved, and perhaps angry, and plan another, and so on; at length, in the course of time, experience and observation begin to convince us, that we are not more able than we are worthy to choose aright for ourselves. Then the Lord's invitation to cast our cares upon him, and his promise to take care of us, appear valuable; and when we have finished planning, his plan in our favour gradually opens, and he does more and better for us than we could either ask or think. I can hardly recollect a single plan of mine, of which I have since seen reason to be satisfied, that had it taken place in season and circumstance just as I proposed, it would, humanly speaking, have proved my ruin; or at least it would have deprived me of the greater good the Lord had designed for me. We judge things by their present appearances, but the Lord sees them in their consequences; if we could do so likewise, we should have exactly the same mind he has, but we cannot. It is an unspeakable mercy that he will manage for us, whether we are pleased with his management or not; and it is spoken of as one of his heaviest judgments, when he gives any person or people up to the way of their own hearts, and to walk after their own counsels.

Indeed, we may admire his patience towards us. If we were blind, and reduced to a desire for a person to lead us, and should yet pretend to dispute with him, and direct him at every step, we would probably soon weary him, and provoke him to lead us to find the way by ourselves if we could. But our gracious Lord is long-suffering and full of compassion; he bears with our forwardness, yet he will take methods both to shame and to humble us, and to bring us to a confession that he is wiser than we. The great and unexpected benefit he plans for us, by all the discipline we meet with, is to tread down our wills, and bring them into subjection to his. So far as we attain to his, we are out of the reach of disappointment; for when the will of God can please us, we shall be pleased every day, and from morning until night about his dispensations. O the happiness of such a life! I have an idea about it; I hope I am aiming at it, but surely I have not attained it. Self is active in my heart, even if it does not hold full sway there. I profess to believe that one thing is needful and sufficient, and yet my thoughts are prone to wander after a hundred more. If it be true, that the light of his countenance is better than life, why am I solicitous about anything else? If he be all-sufficient, and gives me liberty to call him mine, why do I rush around people for their help? If he is about my path and bed; if the smallest as well as the greatest events in which I am concerned, are under his immediate direction; if the very hairs of my head were numbered; then my care (any further than a care to walk in the paths of his precepts, and to follow the openings of his providence) must be useless and needless, yes, indeed sinful, burdensome to myself, and dishonourable to my profession. Let us cast down the load we are unable to carry, and, if the Lord is our shepherd, refer all and trust all to him. Let us endeavour to live to him and for him today, and be glad that tomorrow, with all that it holds, is in his hands.

It is said of Pompey, that when his friends would have dissuaded him from putting to sea in a storm, he answered: 'It is necessary for me to sail, but it is not necessary for me to live!' O pompous speech, in Pompey's sense! He was full of the idea of his own importance, and would rather have died than have taken a step beneath his supposed dignity. But it may be accommodated with propriety to a believer's case. It becomes us to say, it is not necessary for me to be rich, or what the world accounts wise; to be healthy, or admired by my fellow-worms; to pass through life in a state of prosperity and outward comfort; – these things may be, or they may be otherwise, as the Lord in his wisdom shall appoint. What is necessary is for me to be humble and spiritual, to seek communion with God, to adorn my profession of the Gospel, and to yield submissively to his disposal, in whatever way, whether of service or suffering, he shall be pleased to call me to glorify him in the world. It is not necessary for me to live long, but highly expedient that whilst I do live I should live for him. Here, then, I would curb my desires; and here, having his Word both for my rule and my warrant, I am freed from asking amiss. Let me have his presence and his Spirit, wisdom to know my calling, and opportunities and faithfulness to improve them; and as to the rest, Lord help me to say: 'What thou wilt, when thou wilt, and how thou wilt.' – I am, &c.